The C...
of
Oliver Cromwell

By the same author

CIVIL STRIFE IN THE MIDLANDS 1642–1651
Phillimore, London

SUPERPOWER BRITAIN
Willingham Press

The Court of Oliver Cromwell

Roy Sherwood

Willingham Press

Copyright © Roy Sherwood 1977

ISBN 0 9514113 1 4 (paperback)

Paperback edition published in Great Britain 1989 by
Willingham Press
22 Schole Road, Willingham
Cambridge CB4 5JD

First published in hardback 1977 by
Croom Helm Ltd., London, and Rowman & Littlefield, Totowa, NJ

British Library Cataloguing in Publication Data
Sherwood, Roy Edward
  The Court of Oliver Cromwell.
  1. Lord Protector's households. England 1653–1658
  I. Title
  354.4203'12

  ISBN 0-9514113-1-4

Production in association with
Book Production Consultants, Cambridge
Printed in England

Cover: Portrait of Oliver Cromwell by Robert Walker.
Courtesy of the National Portrait Gallery, London

CONTENTS

TO MY MOTHER

FOREWORD

Three main impressions may be drawn from Roy Sherwood's fascinating and thoroughly researched study of the Court of Oliver Cromwell. The first is that it was run extremely economically. It had a fixed revenue allocated to it by Parliament: £64,000 a year, to begin with, and during the last year of Oliver's rule when his status was changed by the constitution known as the Petition and Advice it rose to £100,000 and was always properly controlled.

Neither Charles I nor Charles II was subjected to any such limitation of expenditure which was a precursor of the Civil List. Charles I spent lavishly in collecting paintings and providing masques for his French Queen; Charles II had all sorts of extravagances: the legend that what he spent on his mistresses was not a serious cause of his personal financial difficulties has recently been exposed by Professor Chandaman.

Oliver Cromwell had far fewer servants in Whitehall palace than had the English Kings and none of them were paid excessively. Mr Sherwood draws our attention, for instance, to the case of Sir Oliver Fleming, the Master of Ceremonies. Before the civil war this official was reckoned to earn an income of around £1,000 a year (what might its equivalent be today one wonders — perhaps £30,000 a year?) because his salary was supplemented by handsome gratuities from the ambassadors he looked after; he was also provided with assistants. Now gratuities were frowned upon and he was expected to do all the work himself and to account for every penny he spent. The only gross extravagance of the Protectorate was Oliver's state funeral; and that was hardly his fault.

Secondly, there was little patronage conferred or corruption permitted at the Cromwellian Court. The only instance of nepotism was that Oliver appointed John Claypole, the husband of his favourite daughter, to be his Master of the Horse, which in Stuart times had been a sinecure. Such examples of Court patronage as Mr Sherwood has unearthed are negligible: one relates to a wardrobe keeper, another to a seaman. Perhaps in this respect Oliver was too austere although he did tend to advance his sons-in-law such, for example, as Charles Fleetwood, who he discovered too late was a 'milksop'.

Thirdly, Mr Sherwood shows that it would be a mistake to overstress the puritanical character of Cromwell's Court. Thousands of gallons of French and Spanish wine were purchased for the use of the Protectoral household. We know that Oliver enjoyed his sack or sherry and his glass of ale and that occasionally he smoked a pipe. Fond of music, he enjoyed listening to the Court organists at Whitehall and Hampton Court and to the singing of motets. His tastes in food were traditional; he preferred roast beef to foreign 'kickshaws'. The ambassadors whom Oliver entertained do not appear to have objected to that.

Only when his daughters married did the Lord Protector lash out. Then the trumpets sounded and the violins played while mixed dancing took place in which that shadowy but blameless figure, Oliver's wife, 'the Protectress', joined. Though Oliver did not appoint a Master of the Revels, William Davenant, reputedly the illegitimate son of William Shakespeare, wrote both an opera and a play which were performed during the Protectorate. Thus while neither patronage on any large scale nor corruption nor licentiousness was permitted in the admirably regulated Cromwellian Court, it was by no means rigidly puritanical in the sense in which this adjective is normally understood in our permissive society.

No man, it used to be said, is a hero to his own valet; yet John Maidstone, who was first Oliver's steward and later his master cofferer (or household treasurer) and had been at times both an army officer and a member of parliament, must have known the Lord Protector as intimately as anyone: his tribute to his master has often been quoted, but is worth recalling:

He was naturally compassionate to objects in distress even to an effeminate measure; though God had given him a heart, wherein was left little room for any fear but what was due to himself, of which there was a large proportion, yet did he exceed in tenderness towards sufferers. A larger soul, I think, hath seldom dwelt in a house of clay than his was.

Maurice Ashley
1977

PREFACE

The Cromwellian Protectorate, being 'a Commonwealth in a single person', was in effect a monarchical regime. So much so that many of the trappings associated with the generally accepted concept of a monarchy, that of a crowned head, were attached to the office of lord protector, and hence to the person of Oliver Cromwell.

Probably the most obvious way in which this became manifest was in the establishment of a protectoral court: a court, that is, in the narrow technical sense meaning, collectively, those who were involved in the protector's domestic or household arrangements and gave lustre to his office, rather than the wider application of the term denoting the political figures who surrounded Cromwell, although there were some who were members of both groups.

Until now no attempt has been made to determine either the essential form and structure of the protectoral court, or the extent to which it resembled the royal courts that preceded it. In writing this book I have attempted, I trust with some degree of success, to remedy this, in spite of the fact that there survives little more than a scatter of allusions to the subject.

Furthermore, I have demonstrated (Appendix A) that Cromwell's second investiture under the revised constitution took him beyond the mere assumption of the trappings of monarchy to the actual occupancy of the office of king, while retaining the title protector.

Throughout the book spelling and punctuation in quotations from contemporary sources have largely been adapted to modern usage and the dates indicated are old style but with the year regarded as beginning on 1 January.

I have incurred the usual debts which accrue to a writer of a work of this sort. In particular I am indebted to Mr Maurice Ashley who not only read my manuscript and gave me the benefit of a lifetime's knowledge of the seventeenth century, but has also very kindly provided the book with a foreword. I need hardly add, however, that any errors which may appear in this work are entirely my own.

My thanks are also due to the principals and especially the staffs of the following establishments for the assistance they have afforded to me in consulting material, and for their ready and courteous responses to my enquiries for information: the University Library, Cambridge; the Public Record Office, and in particular Dr J.A. Guy, Assistant Keeper of Public Records, who has been exceedingly accommodating; the British Library; the Cromwell Museum, Huntingdon; Cambridgeshire Libraries, County Library Headquarters, Huntingdon, especially Mr D.A. Dwyer, Deputy County Librarian; the County of Glamorgan Record Office, Cardiff; the Bangor University College Library. Added to these are the marquess of Bath, with particular thanks to the librarian at Longleat House, Miss B.M. Austin, Mr C.W. Scott-Giles, Fitzalan Pursuivant of Arms Extraordinary, who advised me on matters heraldic, and Miss Frances Kelly of Curtis Brown Academic Ltd.

Finally, I owe a very special debt of gratitude to my wife Doreen and to my very good friend Dr R.C. Smail, Fellow of Sidney Sussex College, Cambridge, both of whom have, in their different ways, given me immeasurable encouragement and practical assistance.

Roy Sherwood
1977

ABBREVIATIONS

Aylmer, *K.S.*	G.E. Aylmer, *The King's Servants: The Civil Service of Charles I, 1625-1642* (London, revised edn, 1974)
Aylmer, *S.S.*	G.E. Aylmer, *The States Servants: The Civil Service of the English Republic, 1649-1660* (London, 1973)
Beattie	John M. Beattie, *The English Court in the Reign of George I* (Cambridge, 1967)
Burton, II, VII	*The Diary of Thomas Burton*, ed. J.T. Rutt, Vol. II (London, 1828), Appendix VII
CSPD	*Calendar of State Papers: Domestic Series*
CSP Ven.	*Calendar of State Papers: Venetian*
CJ	*The Journals of the House of Commons*
DNB	*The Dictionary of National Biography*
HMC	Historical Manuscripts Commission
LJ	*The Journals of the House of Lords*
Merc. Pol.	*Mercurius Politicus*
Nichols	John Nichols, *The Progresses, Processions and Magnificent Festivities of King James the First*, Vol. IV (London, 1828)
Perf. Diurn.	*A Perfect Diurnal*
Perf. Proc.	*Perfect Proceedings of State Affairs*
'PCR of RC'	'Privy Council Register of Richard Cromwell, September 3rd 1658–January 18th 1659', in the possession of the marquess of Bath, Longleat House
Pub. Int.	*The Public Intelligencer*
PRO	The Public Record Office
Sev. Proc.	*Several Proceedings of State Affairs in England, Scotland and Ireland.*
SP 18	State Papers 18 (Interregnum – Letters and Papers) in the PRO
SP 25	State Papers 25 (Interregnum – Council of State Draft and Fair Order Books) in the PRO
SP 46	State Papers 46 (Interregnum – Papers of Commissioners for the Admiralty and Navy) in the PRO

He that should see the prevailing party of
these nations . . . cannot but wonder how soon
they have forgot the customs, manners, ways
of their own old people and are cast into
the mould of them that went before them in
the places whereunto they are translated.

John Owen, *Of the Mortification of Sin in
Believers* (1656)

You drew me to accept the place I now stand
in. There is ne'er a man within these walls
that can say, sir, you sought it, nay, not a
man nor woman treading upon English ground.

Cromwell's Speech to Parliament, 4 February 1658

1 THE PROTECTORAL PALACES

I

On 16 December 1653 it was decreed by the Instrument of Government

> that the supreme legislative authority of the Commonwealth of
> England, Scotland and Ireland and of the Dominions thereunto
> belonging, shall be and reside in one person, and the people assem-
> bled in Parliament; the style of which person shall be 'The Lord
> Protector of the Commonwealth of England, Scotland and Ireland
> . . .'. That Oliver Cromwell, Captain-General of the forces of England,
> Scotland and Ireland, shall be, and is hereby declared to be, Lord
> Protector . . . for his life.[1]

Thus the great rebellion against princely authority had assumed a new
dimension. With the judicial execution of an anointed king yesterday's
unthinkable act had already become today's *fait accompli*. It was no
longer inconceivable therefore that an introspective and strangely
magnanimous squire from East Anglia, who had, perchance, become
one of the greatest soldiers of his age, should assume the dignity of an
imperial crown, even though Cromwell was lord protector of what was
nominally a republic, and his sovereign power was theoretically shared
with Parliament and limited by a powerful and omnicompetent central
executive in the form of a Council of State.

The next logical step to the acceptance of princely authority was the
assumption of one of the principal externals of monarchy, a court, and
the primary requisite of a court being a palace, it was resolved by
Protector Oliver's Council, and confirmed by the first Parliament of the
Protectorate, that the ex-royal residences of St James's House, the
palace of Whitehall and the mews there, Somerset House, Greenwich
House, the Manor at York, Windsor Castle and Hampton Court Palace,
together with their parks and other appurtenances, including the
honour and manor of Hampton Court, 'be vested in the present Lord
Protector, and the succeeding Lord Protectors, for the maintenance of
his and their state and dignity.'[2]

Originally, in 1649, after the execution of King Charles I and Parliament's declaration that the 'kingly office' be abolished on the grounds
that it was 'unnecessary, burthensome and dangerous to the liberty,

safety and public interest of the people', it had been decreed that the honours, manors, castles, houses, messuages, parks and lands which had belonged to the late king should be surveyed, valued and sold for the benefit of the new republic, or Commonwealth. The then central executive, or Council of State, however, advised that those residences which five years later were to be put at the disposal of the lord protector ought not to be sold but retained for the use of the Commonwealth and an exempting clause was accordingly inserted into the bill.[3]

But under a subsequent Act of Parliament some of the originally excepted properties had either been sold off or contracted for during the twelve months immediately preceding the establishment of the Protectorate. This necessitated the Council of State* nominating, on 9 February 1654, four of its own members, Sir Anthony Ashley Cooper, Walter Strickland and Colonels Philip Jones and William Sydenham, to take the necessary steps to see that the disposed of houses and lands were reconveyed to the state.[5]

Among such properties were St James's Fields, bought by Mr Woodward, part of Greenwich House which Uriah Babington had, it seems, contracted for and had conveyed to him by the government for £979 3s in February 1653, and Greenwich Park leased to Mr John Parker. There was also the Little Park at Windsor contracted for on 1 March 1653 by Mr Francis Thompson whom Cooper, Strickland and Sydenham were, on 14 April 1654, instructed to treat with, and also others who had bought any of the lands of the late king, his queen or their eldest son which could be of use to the protector and whom, at that time, had not yet been negotiated with.[6]

The process of reacquisition proved, however, to be far from straightforward and not a little expensive. This was especially true of Hampton Court and its appurtenances, the one property that had fallen entirely into private hands. The instruction to Jones, Strickland and Sydenham to deal with the person who had bought the honour of Hampton Court, and with Richard Casewell to whom part of the lands had been conveyed, with a view to getting them to relinquish their interests, was given on 9 February 1654, the same day as the more general Council order to Jones, Strickland, Sydenham and Ashley Cooper covering all of the properties designated for reacquisition.[7]

---

*The Council was also now known as the Council of State to his Highness the Lord Protector, or the Council to his Highness, before finally becoming styled as his Highness's Privy Council in 1656 and officially confirmed as such in the Humble Petition and Advice of May 1657.[4]

But the Council had, in fact, already directed on 20 December 1653, four days after Oliver's investiture as lord protector, that Sir William Roberts and Mr Edward Cressett should treat with those persons who had bought the parks, meadows and the hare warren of Hampton Court, with a view to their repurchase by the Commonwealth at reasonable terms. A report subsequently submitted by Roberts and Cressett revealed that much of the property in question had realised quite profitable returns for their original purchasers. Mr Edmund Blackwell, a goldsmith and jeweller,* who seems to have bought the lease of the bulk of the land attached to Hampton Court, sold, almost immediately after purchase, the lease on 23 acres of New Park to Mr Casewell of Hampton for £53 more than the original cost. Blackwell also sold the meadows, this time to his brother, for £1,550, which was £308 more than the amount he paid for them, and Old Bushey Park to Mr Woolmer at a profit of £100. On top of this Blackwell demanded from the government a profit on the lands still held by him before he would sell the leases back to the state. Accordingly, on 10 March 1654, the Council declared that for the release of land in Hampton Court and Bushey, for which £5,110 19s had been paid, his Highness would allow Blackwell to make a profit of £1,100.[8]

Most of those who had bought leases off Blackwell made similar claims. Blackwell's brother demanded £450 more for the lease of the meadows than he paid for them, and Mr Woolmer asked for £400 more for Old Bushey Park. While Shadrach Brice and John Imwood managed to exact from the government £200 over and above the £1,170 that they had paid to Blackwell to surrender their interest in the hare warren at Hampton Court. They were also successful in realising a further £20 which they claimed for expenses.[9]

The trouble and expense involved in reacquiring these and other properties must have been particularly galling to the government in view of the fact that the decision to sell some of them had been arrived at only a few weeks before repossession was decided upon. And even though by 16 March 1654 the Council felt able to order the government's surveyor of works, John Embree, to see to it that Hampton Court, its lodges, stables and outhouses and the park and its houses were forthwith cleared for the protector's use, certain appurtenances of

---

*There existed at this time a prominent London goldsmith and major government creditor named Edward Backwell (see Chapter 2). It seems possible that these might be one and the same person.

the palace were still legally in private hands. These were the honour, manor and royalty of Hampton Court, the purchasers of which had yet to be dealt with even as late as 14 April 1654, the day before the lord protector took up residence at the palace. Not until 17 May 1654 was it reported to the Council that the repurchase of the manor and royalty of Hampton Court from John Phelps had been agreed to for the figure of £750. Payment was duly made to Phelps out of customs and excise receipts on 10 August.[10]

Added to the apparent tardiness in the completion of the reacquisition process Hampton Court had a squatter problem. On 14 April 1654 which, as already stated, was the day before Cromwell took up residence in the palace, the Council, acting on information received, was compelled to take action against several inhabitants of nearby Kingston-upon-Thames, and places within its proximity, who were fencing off for their own use some of the meadows belonging to Hampton Court.[11]

Squatting also affected Greenwich House. A paper on the subject from Mr Babington, described as keeper of Greenwich House, was presented on 5 October 1654 to the Council. This tells of several persons who were lodging there, apparently without authority, to what Babington terms the prejudice of the property. The matter was referred to Councillors Sir Gilbert Pickering and Walter Strickland for their investigation.[12]

A problem of a different nature confronted the government when it came to deal with one of the properties that had not been allowed to fall into private hands, the mews at Whitehall. In the middle of March 1654 the Council instructed Mr Embree to have the stables cleared forthwith and the rooms and lodgings within a fortnight, for the protector's use, but allowing the horse guard to remain in the mews' barn, and to ensure that Master of the Horse John Claypole received all the keys. Yet five and a half months later, on the last day of August 1654, it was considered necessary to instruct Mr Embree to be particularly diligent over clearing the mews for his Highness's family. In the intervening period there had been a number of petitions addressed to the protector from some of the inhabitants of the mews begging that they may continue to occupy their houses, rooms or sheds, which they had been given notice to quit. These petitioners held their tenure by virtue of the fact that they had either themselves been in royal service, or were the dependents or close relatives of those who had been thus employed. There was Elizabeth, the widow of John Sanderson who had been a waterman to James I and Charles I. Her husband's arrears for his service amounted to £500 and after 1640 he had received a mere £6. The widow's plea was that only by continuing to live in the lodgings which her late husband had erected near the smith's forge could she and her children subsist. Giles Pointer and four other ex-grooms of the late king's stables gave their advanced age, poverty and childlessness as the reasons why they should continue to live in a dwelling they had constructed over the cross stable and riding house adjoining the dunghill yard.[13]

Petitioners who could provide evidence of positive support for the Parliamentary party during the late civil war to assist their cause did so. Mary, the widow of John Alkin, a sumpterman to Charles I, in requesting the continuance of herself, her three small children and a Frances Masters, in their mews accommodation, referred to the fact that two of her sons had fought in the Parliamentary army and that the husband of Frances Masters had died of wounds received in the service. Those who could make no such claims did the next best thing, like Dorothy Woodward and four other aged widows of servants to the late king, whose husbands had built lodgings for themselves and their families over the stables in the dunghill yard. While their husbands had obviously not served on the side of Parliament the petitioners laid considerable stress on the fact that they had not actually fought against Parliament either.[14]

The problem of clearing the mews of its old tenants was apparently still not resolved as late as the middle of November 1655, when the Council issued yet another order, this time to John Maidstone and Nathaniel Waterhouse, the protector's household stewards, to call before them the pretenders to the lodgings and stables there and inform them that the mews must forthwith be cleared for the use of his Highness. This says a great deal, either for the tenacity of those occupants of the mews who still remained a full twenty months after the original instruction to clear them out of their quarters, or for the benignancy with which the order was carried out. If the case of Henry Zinzan is anything to go by even when they were finally ejected the ousted occupants were not exactly left destitute. The 92-year-old Zinzan had been an equerry of the great horse stable to King James I as well as holding a post in the Tower. In February 1656, having been removed from his dwelling in the Round House in the mews, on which he had recently spent £24, he petitioned the Protector for what he called £180 due on his account, plus a pension to preserve him from starving during the short period of life left to him. The pension at least was granted him. This was fixed at twenty shillings a week.[15]

The life guard, or horse guard, who were exempted from the clearing order, occupied the barn in the mews for the next couple of years or so. Then, in August 1656, the Council directed Surveyor Embree to arrange for a stable to be built in the yard at Whitehall to accommodate his Highness's life guard. And in February 1657, the Council further resolved that a stable should be constructed in the mews for the captains and lieutenants of the protectoral life guard, such details as the siting and dimensions of the building being put into the hands of two members of the Council, Major-General John Lambert and Colonel Philip Jones.[16]

The preparation for occupation by the lord protector of the actual palace of Whitehall proved less of a problem. Although John King, a Council messenger, whose rooms, for which he had paid the previous occupier £20, were among those acquired for the protector and his family, did, it seems, require several warnings before he finally quit. Others similarly dispossessed were the committee for approbation of public preachers and the admiralty commissioners. Towards the end of 1654 the latter were required to remove themselves from Whitehall in order to provide quarters for Oliver's eldest son, Richard. These were most likely the rooms once occupied by Charles I. Certainly it was here that Richard lived as lord protector. The admiralty commissioners, together with the committee for approbation of public preachers, eventually secured suitable rooms at Derby House in the Strand. And much later, in February 1658, the Council, by that time known as the Privy Council, ordered the rooms over his Highness's guard in the gallery near the Council chamber to be vacated and prepared as lodgings for some of his Highness's gentlemen. This was followed a month or so later by another Council order authorising the payment of £50 to Captain Edward Dendy, a serjeant-at-arms to the Council, towards the moneys he had expended on his lodgings in Whitehall; this accommodation having been deemed suitable for the disposal of his Highness's family. The £50, which was only half of what Dendy originally claimed for, was eventually paid from the Council's contingencies fund. These last two Council instructions were probably the result of the marked increase in the adoption of the trappings of monarchy by the protector which took place after his second inauguration in June 1657, and the expansion of the protectoral household with the marriages of Oliver's two younger daughters, Mary and Frances, later in the same year.[17]

In spite of the government's generosity in putting as many of the late king's palaces at the protector's disposal Cromwell nevertheless found Whitehall, including the mews, and Hampton Court sufficient for his needs. The palace of Whitehall, which in reality was an agglomorate of many individual buildings, containing altogether some 2,000 rooms and covering an area of about 23 acres, became his official residence. After all Whitehall had gradually become during the reign of James I the principal residence of the monarch and the centre of the national government. It remained so until 1698 when, apart from the Banqueting House, the palace was destroyed by fire. It was natural, therefore, that Cromwell should rule, or 'exercise his sovereign authority', as his Stuart predecessors had done, from Whitehall. Here the protectoral Council met and it was from here that most of the departments of state operated. Here also, in the Banqueting House, designed by Inigo Jones and allegedly described by the French architect, Azout, when he visited England in about 1685, as 'the most finished of the modern buildings on this side of the Alps', Cromwell received the ambassadors accredited to the state of which he was now ruler. Ironically, only a few short years before, Charles I had walked through the self same Banqueting House, under the same ceiling painted by Rubens depicting the apotheosis of the doomed monarch's father, James I, to his death on a scaffold outside. Exactly two years later, in February 1651, the surveyor of works was instructed to have all the portraits and coats of arms of the late king displayed in the chambers, or windows of chambers, or any other public or private place in Whitehall, removed.[18]

Cromwell took up residence in Whitehall Palace on 14 April 1654 on which day it was announced in the press that 'his Highness the Lord Protector, with his Lady and family, this day dined at Whitehall, whither his Highness and family are removed, and did this day lie there, and do there continue'. This had been preceded by an announcement the day before to the effect that 'this day the bedchambers and the rest of the lodgings and rooms appointed for the Lord Protector in Whitehall, were prepared for his Highness to remove from the Cockpit on the morrow'. It was probably to this end that a warrant was issued on 14 April for the payment of £500 to Surveyor of Works John Embree for repairs to, and the fitting out of, the palace of Whitehall. Work had, in fact, been going on for some considerable time. It was reported on 23 December 1653, seven days after Cromwell's investiture, that 'Whitehall is being prepared for his Highness to reside in, and the old Council Chamber is being fitted for his honourable Council to meet in'. Also, on 15 February 1654 it had been decided in Council that the committee appointed to consider the protector's treasuries should examine the bills for furnishing the kitchen and report back.[19]

The cockpit lodgings, in which the Cromwells had lived since Oliver's return from his Irish campaign in 1650, were, as their name suggests, situated next to Whitehall Palace cockpit. Commanding a view of St James's Park the cockpit lodgings had in the past been used as a royal residence (James I's daughter Elizabeth lived there before her marriage), and were part of a cluster of buildings, which also included the palace bowls house, tennis court and tiltyard, set a little apart from the principal buildings of the palace. The progression from these quarters to his relatively more opulent apartments in the palace of Whitehall itself would, one imagines, have been an easy one for Cromwell. After all he was no stranger to the palace of Whitehall. He was, during the pre-Protectorate Commonwealth days, a member of the Council of State which always met there. And he had been lord protector for some months before the move actually took place, during which time the ambassadors of Portugal, Sweden, France and Hamburg received their first audience with England's new ruler at Whitehall, as had the Dutch ambassadors, at whose reception on 4 March 1654 the Banqueting House 'was hung with extraordinary rich hangings' and there were 'divers knights and gentlemen, officers of the army and thousands of people in the said room present'. Cromwell had also slept there. 'This night [17 March 1654]', reported the official newssheet *Several Proceedings of State Affairs in England, Scotland and Ireland*, 'his Highness the Lord Protector lay in Whitehall, who being not well by reason of a cold, lay in one of the chambers formerly the Queen's privy lodgings.'[20]

But it would seem, if the source of the intelligence can be believed, that this singularly dramatic transition from private house to royal palace was not a particularly agreeable prospect to certain members of Cromwell's immediate family. 'He [Cromwell]', so we are informed by what are said to be the memoirs of Edmund Ludlow, 'removed from the Cockpit, which house the Parliament had assigned him, to the possession of Whitehall, which he assigned to himself. His wife seemed at first unwilling to remove thither, tho afterwards she became better satisfied with her grandeur; but his mother, who by reason of her great age was not so easily flattered with these temptations, very much mistrusted the issue of affairs.'[21]

Whether or not the protectress and her octogenarian mother-in-law felt at home in their other abode, Hampton Court Palace, is not known. This residence, built by Henry VIII's most powerful subject, Thomas Wolsey, and which rivalled, if not surpassed, in magnificence the palaces of Wolsey's royal master whose property it became, was to be Cromwell's week-end country retreat (giving rise to the claim that the protector was the inventor of the English week-end), a protectoral Chequers where, it was said, 'the great affairs of the nation are transacted with labour and care, as if they were at Whitehall'.

Here, at Hampton Court, in addition to those at Whitehall, lodgings were provided for certain members of the government, officers of his Highness's household and some of the protector's family. The lord president of the Privy Council, for instance, had at his disposal what had been the late king's dressing room, and a room next to it for a servant. The rooms occupied by the comptroller and cofferer of the protectoral household, and also the master of the horse and Cromwell's second daughter, Bettie Claypole, are described elsewhere. Of the Protector's family, Mary, Oliver's third daughter, who, in 1657, became Lady Falconbridge, lived with her husband in lodgings once occupied by the duke of Richmond, presumably when he was lord steward of Charles I's household. Lady Falconbridge's gentlewoman, a Mrs Grinaways, was allocated part of the armoury, which had been 'hanged round with green and yellow striped stuff', as a private chamber. The rest of the armoury was used as a nursery by Mary's elder sister, Bettie Claypole. The youngest of the Cromwell daughters, Frances, who married the earl of Warwick's grandson Robert Rich, also in 1657, lived in what was formerly the king's cabinet room. This contained five pieces of tapestry hangings depicting the history of Maleager. Frances's gentlewoman 'lay below stairs' in rather more spartan surroundings than the gentlewoman of her elder sister, Mary.[22]

As for the protector himself; his bedchamber, which, incidentally, was not that used by Charles I, was hung with five pieces of fine tapestry hangings illustrating the history of the gods, Vulcan, Mars and Venus, and the window curtains, of which there were two, one of baize and the other made of serge, were scarlet. The furniture included a small couch, two elbow chairs and four back stools upholstered in sky-coloured damask, with a carpet to match. Attached to the bedchamber was a dressing room. The protector also had his own kitchen at Hampton Court.[23]

Not a great deal of the Hampton Court that Oliver would have known survived the rebuilding of the palace, in accordance with Sir Christopher Wren's design, in the 1690s. But the Great Hall built by Henry VIII remains, and in this was installed for Oliver's delectation a large organ, valued at about £300, from out of Magdalen College, Oxford.[24]

Other uses, in some cases similar to those of the preceding years, were found for the unwanted residences. St James's House provided lodgings for the Portuguese ambassador for a short time during the summer of 1654. Unfortunately his stay there must have been somewhat marred by the seizure of his horses and some goods from the quarters he was using. This was possibly the result of an official blunder which the Council attempted to put to rights by issuing an order for the persons responsible to be brought before them and the ambassador's property released from custody and restored. St James's also housed a small garrison which at one time comprised the protector's own regiment of foot and its stores, which included ten barrels of powder. Having soldiers on hand as guards made the house useful as a prison, as indeed the Whitehall mews were. One batch of prisoners in St James's, along with another group who had been incarcerated in the Tower, was commanded by Cromwell to be set at liberty and banished on security not to act in any way prejudicial to the state nor to return without leave. Considering that some of these prisoners were either presumed to have been guilty of high treason, or at the very least held on suspicion of it, their fate suggests that the Cromwellian regime was a singularly benign one.[25]

Somerset House, like St James's, provided quarters for foreign ambassadors, and a Council instruction for some convenient rooms to be set apart for them there was issued in the spring of 1655. This, so it would appear, was not Somerset House's only foreign connection at this time. On 12 January 1655 the Council received the petition from a body calling itself the French Church Assembly at Somerset House chapel, begging leave for its members to exercise their trades in Westminster. And in June 1658 Cromwell gave his approval to a Privy Council order instructing his lord chamberlain to arrange for Somerset House to be fitted out for the entertainment of foreign ambassadors, and to see to it that the people who were currently lodging there were accommodated elsewhere by 29 September. But by 29 September Oliver was dead and Somerset House was the scene of the protector's lying in state, a purpose that this particular residence had served a year previously when, in August 1657, the body of Admiral Robert Blake was brought there prior to burial in Westminster Abbey.[26]

The cost of maintaining the two protectoral palaces of Hampton Court and Whitehall, plus the mews, was, for a time, met out of government funds, or what was termed 'at the public charge'. Responsibility for seeing that maintenance was carried out rested with the state's surveyor of works, John Embree. Then, in November 1655, the Council decided that the state should no longer directly bear the cost of repairs to Whitehall, the mews and Hampton Court. Instead all moneys expended on these properties would, in future, be paid out of the revenue settled on Oliver to cover his household and other expenses. While a committee of councillors was appointed to consider how the ex-royal residences unused by the protector could be kept in good repair with the minimum of expenditure. The purchase of building materials and the employment of men to repair these properties and those occupied by the lord protector continued to be the responsibility of John Embree, only now no work could be carried out on Whitehall, the mews and Hampton Court without his Highness's special warrant.[27]

II

Cromwell having been installed in Whitehall and Hampton Court, it was considered essential that these two protectoral palaces should be furnished in a style befitting their return to the role of residences of what to all intents and purposes was a sovereign prince. To this end certain items of furniture and works of art, totalling in value £35,497 16s 6d, which had once been used in, or had graced, the palaces of the late king, were put at the disposal of the new ruler.[28]

Originally, like the ex-royal residences, the personal effects of the late king, his queen and their eldest son had been ordered to be sold off, the first £30,000 from the sale of curios and works of art at Hampton Court, for instance, being 'lent unto the treasurers of the navy, for supply and present uses of the navy', other proceeds being employed in the payment of debts incurred by the royal family in the running of their households before the war. This was after the goods had been appraised, inventoried and up to £10,000 worth had been reserved for the Council of State. The choice of items to be reserved was left to a committee of councillors which included Sir Henry Mildmay, one-time master of the jewel house to Charles I, and Sir Gilbert Pickering. All that was in 1649 and the sale continued for several years. Then it was stopped. Thereafter instead of the names of purchasers the words 'Reserved: with his Highness', or 'Reserved: in his Highness's service' are subjoined to many entries in the massive copy inventory of the dead king's goods. In fact the Council had issued a warrant to the trustees for the sale of the crown goods on 6 March 1654 authorising them to deliver to the protectoral wardrobe keeper, Clement Kinnersley, for his Highness's use, the rich hangings and other goods still in their possession.[29]

Among the items of a purely domestic nature were carpets, window curtains, and irons, candlesticks, kitchen utensils and a commode, or close-stool, covered in red velvet, which had originally been in employment at Greenwich House but which was now 'in His Highness's service at Whitehall'. There were also quantities of bedding, a number of feather beds, and at least two complete bedroom suites, both of which were designated as being 'in His Highness's service at Whitehall'. One suite, which was valued at £500, comprised a crimson velvet bed with valance and tester, or canopy, of cloth of gold and silver with rich gold and silver embroidery, three carpets, one being of damask, three chairs, six stools and two crimson velvet-covered seat cushions. The other suite consisted of a black satin bed, the principal furnishings of which were of yellow satin, the strings of the tassels being of silver and gold. Three chairs, six stools and a commode were also included. All of this was valued at £120. There were also two rich canopies, three chairs of state, one footstool, six high stools, one suite of crimson velvet furnishings for a bed, plus a number of silk curtains, all of which had been deposited in the Tower after being seized when Stirling Castle was taken following the abortive Scots' invasion of England under Charles II in 1651.[30]

Numerous hangings were assigned to the lord protector. Containing up to ten pieces to the set or suite these tapestries had woven into them, as the titles given to them suggest, dramatic representations of mythological, classical and biblical themes and events such as *The Seven Deadly Sins, The History of Vulcan, Mars and Venus* which, as already stated, decorated the protector's bedchamber at Hampton Court, *The Story of King Hezekiah, The History of the Siege of Jerusalem, The Triumph of Julius Caesar, The History of Charlemagne* and, hanging in Frances Cromwell's Hampton Court apartments, what was described as *The Glory of Maleagar*. Three more suites portrayed *Hannibal and Scipio, Joseph and Pharoah* and *Titus and Vespasian*. Except for *The Seven Deadly Sins*, which was not valued, none of these particular items was rated at more than £1,500 and the value of most of them had been assessed at under £500. In contrast stands the ten piece set dealing with the history of Abraham, assessed at £8,260. Originally the property of Henry VIII it is thought to have been woven about 1540 by the Brussels weaver Wilhelm Pannemaker who also made *Abraham* tapestries for the king of Spain and the Austrian emperor, all three sets being richly embellished with gold and silver thread. Each piece measuring between 15 feet 8 inches and 16 feet 1 inch in height and 25 feet 6 inches and 30 feet 8 inches in length, the suite had, since the time of its purchase, decorated the walls of Hampton Court as, indeed, it does to this day. Rated at a little less than the *Abraham* tapestries were three other suites depicting the story of Tobias, the history of Julius Caesar and the story of St Paul, comprising, respectively, nine, ten and nine pieces, and valued at £3,409, £5,022 and £3,065.[31]

These tapestries were as often as not described as 'arras hangings' and most of them were woven by Flemish weavers at Mortlake in Surrey. Established in 1619 to cater for the then growing demand in England for tapestries, the Mortlake factory became, in the late 1630s, the property of the crown. With the establishment of the Commonwealth in 1649 the state assumed responsibility for this now long ailing enterprise and attempted to foster it. In 1651 the factory was placed under the control of a new director, Sir Gilbert Pickering, a member of the powerful central executive or Council of State, who was eventually to become Protector Oliver's lord chamberlain. During Pickering's directorship a number of ex-weavers among the Dutch prisoners of war were put to work at Mortlake. In August 1653 the Council of State ordered that cartoons of Andrea Mantegna's great picture cycle, *The Triumph of Julius Caesar*, be made, presumably for the purpose of producing tapestries to that design. And a warrant was subsequently issued authorising the wardrobe keeper at Hampton Court to deliver up *The Triumph* to Sir Gilbert Pickering for copies to be made. Later on, in May 1657, the workers at Mortlake asked what was by then the Protector's Privy Council if they might begin work on tapestries depicting the story of Abraham or another triumph of Julius Caesar, or both, according to his Highness's wishes. Both were, it would appear, commissioned by the government on an initial payment of £150. As Oliver was already in possession of an *Abraham* and a *Triumph* these were probably destined for employment by, or in, some department of state.[32]

Just as some, or parts, of the ex-royal residences which the government wished to put at the protector's disposal had to be bought back from private purchasers, so it was with some of the dead king's tapestries and other furnishings that it was desired should once again adorn these properties. In May 1654 Wardrobe Keeper Clement Kinnersley was given the sum of £11 8s 0d by Gualter Frost, treasurer for council contingencies, to repurchase four pieces of tapestry hangings from three individuals. Five months later, in October 1654, Frost made a direct payment of £375 to John Bolton for a five piece suite of rich arras hangings called *The Five Senses* and another payment of £350 to John Stone, or Stowe, for the six piece suite of tapestry hangings of *The Story of Vulcan, Mars and Venus* which hung in the protector's lodgings at Whitehall. And in the same month Kinnersley received the sum of £168. 6s 0d for hangings portraying *Cupid and Venus, Elijah the*

Prophet, and *The Story of Jacob*, plus 20 Turkey carpets, 15 of damask and one of taffeta. They had in all probability originally been purchased by the wardrobe keeper for himself. Sir Gilbert Pickering and Walter Strickland, the two councillors who had been nominated to see to it that the prices of the goods to be repurchased for the protector were reasonable, appear to have had reservations about another Turkey carpet, and *The Story of Hero and Leander*, a six piece suite of hangings for which a Ralph Grafton was asking £180.[33]

Also retained for Protector Oliver were a number of paintings once part of King Charles I's renowned, and now largely disposed of, collection. These included a number of landscapes and such individual items as a full length portrait of King Louis XIII of France, valued at £15 and, to use the titles given in the copy inventory of the late king's goods, *A Madonna with Many Angels and One with a Scourge, Mary's Ascension with the Apostles looking on, A Young Woman with Goliath's Head, The Judgement of Venus*, and *A Shepherd and a Nymph*, valued respectively at £20, £10, £15, £25 and £3. There was also a picture by Van Somer entitled *An Ambassador of France* and Titian's *Herodias with the Head of John the Baptist*. The prices put on these were £10 and £150. By Raphael's favourite pupil, Giulio Romano, there were *The Burning of Rome by Nero, A Dictator, or Julius Caesar, with an Eagle above his Shoulder*, and *Temperance putting Water in a Glass*. The worth of these was given as £24, £34 and £15. But most impressive of all the works of art put at Cromwell's disposal were undoubtedly the Raphael cartoons of *The Acts of the Apostles* and Mantegna's almost as immense and equally as renowned masterpiece *The Triumph of Julius Caesar*. The seven Raphael cartoons, measuring approximately eleven and a quarter feet in height and between about fourteen and a half feet and seventeen and three quarter feet in width, were, and indeed still are, all that remains of a set of ten such works, representing subjects drawn from the lives of St Peter and St Paul, which were commissioned by Pope Leo X in the second decade of the sixteenth century for tapestries to complete the decoration of the Vatican's Sistine Chapel. In spite of the fact that they were meant to be designs for something else the cartoons are, nevertheless, regarded as works of art in their own right and among the greatest to have survived from the period of the High Renaissance. 'Their intrinsic qualities', it is said, 'are matched both by their subsequent influence on the history of art and by the extent to which they have moulded the mental image of the New Testament story for generation after generation.' Certainly Charles I, as Prince of Wales, must have been impressed by their excellence for it was he who, in 1623, acquired them for the royal collection, where they remain to this day, in order that tapestries could be made from them at Mortlake. In earmarking them for the delectation of the lord protector the government of the Commonwealth too were obviously not insensible of the merits of Raphael's work, which the trustees for the sale of the late king's goods had valued at its 1623 purchase price of £300. The same could be said of Mantegna's *The Triumph of Julius Caesar*. This pre-dates the Raphael cartoons by twenty or thirty years and received instant recognition as a masterpiece. Also, we are told, 'not only is it Mantegna's most remarkable achievement but it is one of the works which signalled a new art, the art of what we call the High Renaissance'. Consisting of nine canvasses, each nine feet square, *The Triumph* was bought by Charles I in 1627 for display at Hampton Court Palace. Here it remained throughout Oliver's rule, decorating the Long Gallery, having been valued in 1649 at £1,000. Now regarded as worth £9,000,000 the work is still to be seen at Hampton Court.[34]

Some of the ex-crown goods which had, since 1649, been in the service of the republic were also put at Cromwell's disposal. Thus the Council wished to know of all the hangings, bedding, carpets, chairs and stools and other furniture and household stuff which had been designated as now belonging to the protector, but which had previously been lent out and not returned, so that steps could be taken to call it all in. This, presumably, was meant to include the hangings, plate, pewter, linen and other goods belonging to the state which had been sent to Sweden with the Commonwealth's ambassador there, Bulstrode Whitelocke, and had since been returned, and also two pieces of tapestry hangings depicting *The Story of Hercules*, lent to Colonel Walton, together with other items from Somerset House. All of these were to be delivered up to the keeper of the protectoral wardrobe, Clement Kinnersley. Also to be handed over to Kinnersley for his Highness's use were all the hangings and other wardrobe goods from the Parliament House, and those which still remained in the hands of the ex-keepers of the now defunct wardrobes at the palace of Whitehall and Windsor Castle. As it happened this was easier said than done because a year later the Council was still ordering the ex-wardrobe keeper of Windsor Castle, William Thomas, to deliver up to Kinnersley all the hangings belonging to the Commonwealth which remained in his keeping. Thomas's apparent dereliction was due, in the most part, to the fact that some of the contents of the Windsor wardrobe had been loaned out and not returned.[35]

In furtherance of the provision of domestic necessities and luxuries for Cromwell and, through them, the attachment of lustre to the office of lord protector, Oliver's two household stewards, John Maidstone and Nathaniel Waterhouse, were authorised on 13 April 1654 to receive into their charge the plate bought on the Commonwealth's account for the protector's use. An inventory giving the exact weight and a description of each item was to be made out by the stewards and presented to the Council, three members of which, Sir Gilbert Pickering, Walter Strickland and Colonel Philip Jones, were to consider the best means of maintaining a schedule of all the plate and other goods bought for the lord protector. Among the bills presented to the Council for goods provided for what was described as the first furniture of Whitehall and the mews were those of four upholsterers, a brazier, a silkman, a turner, three linen drapers, Mr Robert Crofts and two others for plumes of feathers and gilt nails and the lord mayor of London for 'two services of plate for the Protector and his Lady' worth £3,183 14s 1d. The cost of this initial expenditure was in the region of £6,000. There was also the sum of £50 paid to Alexander Rowley for setting up a sphere in Whitehall for the use of his Highness. This is what the warrant for payment states that the fifty pounds was for. But according to a petition from Rowley addressed to the protector the sum covered other items as well, the suppliant having 'served you [Cromwell], your sons, your court and family with a sphere and books, which cost me £30 and one and a quarter years labour'. And it was in response to this petition that the Council authorised the payment of the £50. It was presumably intended that Rowley's sphere should complement the 'globe, or sphere of the world' valued at £5 which had once belonged to Charles I and was now 'Reserved: in his Highness's service' at Hampton Court.[36]

The desire to surround Cromwell in this way with some of the grandeur normally associated with sovereignty was not simply confined to an initial burst of enthusiasm on the establishment of the Protectorate. It continued throughout the period of Oliver's rule. In January 1656 the prize goods commissioners were instructed to deliver out of the prize office to Surveyor of Works John Embree nine marble pillars and six tables for his Highness, the lord protector's use. In the same month the customs commissioners were asked to permit an organ to be brought from Exeter to London by sea for Cromwell. And in March 1656, Henry Browne, the housekeeper at Somerset House, was told to deliver up to John Embree the fountain in Somerset House garden, together with its brass figures by Fanelli, lead pipes and marble and stone cisterns, all of which were to be removed to Hampton Court for the service of his Highness. The fountain joined the other works of art which adorned the exterior of Protector Oliver's out-of-town residence.

These included statues of Venus, Adonis and Apollo and a statue of Cleopatra. It was these 'monsters which are set up as ornaments in the privy garden' that a Mrs Mary Netheway implored Cromwell to destroy, 'for whilst they stand, though you see no evil in them', she reasoned, 'yet there is much evil in it, for whilst the groves and alters of the idols remained untaken away in Jerusalem, the wrath of God continued against Israel'. Later in 1656 two suites of tapestry hangings, one of eight pieces depicting *The Story of Noah* and the other containing seven pieces, together with four more pieces telling of *The Labours of Hercules*, plus seven Turkey carpets, four feather beds, four rugs, four blankets, three bolsters and one quilt, were ordered to be sent from Scotland to Wardrobe Keeper Kinnersley.[37]

Such was the extent of the money, time and effort expended on attaching to the post of lord protector, by means of all these and many other material aids, the majesty hitherto associated only with the office of king, that the diarist, John Evelyn, was able to record on 11 February 1656 that: 'I ventured to go to Whitehall, whereof of many years I had not been, and found it very glorious and well furnished.'[38]

Notes

1. *The Government of the Commonwealth of England, Scotland and Ireland, and the Dominions thereunto belonging; as it was publickly declared at Westminster the 16th day of December, 1653. Published by His Highness the Lord Protector's special commandment.* (London, 1653).
2. *CJ*, Vol. VII, p. 404.
3. *Acts and Ordinances of the Interregnum, 1642-1660*, ed. C.H. Firth and R.S. Rait, Vol. II (London, 1911), pp. 18, 19, 168; *CSPD, 1649-50*, p. 155.
4. E.R. Turner, *The Privy Council of England in the Seventeenth and Eighteenth Centuries, 1603-1784*, Vol. I (Baltimore, 1927), pp. 313-14.
5. *CSPD*, 1653-4, p. 397.
6. Ibid., pp. 354, 355; 1654, p. 99.
7. Ibid., 1653-4, pp. 396, 397.
8. Ibid., p. 300; 1654, p. 18.
9. Ibid., 1653-4. pp. 300, 363, 419.
10. Ibid., 1654, pp. 32, 99, 180, 223, 452.
11. Ibid., p. 99.
12. Ibid., p. 373.
13. Ibid., pp. 32, 137, 138, 347.
14. Ibid., pp. 137, 139.
15. Ibid., 1655-6, pp. 28, 197.
16. Ibid., 1656-7, pp. 77, 267, 268.
17. Ibid., 1654, pp. 395, 401; 1655, p. 24; 1655-6, p. 85; 1657-8, pp. 286, 339, 558; 1658-9, p. 355.
18. W.J. Loftie, 'Whitehall: Historical and Architectural Notes', *The Portfolio*, No. 16 (April, 1895), p. 30; *CSP Ven.*, 1653-4, p. 164; *CSPD*, 1651, p. 57.

19. *Sev. Proc.*, 22-29 December 1653; 13-20 April 1654; *CSPD*, 1654, pp. 400, 457.
20. *Sev. Proc.*, 2-9 March 1654; 16-23 March 1654.
21. *Memoirs of Edmund Ludlow, 1625-1672*, ed. C.H. Firth, Vol. I (London, 1894), p. 379.
22. SP 18/203, fos.84, 85, 87.
23. Ibid., fos.84, 94.
24. Ibid., fo.89.
25. *CSPD*, 1654, pp. 260, 353, 354; 1655, p. 148.
26. Ibid., 1655, pp. 15, 127; 1657-8, p. 61; 1658-9, p. 57.
27. Ibid., 1655, p. 282; 1655-6, p. 14; 1656-7, p. 285.
28. Ibid., 1654, p. 360.
29. Ibid., 1649-50, pp. 157, 158, 276; *Acts and Ordinances of the Interregnum*, Vol. II, p. 167; 'The Inventories and Valuations of the King's Goods', ed. Oliver Millar, *Walpole Society*, 34th Vol., 1970-72; *CSPD*, 1654, p. 433.
30. 'Inventories and Valuations', pp. 55, 57, 128, 384; *CSPD*, 1654, p. 291.
31. 'Inventories and Valuations', pp. 4, 73, 74, 158, 160, 162, 290, 357, 358; SP 18/203, fo.84; H.C. Marillier, *The Tapestries at Hampton Court Palace* (HMSO, London, 1962).
32. Alan Haynes, 'The Mortlake Tapestry Factory, 1619-1703', *History Today*, Vol. XXIV, No. 1 (January, 1974); *CSPD*, 1653-4, pp. 111, 435; 1656-7, p. 385; 'Inventories and Valuations', pp. 158, 160.
33. *CSPD*, 1654, pp. 291, 447, 456, 457.
34. 'Inventories and Valuations', pp. 72, 151, 186, 190, 193, 314, 327, 328, 417, 418; *The Raphael Cartoons*, Introduction by John White (HMSO, London, 1972), p. 3; *Andrea Mantegna: The Triumph of Caesar: Hampton Court*, Notes by Anthony Blunt (HMSO, London, 1975), p. 3; SP 18/203, fo.84.
35. *CSPD*, 1654, pp. 69, 70, 291, 412, 413, 414, 433; 1655, pp. 27, 62, 113, 114.
36. Ibid., 1654, pp. 92, 93, 203, 208, 383, 402, 403, 449, 454, 457; 1655, p. 139; 'Inventories and Valuations', p. 178.
37. *CSPD*, 1655-6, pp. 23, 117, 118, 228, 315, 580; 1656-7, p. 36; John Nickolls, *Original Letters and Papers of State addressed to Oliver Cromwell*, Found among the Political Collections of Mr John Milton (London, 1743).
38. *Diary of John Evelyn*, ed. William Bray, new edn, with life of the author by Henry B. Wheatley, Vol. II (London, 1879), p. 82.

2 THE HOUSEHOLD, OR HOUSEHOLD BELOW STAIRS

Having accommodated Cromwell in a condition of regal splendour the Council felt that a corresponding adjustment should be made to the lord protector's household arrangements. In place of a commissary, Mr Fowler, and the few servants due to him as Lord General of the Army when he lived in the cockpit lodgings, Oliver was to have a household, or 'family' as the Council called it, modelled on, though not quite in the same order as, that of the late king. Six of the then 15 Council members (excluding Cromwell), Major-General John Lambert, Sir Gilbert Pickering, Viscount Lisle, Walter Strickland, Colonel Philip Jones, and Colonel Edward Montague were nominated to give some consideration to the matter, and of these Jones was eventually to become an important officer of the household, or household below stairs, while Pickering and Strickland were to be similarly placed in another department of the protectoral court.[1]

The household below stairs was one of the three principal departments that went to make up a royal court. The other two departments were the stables, over which jurisdiction was exercised by the master of the horse, and the chamber, or household above stairs, the chief officer of which was the lord chamberlain, who was also the effective head of the entire court. Heading the royal households was a lord steward who, like the lord chamberlain and the master of the horse, was invariably a great magnate and a favourite of the monarch. Under James I Lewis Stuart, duke of Lennox, held the office of lord steward of the household. William Herbert, third earl of Pembroke, was Charles I's lord steward from 1626 to 1630. The office was then left vacant for the next decade. After the Restoration James Butler, marquis and duke of Ormonde, became Charles II's lord steward. Besides their court post these men held high political office. They also had under them a treasurer, a comptroller, a cofferer and a master of the household who, collectively, in effect carried the main burden of running the royal household below stairs, which was really a rather large catering establishment.

By contrast the protectoral household below stairs was, for the greater period of its existence, run by, through Council directives, two relatively insignificant individuals, John Maidstone and Nathaniel Waterhouse. Both were known as simply his Highness's steward and they worked in double harness, although Maidstone was undoubtedly the senior of the two, until the autumn of 1657 when Cromwell's household adopted a hierarchical structure which contained elements that had existed in the households of Oliver's royal predecessors, but which had hitherto been absent in the household of the protector.

Little is known of either of the two stewards of the protectoral household, except that Waterhouse had a brother, Dr Joseph Waterhouse, who was one of the state's physicians, and that they were both representatives of the uninfluential so-called socially 'middling sort' who had also received little in the way of formal training and higher education, for whom opportunities to exercise their innate talents presented themselves during the civil war and its aftermath.[2]

As in the case of all of the officers and servants of the protector's court no record or account books belonging to the two household stewards have survived. All we are left with are a few scraps of material among the state papers of the period. According to these the first few months of the Protectorate saw Maidstone and Waterhouse employed in the task of setting up the protectoral household. The receipt of plate, provided at the state's expense for the employment of the lord Protector, into the stewards' charge, and the provision of furnishings for Whitehall, for which Maidstone presented bills totalling just over £6,000, have already been dealt with (see Chapter 1, II).[3] There was also an investigation into the claims of those who held privileges at Hampton Court, by virtue of letters patent from the late king, in preparation for the palace's new role as the protectoral country residence, carried out by Waterhouse, aided by Surveyor of Works John Embree. Later both Waterhouse and Maidstone were involved in seeing that the stables at Whitehall Palace mews were cleared for the protector's use.[4]

In the meantime Maidstone and Waterhouse would also have been carrying out their usual everyday duties as stewards, that is seeing to the efficient running of the household below stairs, which was principally responsible for the collection, storage, preparation and distribution of food and wine; the recipients being the lord protector, his court and its servants. In May 1655, for instance, the two protectoral stewards requested that the Council allow a quantity of duty free wine to be procured for the protector and the household. A year later a licence was issued for Maidstone to obtain, again, like all such commodities acquired for the protector, free of customs and excise duty, 30 tuns (7,560 wine gallons) of Spanish and 20 tuns (5,040 wine gallons) of French wines for his Highness's household. And on 20 January 1657 a licence was issued for the nominee of John Maidstone to take up a further 40 tuns (10,080 wine gallons) of Spanish and 30 tuns of French wines for his Highness's household for the ensuing year. Other consignments of wine which would also have been handled by the protectoral steward's department included 5 tuns (1,260 wine gallons) of French wines, which the commissioners for prize goods were ordered, in March 1654, to deliver to Mr Kirby his Highness's servant and, during the same period, three shipments of French wines for the protector's use, one of 40 tuns from a French nobleman, another of the same quantity, for the transport of which the *St Katherine* was given a pass to come from France into the port of London, plus four casks sent to Cromwell by Monsieur de Montigny, governor of Dieppe.[5]

The exact number of below stairs personnel in the protector's court is not known. A list of such servants appears in the Reverend John Prestwich's description of Cromwell's funebrial cortège, which is obviously based upon the order of procession drawn up before the ceremony. But these may have been a chosen number designated to represent the whole department. The ten general duties servants of the protectoral wardrobe, for instance, were represented by four of their number in Cromwell's obsequies. But it would be reasonable to assume that although the functions of the protectoral household were the same as those of its royal predecessors its staff numbered only a fraction of those employed in the vast lord steward's department of the court of, say, Charles I. Nevertheless all the more essential of the numerous sub-departments of a royal household below stairs existed in that of the lord protector, probably throughout the entire period of Oliver's rule and most certainly at the time of his death, albeit on a reduced scale.[6]

As in former times the household kitchen was the largest of these. Its business was to prepare food for all the court tables except the protector's. For Oliver there was a privy kitchen, the staff of which would have removed themselves from Whitehall to Hampton Court whenever the protector did. There was also a privy cellar and the posts of butler to his Highness and to her Highness. The establishment of the household kitchen included, in order of rank, a number of clerks (probably two, one of whom may have been a Mr Smily), three cooks and eight inferior servants. While the protector's own kitchen comprised two clerks, cooks and seven inferior servants. Authority over the kitchen would have been exercised by the clerks working turn and turn about. The clerks kept the kitchen accounts as well as ordering provisions, probably through another household office, that of caterer, whose counterpart under Charles I would have been the clerk of the market. This means that the kitchen clerks most likely had some degree of jurisdiction over the larder, the bakehouse and the pastry department, which unlike their royal equivalents appear to have possessed no clerks of their own, as well as the pantry, buttery and cellar.[7]

Three men of whom it could be reasonably supposed served either in the household kitchen or in that of the Protector were Mr Mushee, Philip Starkey and Mr Ashwell. All, at one time or another, officiated at the entertainments of foreign ambassadors, Mushee and Starkey as master cooks, for which they usually received £20 for each banquet, and Ashwell as clerk of the kitchen, for which services he was paid £10.[8]

The identity of the protector's *chef* requires no speculation. It was a Mr Hamor. This we know because Hamor is described as 'his Higness's chief cook' in a letter recommending his son, Thomas, for a post as seaman. The success of this solicitation, which was accompanied by one from the then protectoral household steward John Maidstone, was, according to its author, destined to 'gratify the greatest wish of his Highness's family'.[9]

Other sub-departments of the protectoral household below stairs included a spicery and a wine cellar, both of which possessed their own clerks, a great beer cellar with a complement of ale-brewers (every single member of a royal court had been entitled to a daily wine or beer ration and there is no reason to suppose that this situation did not obtain during the Protectorate), a slaughterhouse, a scullery and a woodyard, and a department called the hall-place. Added to these, in the autumn of 1657 when the structure of the protector's household became more closely assimilated to that of a crowned head, were the servants of officers of the household, such as the gentlemen who waited at the comptroller's table, together with inferior waiters and the comptroller's butler (the comptroller had his own kitchen at Hampton Court and probably also at Whitehall), and the waiters and inferior waiters of the cofferer. All were present at Cromwell's obsequies, their positions in the funeral procession being determined by their rank, the highest having a place near the rear, and therefore close to the bier, the more lowly being positioned near the front of the cortège and therefore further away from the bier.[10]

The household was the only department of the protectoral court for which money was specifically assigned and from which payments were made. In February 1654 a committee of four councillors, Major-General John Lambert, Colonel William Sydenham, Sir Anthony Ashley Cooper and Colonel Philip Jones, was convened to consider what revenue should be settled on the protector to cover his household and other, unspecified, expenses. The committee's judgement, delivered the following April by Jones, 'to his Highness as the advice of the Council', was that the sum of £100,000 should be charged against receipts of customs for this purpose.[11]

By settling on the ruler a set sum of money expressly for the maintenance of the household the protectoral government had broken with tradition. Hitherto the monarch had been expected to 'live of his own', that is he had to maintain not only the household and the remainder of the court, but he also had to bear the expenses of government out of his revenue. This arrangement was reintroduced at the Restoration and the concept of a true civil list, exclusive of the cost of maintaining every department of government, including the civil service, as was the case at the time of the Protectorate, did not re-emerge until the reign of George III more than a century later.

Initially payments for the upkeep of the protectoral household, or steward's department, which were based on the basic allowance of £16,000 a quarter, were made directly to John Maidstone under warrants issued by Gualter Frost, treasurer for council's contingencies, from moneys paid into the fund by the commissioners of customs for that specific purpose. The money was not issued in regular, uniform payments but in irregular amounts at varying intervals usually in response to a prior request by Maidstone. One such request made by Maidstone in July 1654, and supported in this instance by Mr Barrington, described as his Highness's auditor, concerns money to enable winter stores to be got in for the household.[12]

A payment of £5,000 had, in fact, been made to Maidstone from moneys received from the customs commissioners by the protector's own warrant, as early as 31 December 1653, fifteen days after Oliver's installation as lord protector. A further £5,000 was paid to Maidstone in March 1654. This time the money came out of £6,000 transferred to the Council's contingencies from the state's treasury in the Tower of London during the same month. The payment of these two sums was presumably meant to tide Maidstone over until the special committee of councillors, nominated to consider the protector's revenue and to confer with him as to a convenient way of signing warrants for payments for moneys, could be convened and its findings made known.[13]

The cost of running the protectoral household during the first year of Oliver's rule, that is 16 December 1653 to 15 December 1654, amounted to £70,000 and it was on this figure that Maidstone based his assessment for the likely cost of running the household during the succeeding half year, which he gave as £35,000. This estimate looked like being more than realised in September 1655 when it was decreed that Maidstone should be paid an annual sum of £80,000. But the following February this was substituted for the smaller, and original, amount of £64,000 to be paid to 'John Maidstone, Esquire, Steward of his Highness's Household . . . for the defraying of the necessary charges and expenses thereof' at the rate of '£16,000 quarterly, on the 20th day of the months of September, December, March and June'.[14]

In September 1654 an Ordinance of 21 June of the same year, by which all revenues of the Commonwealth were to be brought into a single treasury, namely the exchequer at Whitehall, so reducing the expense incurred in maintaining a multiplicity of treasuries, became effective, though not fully. Consequently payments to Mr Maidstone ceased to be made exclusively out of the receipts of customs and were instead made by the exchequer from funds which, for a time at least, emanated from a different source than hitherto.[15]

Some time later Cromwell began suffering from the same chronic lack of funds that his Stuart predecessors had. Evidence of the government's steadily waning financial condition, in addition to the cut-back in payments to Steward Maidstone to the 1654 figure, is reflected in a number of expedient acts, of robbing Peter to pay Paul, which involved the expenses of the protectoral household during 1656 and 1657. In March 1656, in a note to the admiralty commissioners, Maidstone's colleague Nathaniel Waterhouse makes mention of a £2,000 loan made to the protector out of moneys originally allocated for the use of the navy. And in September of the same year, after consultation between certain members of the Council and the admiralty commissioners, the navy treasurer was instructed to transfer £4,000 from his department's allotment out of the 'Portugal money' to John Maidstone for his Highness's household, the sum to be repaid by Maidstone out of the first money he received from the exchequer.[16]

'Portugal money' refers to the £50,000 which Portugal promised to pay England under the terms of a peace treaty agreed to in July 1654. For nearly two years the king of Portugal vacillated over the ratification of the treaty and the payment of the money, until, in June 1656, Admiral Blake positioned a number of warships off Lisbon 'and then', goes a contemporary report, 'the king, not knowing what their intentions might be, signed the peace and paid the £50,000'.[17]

December 1656 saw the admiralty commissioners in urgent need of funds to pay for naval stores which had been bought on promise of ready money, the government obviously being regarded as no longer credit-worthy by the suppliers, and so the treasury commissioners were ordered to pay £4,000 to Maidstone so that he could repay the loan made by the navy treasurer. In the meantime, in October 1656, the admiralty commissioners were instructed by the Council to lend Maidstone a further £2,000, this time out of the moneys that they had received from excise receipts, which the exchequer promised to repay at the first opportunity. A few days later the Council ordered that this sum should be paid out of the proceeds of the contract for captured Spanish plate instead of customs revenue. It was further directed 'that none of the money payable by Sir Thomas Vyner, and Mr. Backwell upon their contract be disposed to any other uses but of the navy, the army and his Highness's household'. At about the same time another £1,000 was ordered to be paid to Maidstone out of £2,000 lent to the state by Sir Thomas Vyner and Edward Backwell. Both Vyner, who was knighted by Cromwell in 1654 when he was lord mayor of London, and Backwell, a prominent London goldsmith, were major government creditors. The money had been 'procured' by William Sydenham, councillor and treasury commissioner, 'for answering some present emergencies'. Francis Hodges, the treasurer for the protector's forces in Jamaica, was the recipient of the other half of the loan. More funds for the protector's household were to come to Maidstone from the rents and arrears of rents in Scotland, which had formerly belonged to the kings of Scotland and which were now ordered to be paid into the English exchequer.[18]

In January 1657 the Council again decided to attempt to regularise the payment of moneys for the upkeep of the protector's household. In future, of the basic £16,000 a quarter allowance made to Maidstone, £4,000 would be paid at the beginning of the quarter from the exchequer and the remainder in weekly instalments of £1,000 from customs and excise revenue. The initial £4,000 emanating from the exchequer was to come out of the proceeds from a consignment of silver worth '£600,000 sterling and upwards', taken by a squadron of the Commonwealth navy after an attack on a Spanish fleet outside Cadiz the previous September, which Vyner and Backwell had contracted for.[19]

This resolve remained unfulfilled, however. In April 1657 Maidstone was complaining to the Council about the straits he was in for want of money, the current quarter's initial £4,000, for which payment had been arranged early in March, not having materialised. This was in spite of the fact that money for the protectoral household was on the priority list as it were, the treasury commissioners being ordered to pay

Maidstone out of the first money coming in on Vyner and Backwell's contract. Presumably the cash which the captured Spanish silver was supposed to realise was not flowing into the exchequer at sufficient speed and in large enough quantities to meet the demands made upon it.[20]

Precedence was still being granted to the protector's household in July 1657 when it was ordered that Maidstone should have first call on prize money coming into the exchequer. Next after Maidstone, who was to receive £5,000, came repairs to his Highness's houses, for which Mr Embree was to be paid £3,000, and then came Admiral Blake, to whom a payment of £3,815 16s. was to be made on his Highness's Privy Seal.[21]

The prize money referred to may not have been from the proceeds of the action at Cadiz in September 1656 but from the anticipated spoils of similar engagements in the future, in pursuance of Oliver's policy of severing Spain from its colonies in the West Indies or South America, so smashing the Spanish Empire. To this end a powerful Commonwealth fleet under Admiral Blake had already attacked a Spanish treasure fleet, sinking sixteen ships lying off Santa Cruz in the Canaries in April 1657. But no part of the Spaniards' valuable cargo was taken on this occasion.[22]

At the end of August the Council instruction was that Maidstone should receive £5,380 from the money earmarked for the Commonwealth's forces in Ireland, or out of the first money coming into the exchequer. But Maidstone only received £1,000 out of this particular allotment; the remainder had to be made up the following month from a further apportionment out of moneys paid into the exchequer from excise on beer and ale in the cities of London and Westminster.[23]

Adding to the difficulties involved in securing regular payments for the maintenance of the protector's household at this time was the problem of a debt, or 'an overplus of expense . . . above the ordinary allowance for the expenses of his Highness's household', amounting to nearly £12,000, which Maidstone claimed that he had incurred in his efforts 'to carry on the necessary expenses of his Highness's family' during the first three years of the Protectorate, that is from December 1653 to December 1656. It was eventually decided that the debt should be cleared out of Spanish prize money under Privy Seal warrants.[24]

Two months after Cromwell's second installation as lord protector under the revised constitution on 26 June 1657, the subject of Oliver's household expenses was again discussed by the Council. Out of these deliberations emerged the decision to allow the sum of £100,000 a year expressly for the purpose of 'defraying the expenses of his Highness's household, and for answering the disbursements for repairs to his Highness's houses', and nothing else. The cost of maintaining the protectoral palaces had been transferred from the public coffers to the protector's household expenses account in November 1655, one sum of £2,000 for repairs about his Highness's houses being allocated some little time later from the profits of a consignment of cocoa brought over from the West Indies. There was also the purchase of a parcel of cedar, which had been brought over from the Bermudas, to be used for ceiling at Hampton Court. Payment of the new allotment of £100,000 was to have been made under the Great Seal in 'weekly proportions' of £1,923 1s 6d by the exchequer out of the revenue from customs and excise, beginning 16 September 1657. But once again adverse economic circumstances supervened, the money apportioned under the original warrant having to go to the navy. A new warrant under the Great Seal was drawn up with alterations submitted by Colonel Philip Jones. The weekly payments would now take effect from 21 October 1657. As before, these would be made from customs and excise receipts. Arrears up to that date would, however, be paid out of any available revenue except that of customs and excise. But by March 1658 the exchequer was being instructed to disregard the order limiting to one source moneys to be paid for the upkeep of the protectoral household and to pay out of whatever funds were currently available. It was a time when every public treasury was being searched for money 'though', recorded Cromwell's secretary of state, John Thurloe, 'not with all that success as was desired'. The £100,000 required represented about three per cent of the government's expenditure for that year and the percentage hovered around this figure for the entire period of Oliver's rule. Charles I's court, inclusive of all departments, accounted for over 40 per cent of peacetime government, or royal (they were, of course, synonymous), expenditure.[25]

As already stated, in the autumn of 1657, the protectoral household adopted a hierarchical structure which contained elements found in the households of its royal predecessors. This could be seen as an essential part of a policy designed to assimilate further the Protectorate to the traditional form of a monarchy, that of a crowned head, in order to give the regime stability. It could also be taken as evidence that although the crown had been refused by Cromwell its acceptance by him nevertheless remained a possibility. There was certainly a resurgence of rumours to this effect at that time. Either way the result was the emergence of the posts of comptroller and cofferer of the protector's household. In the case of previous royal courts these were two of the five offices whose occupants in effect ran the household below stairs. These posts were, it will be remembered, in order of precedence, those of lord steward, treasurer, comptroller, cofferer and master of the household.

Unlike those of comptroller and cofferer the posts of lord steward, treasurer and master of the household were not revived under Oliver. The office of protectoral comptroller was given to one of Oliver's privy councillors, Colonel Philip Jones, while that of cofferer fell to John Maidstone. The post of household steward, which Maidstone had held jointly with Nathaniel Waterhouse, was abandoned. In the Reverend John Prestwich's description of the protector's funeral procession Waterhouse's office is given as 'Steward of the lands', which probably explains his involvement, in December 1657 and February 1658, in the leasing of properties in Scotland Yard, which was situated within the confines of the Palace of Whitehall, 'in trust for his Highness', for the use of the protector's life guard.[26]

The role of steward appears to have devolved upon Comptroller Jones because in December 1657 he was undertaking one of the responsibilities that had hitherto fallen to John Maidstone when he was senior of the two protectoral household stewards. On the twenty second of that month the Council instructed the excise commissioners to allow whomsoever Mr Comptroller should appoint to take up to 40 tuns (10,080 wine gallons) of sack, 40 tuns of French and Rhenish wine, and 10 tuns of vinegar, customs and excise free for his Highness's use. For this a warrant, to which was added 6 tuns (1,512 wine gallons) of Flemish wine, was made out to Colonel Philip Jones.[27]

Jones's function as comptroller of the protectoral household is exemplified by an entry in the Council order book dated 18 February 1658, from which we learn that it was through the comptroller that the estimate of £30 15s 0d for 'carpenter and bricklayer work to be done about the guards at Whitehall' was presented to the Council which then ordered 'Mr Embree, his Highness's Surveyor' to carry out the necessary repairs.[28]

Although the office of comptroller dates from late 1657 (the first extant official record of its existence is dated 22 December of that year, though the creation of the post was remarked upon in a piece of private correspondence of 8 December) Jones had been among those particularly concerned with the subject of the protectoral household and its finances throughout Oliver's rule as, to a certain extent, we have already seen. He was nominated, together with Walter Strickland, to draw up a blue-print for the protector's household and present it to a group of fellow councillors for discussion, as well as being a member of, and spokesman for, the committee of four councillors, set up in February 1654 to consider what revenue the household should have allocated to it. This was followed by his designation, together with Sir Gilbert Pickering and Strickland, to consider the best means of keeping an account of all the plate and other goods bought on the Commonwealth's account for the protector's use. The scrutiny of the bills for some of these items, which had been submitted by tradesmen and others and subscribed by Maidstone, was carried out by a committee comprising Jones, Strickland and another councillor, and payment was eventually made on the strength of the committee's recommendation as submitted by Jones. When the problem of the government's economic difficulties began to manifest itself it was Jones, in company with Pickering and two other councillors, whom the Council nominated to speak with the admiralty commissioners about a convenient sum to be paid for supplying his Higness's household out of the 'Portugal money' originally assigned to the use of the navy. Jones was also a member of the Council committee for 'settling the expenses of his Highness's household' which, on Maidstone's recommendation, attempted, early in 1657, to bring order to the haphazard way in which the financial aspects of the household had hitherto been managed by recommending that Maidstone be paid in regular instalments. This same committee also considered how Maidstone's £12,000 'overplus of expense' could 'be satisfied with most conveniencey'. And the draft patent passed by the Council on 20 October 1657 'for the payment of £100,000 per annum for his Highness's family' was subjected to amendments and alterations recommended by Colonel Jones before it was finally 'offered to his Highness as the advice of the Council'.[29]

Traditionally, but with some exceptions, the offices of comptroller and cofferer had been career posts rather than political appointments. As such they represented the middle two rungs on an officially recognised and frequently ascended ladder of promotion from master to treasurer of the royal household, the last two posts on which ladder, those of comptroller and treasurer, giving the occupants *ex officio* admission to the king's Privy Council. Also, like those of other court officials, the salaries of the comptroller and cofferer had been supplemented by 'diet', or free board, which necessitated them maintaining their own servants at court.[30]

The provision of 'diet' obviously obtained in the court of the Protectorate. (It is not known what salaries went with the more important offices in the Cromwellian court.) This is exemplified by the presence of waiters at the comptroller's and cofferer's tables, the comptroller's butler and gentlemen who waited at the comptroller's table, at the obsequies of the lord protector. But unlike their royal predecessors neither the comptrollership nor the cofferership in the protectoral court could be regarded as non-political career posts. The office of comptroller was filled, as it were, from above, by one whose political power was considerable and, being already a member of the central executive, his entrée to the ruler's Privy Council was not dependent upon him holding the post of comptroller. While Cofferer Maidstone sat as one of the members for Colchester in both of Protector Oliver's Parliaments, thus adding to the already substantial group which represented the protector's interests in those assemblies, a group that can justifiably be called the court party. Maidstone, together with Clerk of the Greencloth Abraham Barrington, was also returned as one of the members for Colchester in Protector Richard's Parliament, but the parliamentary committee of privilege and elections discovered a technical irregularity in the way in which these two men were returned and their election was declared void, their places going to two others. Another member of the household below stairs who sat in the parliaments of the Protectorate was the master of the greencloth or, as he appeared on the returns, 'Nathaniel Waterhouse of the City of Westminster, Esquire', who represented the county of Monmouth in Oliver's second Parliament and the borough of Monmouth in that of Richard.[31]

As officers of the protectoral household Jones and Maidstone had rooms at both of the protector's palaces. At Hampton Court Comptroller Jones was given the lodgings last occupied by the royal lord chamberlain. These comprised five rooms. There were two bedrooms, a large one with liver-coloured (i.e. dark reddish brown) hangings, a carpet to match and a suite of furniture, and a smaller and somewhat more sparsely furnished bedroom adjoining. The withdrawing room was hung with three tapestries, two of Hercules and one depicting the Triumph of Julius Ceasar. The dining room was furnished with two Spanish tables, one deal side table, and what were described as 'two dozen Turkey work chairs'. Adjoining the dining room was a room for the servants to eat in. The furniture in this was confined to three long forms made of deal and a large table which stood on trestles. A bedroom was also provided for the comptroller's servants who, as seems to have been the custom, all slept together. Comptroller Jones also had his own exceedingly well equipped kitchen at Hampton Court. Cofferer Maidstone occupied a three room suite comprising a bedroom, a dining room and 'The Blue Room', which was probably his withdrawing room. These lodgings had formerly belonged to the earl of Holland whose household appointments had included the captaincy of the guard and that of high steward of the queen's (Henrietta Maria's) revenues. Maidstone's manservant also had a room at the palace. What apartments Nathaniel Waterhouse had at Hampton Court is not known. Mrs Waterhouse, however, is known to have occupied what had formerly been the queen's robe room 'hung round with French green serge' with a matching bedroom suite, plus an adjoining room containing a table and a bed, presumably for her maidservant.[32]

One role that the comptroller and cofferer performed in a royal court was that of member of what was known as the board of green-cloth, so named from the green-covered table at which its business was originally transacted. This was, as it were, the administrative committee of the court which scrutinised the expenditure of the household and arranged for the purchase of supplies. Besides the comptroller and cofferer the board comprised the treasurer of the household and, for the more important meetings only, at which times he always presided, the lord steward, plus two clerks of greencloth and two clerk comptrollers.

Like the posts of comptroller and cofferer the board of greencloth was reconstituted during the last year of Protector Oliver's rule. The earliest direct official evidence of this is contained in a Council order dated 19 January 1658, by which one of the Council clerks, Henry Scobell, was assigned new accommodation over the Council chamber and the rooms which Scobell had vacated were commanded to be 'applied for the use of the Greencloth, as formerly'. Also, marching in the protector's funeral procession in order of precedence, with Cofferer Maidstone and Nathaniel Waterhouse, were Mr Barrington and Mr Ewer, described as clerk of the greencloth and clerk comptroller respectively. Abraham Barrington, it will be remembered, had been known as his Highness's auditor before the reconstitution of the board of greencloth.[33]

The board of greencloth, of which Comptroller Jones, Cofferer Maidstone and Nathaniel Waterhouse were officers, was, as the business centre of the whole court, which it had been formerly, responsible for the financial aspects of the protector's state funeral. Following the demise of Oliver, the Privy Council (now that of Protector Richard) decreed that the business of fitting out rooms in Whitehall and Somerset House with funebrial furnishings should be 'committed to his Highness's officers of the Greencloth who are to take orders that velvet, cloth and baize etc. be provided for the said several services and that the same be done with the best husbandry and advantage for the public'. That was on 7 September 1658, four days after Cromwell's death. And there exists an invoice made out to Philip Jones for £1,573, dated 9 September, for the furnishing of such materials. There was, too, 'work bespoke, provided and done' to adorn the framework of 'the standing hearse at Westminster to receive the effigy of his Highness'. The cost of this was agreed between two officers of the greencloth, Cofferer Maidstone and Nathaniel Waterhouse (described in this instance as steward), Clerk of the Greencloth Mr Barrington and 'Mr. Kinnersley, Wardrobe-Keeper-Assistant' (i.e. John Kinnersley, son of Clement Kinnersley, keeper or master of his Highness's wardrobe).[34]

The subject of mourning to be allotted to certain of those taking part in the obsequies, and others, also commanded the attention of the greencloth. There is an entry in the Privy Council register of Richard Cromwell, dated 25 September 1658, concerning Comptroller Jones's disbursements, totalling £11,062 13s 0d for 11,169 yards of mourning for distribution to those whom 'the Commissioners of the Council' for 'the consideration of matters requisite for the funeral of his late Highness . . . think fit mourning should be given'. Appended to the entry is the marginal note 'Att. Mr. Ab. Barrington'. And on 27 September we have Barrington writing from 'Whitehall, at the Greencloth' authorising 'Mr. Clerk Comptroller . . . to direct the delivering of nine yards of black cloth . . . for John Pell', the Commonwealth's envoy to Switzerland.[35]

Two Council instructions were also marked for the attention of Clerk of the Greencloth Barrington. The first refers to a warrant issued by the new protector to the lord commissioner of his Highness's treasury for the payment of £10,000, out of his Highness's exchequer, to John Maidstone, cofferer of his Highness's household, 'on account, towards the charges of the funeral of his late Highness'. The second instruction concerns 'what diet will be convenient to be kept at Somerset House for those that attend his late Highness's body after it shall be reposed there'.[36]

Something of an enigma surrounds the protectoral board of greencloth. This arises from the existence of two letters. The first, dated London, 8 December 1657, from Andrew Newport to a fellow royalist Sir Richard Leveson, reports that 'His Highness hath made lately several officers of his House, Sir Gilbert Pickering, Chamberlain, Colonel Philip Jones, Mr. Comptroller, Mr. Waterhouse, Master of the Greencloth'. The second letter, dated Westminster, 11 January 1658, from John Payne, steward to Lord Nieuport, the Dutch ambassador to the

Commonwealth, and addressed to Nieuport at the Hague, confirms, in part, what the first letter says: 'The Lord Protector hath lately bestowed three new places in his court, namely to his Steward, Captain Maidstone, a place called Master-Cofferer, to Mr. Waterhouse, Master of the Green-cloth, and to the Auditor, Substitute-Comptroller of the court [i.e. clerk of the greencloth]; which were in the time of the King'. Now while there was undoubtedly a comptroller and a cofferer of the house-hold 'in the time of the King', the same cannot be said of a master of the greencloth. In fact there would seem to be no precedent for the existence of such a post as this in previous royal courts. Furthermore, apart from in these two pieces of private correspondence, there is, as far as can be reasonably ascertained, no mention in any other extant document, private or official, of the existence of the office in the pro-tectoral court. So exactly what was meant by master of the greencloth is impossible to say. One feasible explanation is that it was a substitute title for master of the household. Certainly Waterhouse's position in the protector's funeral procession, in the account of which, it will be called to mind, Waterhouse is described as 'Steward of the lands', corresponds exactly with that occupied by the master of the household in the cortège of James I. This had been the one officer of the upper echelons of the royal household below stairs who was not a member of the board of greencloth. But Waterhouse was, it seems, a member of the protectoral board of greencloth (in the document, dated autumn 1658, which suggests this he is for some reason described as steward) together with Cofferer Maidstone. Comptroller Jones's role in relation to the board was probably similar to that of a royal lord steward. The master of the household was principally responsible for discipline among the servants of the household, a role which Charles I's board of greencloth had assumed when the mastership of the household was in abeyance after 1632. It is therefore possible that in addition to being steward of the lands Waterhouse also functioned as a master of the household, not with autonomy though but as an agent of the board of greencloth, hence the title, master of the greencloth.[37]

If this was so then Waterhouse possessed all the assistance in main-taining order within the court that had been afforded royal masters of the household. This aid came in the form of the knight marshall, a kind of aulic chief of police, and the knight marshall's men who policed the court. Under Charles I the knight marshall had been the ill-fated Sir Edmund Verney who, as his master's standard-bearer, had been slain at the battle of Edgehill.

Protector Oliver's knight marshall was a Colonel Biscoe. Under him he had a deputy, Richard Gerald, and thirteen marshall's men or 'tipstaves'. At the protector's obsequies Biscoe, carrying a black truncheon tipped at both ends with gold, rode at the head of the cortège. He was followed by his deputy, Gerald, bearing a black truncheon, only his was tipped with silver, and the marshall's men, all of whom were mounted and wearing the mourning allotted them for the occasion. The function of the knight marshall and his men on this occasion was, as a contemporary account of the protector's obsequies tells us, 'to clear the way'. This was their traditional role at the state funeral of a monarch, that of James I, the last king at the time of Cromwell's death to have received such honours, also being led by 'the Knight Marshall on horseback', whose instructions were 'to ride to and fro, and his men on foot [which numbered fifty], to make way and keep the streets clear for the proceeding'.[38]

The protectoral household below stairs remained unchanged under Richard Cromwell during whose rule Comptroller Philip Jones, as a member of the wider political court, became one of the small inner circle of trusted advisers that the new protector gathered around himself. Naturally Jones was the object of the ire of those who contrived at the fall of Richard and the Protectorate. Within a month of this happening Jones found himself facing impeachment before the reconstituted Rump Parliament for what were described as 'transcendent crimes, injuries, misdemeanours, oppressions and high breach of trust' some of which dated back to the civil war. Among these charges, which appeared under twenty headings or 'articles', was one claiming that 'few or none of those that spent their blood and time in asserting the public cause of the nation can shew the like improvement of estate', Jones 'having in 10 years brought £81 per annum to about £5,000'. This, according to the indictment, was in spite of the fact that Jones had 'no trade to increase his fortune, nor any visible lawful, honest means to accomplish the same, having the £1,000 per annum stipend as a Privy Councillor, which he did yearly expend with an over-plus in the support of himself and his family who lived at excessive high rates'.[39]

From his place in Parliament, to which he was entitled by virtue of the fact that he had been a member of the Rump at the time of its dissolution in 1653, although he had been stripped of his government posts and in August 1659 forced to deliver up the keys to his lodgings in Whitehall, Jones denied the charges laid against him and requested that 'this House would be pleased to put the business into a speedy way of examination'. A committee of MPs was convened for this purpose, a committee which Jones managed to get himself on, much to the chagrin of Bledry Morgan, the fellow countryman of Jones who had 'exhibited' the indictment. In a petition to Parliament Morgan complained that this would 'daunt and discourage the evidence' produced against the defendant. Morgan also suggested that Jones should be 'suspended from sitting in this Parliament until the whole charge against him be fully examined'. The outcome of this, Morgan's petition, and the deliberations of the parliamentary committee on the charges brought against the ex-comptroller of the protectoral household are unknown. Presumably they were resolved in Jones's favour.[40]

What is important about these charges is that although they were laid by an obscure South Walian it is very likely that they were the result of the machinations of the more violent and vengeful members of the military and republican factions. And it is unlikely that Jones lost much sleep over the affair. After all, as a man who had undoubtedly profited one way and another from the civil war and its aftermath (Cromwell is regarded as having been fairly liberal in his gifts of lands and fees) he must have become accustomed to such things. Round about 1650, for instance, he had been unsuccessfully charged with corruption, while in a condemnatory pamphlet published in 1658 he is said to have 'made hay while the sun shined, and improved his interest and revenue in land, well gotten (no question), to £3,000 per annum'.[41]

In spite of his close identification with the Cromwellian regime Jones survived the Restoration; he was, after all, not a regicide. But another legal action was brought against him, this time by the attorney-general who challenged Jones's receipts and disbursement of public money when he was a political figure. Once again the case came to nought. Another piece of good fortune at this time was the ruling in Jones's favour by the House of Lords by an order of 17 February 1661. This concerned the petition originally submitted to Protector Oliver in 1654 for the recovery, by its previous owner, of the manor of Wrinston in Glamorgan. Jones had, it seems, purchased Wrinston, together with three adjoining manors, from Colonel Horton's brigade, to whom they had been given as a reward after the battle of St Fagans out of the forfeited estates of the marquis of Worcester. Jones was not only to strengthen his title to his other estates by purchasing the reversion from the original owners but he was also able to add to them by buying, in 1664, Penmark Manor, which included what was to be his home until his death in 1674, Fonmon Castle in his native Glamorgan.[42]

Thus Jones was able to steer a course through the turbulence that followed the collapse of the Cromwellian Protectorate, surviving one attack made upon him during the period of the post-Protectorate Commonwealth and another under the restored Stuart monarchy, both regimes being openly hostile to old Cromwellians. But he was never again to be involved in national politics or to hold high government office. He did, however, remain a powerful local magnate and was the sheriff of Glamorgan in 1671.

With the demise of the Protectorate (on the eve of which it was reported that 'the Protector's servants at Whitehall remove their goods into the City, for fear of plunder') a return to the total obscurity whence they came was eventually to be the fate of Nathaniel Waterhouse and John Maidstone. Waterhouse, one time steward of the protectoral household and later master of the greencloth, continued for a while to be concerned with the affairs of the abdicated Protector Richard. He was authorised, in July 1659, to receive from the government the sum of £2,000 on behalf of Richard Cromwell, referred to by the restored Rump Parliament as the son of the late General Cromwell, in accordance with its policy of regarding as an aberration most of what had occurred between Cromwell's dissolution of the Rump by force in April 1653 and its restoration in May 1659. The £2,000 was 'advanced for the present occasions of Richard Cromwell' upon his removal from Whitehall, in accordance with a Parliamentary order of 25 May 1659.[43]

In addition to this sum it was resolved that there should be 'the settlement of a comfortable and honourable subsistence on Richard Cromwell', the Parliamentary committee that convened to consider 'how and in what manner the same may be done' having among its members the ex-lord chamberlain of the protectoral household, Sir Gilbert Pickering, and ex-Comptroller Philip Jones. But this came to nothing, as did Parliament's undertaking on 25 May 1659 to 'put in oblivion all matters concerning the said Richard Cromwell, and to take upon them his just debts' which, according to a schedule drawn up on 15 May, amounted to a total of £29,640. This figure included a debt which Richard had inherited from his father that had originally stood at £28,000 but which the young Protector had managed to reduce to £23,550. The sum 'was due unto several persons for diet, fuel, lights, household stuff, apparel and several other contingent charges thereunto relating, for provisions and furniture relating to the mews, as also for wages to officers and servants'. There was also £3,700 for the purchase of winter coats for the army paid for 'out of moneys assigned to the family'.[44]

Creditors hounded Richard for the settlement of these debts, some of which were in effect governmental, not personal, liabilities, and it was this which eventually forced the ex-protector into exile in July 1660, two months after the Restoration. As Charles II had succeeded to a Cromwell's sceptre so ex-Protector Richard had succeeded to a Stuart's exile, and one which was to last for twenty years.

One suggestion for the assuagement of Richard's difficulties was made by a committee appointed by Parliament to discover what moneys were still outstanding for mourning bought for the funeral of the late protector. The committee revealed, in August 1659, after a perusal of bills signed by Cromwell's servants and the accounts of Abraham Barrington, that £19,303 0s 11d was still owed to eleven mercers and drapers, and recommended that Nathaniel Waterhouse, described as servant to Richard Cromwell, should be authorised to sue, for the recovery of the debt, the individuals who had received the mourning.[45]

Abraham Barrington, incidentally, the now ex-clerk of the greencloth, was nominated in July 1659 as one of the auditors of imprest. But he had to quit his lodgings in Whitehall which were reassigned to Sir Anthony Ashley Cooper, a member of the new Council of State.[46]

On the very same day that the recommendation regarding the outstanding moneys due for mourning was made, the Council of State ordered that Waterhouse's house in Spring Gardens be reallocated to two members of Parliament. The following January (1660) Waterhouse's lodgings in Whitehall were also reallocated. The last we hear of Waterhouse is in May 1662 when two individuals petitioned Charles II for authority to recover from this officer of the defunct protectoral household the sum of £6,000 or £7,000 which they considered rightly belonged to the crown. This money was intended to relieve the destitute condition of the two men, which had been brought about by the sufferings of their late fathers during the civil war. The outcome of this affair, like Waterhouse's eventual fate, is not known.[47]

John Maidstone, Waterhouse's senior partner as joint protectoral steward and also sometime cofferer of the protector's household under its comptroller Philip Jones, was, as late as 9 March 1660, just over two months before the Restoration, still in a position to write from Whitehall to Admiral Montague recommending a soldier, who had fought for the late Protector Oliver in the Anglo-Dutch wars, for employment aboard some ship as a corporal. Obviously, notwithstanding the events of the previous ten months, he had retained his lodgings at Whitehall and his influence remained considerable, or at least he thought it had. After this Maidstone vanishes into the shadows. But not before bequea-

thing to posterity what must be one of the finest epitaphs to his late
master, the great Protector Oliver: 'A larger soul hath seldom dwelt in
a house of clay.'[48]

Notes

1. *CSPD*, 1652-3, p. 588; SP 25/75, pp. 177, 181.
2. Aylmer, *SS*, pp. 204, 398, 399, 419.
3. See also *CSPD*, 1654, pp. 92, 93, 403; 1655, p. 139.
4. *CSPD*, 1654, p. 203; 1655-6, p. 14.
5. Ibid., 1654, pp. 66, 83, 433, 434; 1655, pp. 191, 588; 1655-6, p. 581; 1656-7, p. 586.
6. *Burton*, II, VII; SP 18/182, fo.303; Aylmer, *KS*, pp. 472, 473.
7. *Burton*, II, VII; Aylmer, *KS*, p. 472.
8. *CSPD*, 1655, pp. 602, 605, 607; 1657-8, pp. 124, 556.
9. SP 46/117, fos.71, 72a.
10. *Burton*, II, VII.
11. *CSPD*, 1653-4, p. 381; 1654, p. 217; SP 25/75, fo.227.
12. *CSPD*, 1654, pp. 254, 290, 396, 446, 447, 449, 450, 452, 453, 457, 458; 1655, pp. 76, 100.
13. Ibid., 1653-4, pp. 381, 457; 1654, p. 444.
14. Ibid., 1654, pp. 254, 290, 396, 446, 447, 449, 450, 452, 453, 457, 458; 1655, pp. 76, 100; *Fifth Report*: Deputy Keeper of the Public Records, Appendix II, p. 250.
15. *CSPD*, 1654, p. 215.
16. SP 18/125, fo.26; *CSPD*, 1656-7, pp. 90, 98, 427.
17. Bulstrode Whitelocke, *Memorials of the English Affairs* (London, 1682), p. 577; *The Protectorate of Oliver Cromwell and the state of Europe during the early part of the Reign of Louis XIV*, ed. Robert Vaughan (London, 1838), Vol. I, pp. 144, 406, 432, Vol. II, p. 4.
18. *CSPD*, 1656-7, p. 193; SP 25/77, pp. 456, 457, 471.
19. *CSPD*, 1656-7, pp. 237, 262; *The Protectorate of Oliver Cromwell*, ed. Robert Vaughan, Vol. II, pp. 26-9, 42, 46, 76.
20. *CSPD*, 1656-7, pp. 262, 304, 381.
21. Ibid., 1657-8, p. 33.
22. *The Protectorate of Oliver Cromwell*, ed. Robert Vaughan, Vol. II, pp. 175-9.
23. *CSPD*, 1657-8, pp. 83, 94, 100.
24. SP 25/77, pp. 746, 808; *CSPD*, 1657-8, pp. 51, 128.
25. *CSPD*, 1655, p. 282; 1655-6, p. 14; 1656-7, p. 115; 1657-8, pp. 83, 113, 130, 132, 140, 149, 330, 373; SP 25/78, p. 183; *Fourth Report*: Deputy Keeper Public Records, Appendix II, p. 250; John Thurloe, *A Collection of State Papers of JT. To which is prefixed the life of Mr. Thurloe by Thomas Birch*, Vol. VII (London, 1742), p. 99; Maurice Ashley, *Financial and Commercial Policy Under the Cromwellian Protectorate*, 2nd edn (London, 1962), p. 48; Aylmer, *KS*, p. 27.
26. *Burton*, II, VII; *CSPD*, 1657-8, pp. 218, 290.
27. *CSPD*, 1657-8, pp. 225, 551.
28. SP 25/78, p. 458.
29. HMC, *Fifth Report* (1876), Appendix, p. 152; *CSPD*, 1653-4, p. 381; 1654, pp. 93, 403; 1655, p. 139; 1656-7, pp. 90. 237; 1657-8, pp. 225, 551; SP

25/75, pp. 177, 181, 227; SP 25/77, p. 746; SP 25/78, p. 246.

30. Aylmer, *KS*, pp. 21, 111, 168.
31. *Burton*, II, VII; Willis Browne, *Notita Parliamentaria*, Vol. III (London, 1750), pp. 261, 274, 288; *Members of Parliament*: Part I, *Parliaments of England, 1213-1702* (London, 1878), pp. 504, 508, 509; *CJ*, Vol. VII, pp. 617, 618.
32. SP 18/203, fos.86, 87, 89, 90, 94.
33. SP 25/78, p. 408; *Burton*, II, VII.
34. 'PCR of RC', p. 20; 'Fonmon Castle Mss. – Papers of Philip Jones', (Document D/DFF/177), Glamorgan Record Office; Sir John Prestwich, *Respublica* (London, 1787), p. 199.
35. 'PCR of RC', p. 50; *The Protectorate of Oliver Cromwell*, ed. Robert Vaughan, Vol. II, p. 341.
36. 'PCR of RC', pp. 24, 32.
37. HMC *Fifth Report*, App., p. 152; *Thurloe State Papers*, Vol. VI, p. 722; *Burton*, II, VII; Nichols, p. 1044; *Respublica*, p. 199.
38. *Burton*, II, VII; SP 18/182, fo.228; Henry Fletcher, *The Perfect Politician: or a full view of the Life and Actions (Military and Civil) of O. Cromwell*, 2nd edn (London, 1680), p. 277; Nichols, p. 1040.
39. *Articles of Impeachment of Transcendent Crimes [etc.]... committed by Col. Philip Jones... Together with Col. Philip Jones' Answer thereunto* (London, 1659).
40. *CSPD*, 1659-60, p. 75; *CJ*, Vol. VII, p. 663; *Articles of Impeachment; The Humble Petition of Bledry Morgan.*
41. *DNB*; A.G. Vesey, *Colonel Philip Jones, 1618-74*, unpublished MA thesis deposited in the University College of Wales, Bangor (1958); *A Second Narrative of the late Parliament (so called)* (London, 1658), reprinted in *The Harleian Miscellany*, Vol. III (London, 1745), p. 479.
42. *DNB*; Vesey, *Colonel Philip Jones.*
43. *Thurloe State Papers*, Vol. VII, p. 667; *CJ*, Vol. VII, p. 665; *CSPD* 1659-60, p. 576.
44. *CJ*, Vol. VII, pp. 664, 665.
45. *CSPD*, 1659-60, p. 146.
46. Ibid., pp. 11, 29.
47. Ibid., pp. 144, 300; 1661-2, p. 371.
48. Ibid., 1659-60, p. 531; W.C. Abbott, *The Writings and Speeches of Oliver Cromwell*, Vol. IV (Cambridge, Mass., 1947), p. 879.

3 THE STABLES

Unlike the household the protectoral stables had had an existence before the Protectorate was established, as a department of state. Within a year of the birth of the Commonwealth the government was giving its attention to the need for coaches and horses for the use, to and from audiences and receptions, of the representatives of foreign powers accredited to the new republic. Such facilities were, it seemed, afforded to ambassadors in other states and the new government of England was, quite naturally, anxious to observe accepted diplomatic customs and practices. The coaches and horses were meant to complement the state's barges' department which had been set up in the autumn of 1649 also, primarily, for the conveyance of ambassadors, in this instance on the main transport artery of the metropolis, the River Thames. The upshot of the matter was a Council of State instruction that £100 be expended on the purchase of a suitable coach to be upholstered with crimson velvet. Horses were also to be bought and there was to be a coachman and a postilion, both of whom would wear livery bearing the badge of the Commonwealth, which comprised two separate shields side by side, one containing the cross of St George and the other the Irish harp, and the motto God With Us. (The St Andrew's cross of Scotland was not received into the arms of the Commonwealth until April 1654.)[1]

The conveyance of plenipotentiaries, and also state dignitaries on government business, continued after what had been in effect the state's stables became the more extensive and considerably grander stables of the lord protector, which resembled those of the previous monarchs.

When representatives of foreign powers came with their entourages from their lodgings to Whitehall for an audience with the lord protector in the Banqueting House, or to Sir Abraham Williams's house in the precincts of the palace of Westminster, where they were most often entertained by members of the government, the protector's 'chief coach', which was a six-horse 'rich' affair, was furnished for the ambassadors' own use. It was driven by his Highness's coachman and postilion. Also in attendance, and running alongside the carriage when it was in motion, were the ambassadors' own footmen accompanied by ten others belonging to, and wearing the livery of, the lord protector, which

was a velvet collared coat of grey cloth welted with velvet, silver and
black silk lace. These protectoral 'pages laquies', as one contemporary
news-sheet called them, would have been part of the stables establishment as their royal predecessors had been.[2]

As has already been said the provision of 'stately equipage' by the
protectoral stables was also accorded in certain instances to state dignitaries. When some members of the Council, together with a Council
clerk, Henry Scobell, and Secretary of State John Thurloe, visited the
representatives of the Dutch government on the evening of 5 April
1654 in order to ratify a peace treaty between the United Provinces
and the Commonwealth, they travelled from Whitehall to Sir John
Trevor's house, where the ambassadors were, 'in the Lord Protector's
coaches'.[3]

Like that of its royal predecessor then, the work of the protectoral
stables department involved the acquisition and maintenance of the
ruler's horses and carriages, and the supplying of these, plus the necessary attendants, when they were required. The most regular of these
duties would have been to supply the coaches to transport the protector and his retinue from Whitehall to the protectoral country retreat
at Hampton Court and to furnish Cromwell with a suitable mount when
he went out riding in St James's and Hyde Parks. There was also haw-
king and deer-hunting, for which Oliver possessed a particular and well-
known liking. Among the many gifts sent to the protector by well-
wishers were some hawks from the prince of East Friesland and a young
deer from the president of Providence Plantation, New England.[4]

Less frequent was the provision of coaches and horses for ceremonial
or state events. These included the entertainment, 'in very magnificent
manner', of the newly proclaimed Oliver by the City of London, as had
been the custom on the accession of a new monarch. On this occasion
the protector, dressed in a musk coloured suit and coat richly embroidered with gold, travelled from Whitehall to the City boundary at
Temple Bar in the protectoral coach, which was attended by twelve
footmen 'in rich liveries', and two pages. Then, after the lord mayor
had delivered up his sword to Oliver and had it returned, the protector
transferred himself to a horse for the ride to the Grocers' Hall for the
City's reception. There were also the openings of the two Parliaments
of Oliver's Protectorate, Cromwell's investiture as lord protector, in
June 1657, when he used a 'coach of state', and Oliver's state funeral,
for which a carriage 'adorned with plumes and escutcheons and . . .
drawn by six horses covered with black velvet, each of them likewise
adorned with plumes of feathers', was furnished for the conveyance of

the protector's effigy from Somerset House, where it had lain in state, to Westminster Abbey. Coaches would also have been supplied for some of the very many dignitaries that attended these events.[5]

The two pages who, together with the footmen, are mentioned as having attended the protector at the reception given in his honour by the City of London, were probably the protectoral equivalent of what in a royal stables had been pages of honour whose attendance on the monarch was somewhat more personal than that of the footmen, their role being more like that of very junior equerries (see below). Mention of the office of page is made again in an account, by the Dutch ambassador, of the protector's death and the succession of his son.The tidings were brought by the master of the ceremonies, Sir Oliver Fleming, who travelled to the ambassador's residence in a six horse coach attended by 'some lackeys of my Lord Protector'. And at the audience itself Fleming was accompanied by 'a gentleman and a page of the Lord Protector'.[6]

Exercising jurisdiction over the protectoral stables was the master of the horse. In previous royal courts the master of the horse had been the third ranking aulic officer after the lord chamberlain and lord steward. And, like these other two senior royal court officials, he was a powerful magnate. James I's masters of the horse were Edward Somerset, earl of Worcester, and the supremely powerful but ill-fated George Villiers, first duke of Buckingham (of the second creation), who continued in the post of master of the horse after the accession of Charles I in 1625, until his assassination three years later. The reins of the office were then taken up by James, marquis of Hamilton.

Protector Oliver's master of the horse, or chief court officer out of doors as it were, was his son-in-law, John Claypole, the husband of Bettie Cromwell, Oliver's second, and some say favourite, daughter. Unlike his royal predecessors and the other high-ranking officers of the protectoral court, such as the comptroller and the lord chamberlain, Claypole was not a member of the Privy Council. He did, however, constitute one of the elements of the court party in the first and second Protectorate Parliaments, in which he sat as the member of the county of Northampton.

John Claypole's connection with the protectoral stables seems to have been established quite early on in the Protectorate. In March 1654 one news-sheet describes him as the gentleman of the horse, a post which, in royal households, ranked next to the master of the horse, the occupant being responsible specifically for the horses and little else. It could well be that at that time the office of master of the horse to the lord protector did not yet exist and that Claypole was managing the protectoral stables with a slightly less exalted title. Or it could simply be that the news-sheet had got Claypole's title wrong. When the same journal next mentions Claypole, however, in September 1654, it refers to him as master of the horse.[7]

In November 1657 the designation gentleman of the horse again crops up, Nicholas Baxter his Highness's gentleman of the horse being reported as having been to Rotterdam to pick up an Arabian horse for the lord protector. There is reason to believe that at that time the office had only recently been re-constituted, providing yet another example of the greater proliferation of court posts and the establishment of a ritualistic looking hierarchy so characteristic of previous royal courts which became evident in the protectoral court towards the end of 1657 and the beginning of 1658. Such a person would in any case have been needed to cater for Oliver's equine fancies, which included the desire to establish the Arabian breed of horse in England. This is exemplified by Baxter's trip to Rotterdam. There was also a request made to Sir Thomas Bendish, the Commonwealth's ambassador to Turkey, by the Levant Company on behalf of his Highness, to procure at Constantinople two Arabian horses of the best kind in order that England may possess this breed. A further two horses had already been acquired for the company at Aleppo, for which the ambassador was asked to furnish a licence, if this was necessary, for their despatch to England. Oliver also received gifts of horses from admirers, usually foreign princes. Six geldings had accompanied the present of hawks from the prince of East Friesland which was mentioned earlier. At about the time of the East Friesland gift some other horses sent to Cromwell by the count of Oldenberg fell prey *en route* to English privateers, and two of them were 'spoiled', even though they were travelling under a safe conduct pass. Cromwell ordered that the perpetrators of this crime should be prosecuted severely in the Admiralty Court.[8]

One office under the master of the horse which, like the mastership itself, was in existence for most of the Protectorate, was that of his Highness's avenor. The word avenor is a corrupt form of avener derived from the Latin *avenarius*, which means pertaining to oats. It comes to us through the Old French for an oat-merchant, *avenier*. In royal courts and, from late 1657 onwards in the protectoral court, this was the third ranking stables office after the master and gentleman of the horse. The occupant was head, under the master of the horse, of administration. As such he had charge of provender for the horses.

He was also, with the assistance of the clerk of the office, known as the clerk of the avery, together with the clerk of the stables, concerned with certain financial aspects of the stables, including the issue of debentures for the wages of the department's servants, whom he also swore in. In July 1655, for instance, a paper certified by Charles Rich, his Highness's avenor, was passed to William Jessop, clerk to the Council and treasurer for the protector's contingencies, for scrutiny, on the strength of which a payment of £145 3s 6d was made by the treasurer for Council's contingencies, Gualter Frost, to Rich to cover the moneys due to the coachmen, footmen and trumpeters who had attended the Spanish and other ambassadors when they had been entertained at Whitehall some time earlier. Another payment was made by Frost to Rich on 20 November 1656. This time the amount was £302 6s 6d, which represented the expenses incurred by Rich between 11 December 1655 and 4 September 1656. These covered the coaches and footmen provided for the reception/audience of the Swedish and Venetian ambassadors, for the leave-taking of the Swedish ambassador and agent, and for bringing the French ambassador to dinner, as well as conveying the Brandenburg agent to his audience with the lord protector, and carrying his Highness's commissioners to conferences with ambassadors. They also covered the furnishing of trumpets, torches, coaches and a hearse, plus innkeeper's bills for Major-General Worsley's funeral.[9]

The next rank after avenor in the upper echelons of the stables hierarchy in a royal court was that of equerry. There were sixteen of these in the stables of Charles I, the post of first equerry usually being held by the gentleman of the horse. The function of the equerries was primarily to wait in attendance on the monarch in the same way that the gentlemen of the privy chamber and such like other court servants did (see Chapter 4, II), the one difference being that the equerries would also have accompanied the king whenever he went riding or hunting.

The only extant mention of the existence of equerries during the Protectorate is in relation to Cromwell's obsequies. In the official memoranda concerning these it was ordered that in the funeral procession there should be four standards, a guidon and six banners representing England, Wales, Scotland and Ireland, the Union and Cromwell himself. These were to be borne by persons of 'honour and quality', and in the case of the protector's own 'great' banner, by a Cromwell. Attending each of these standards and banners, and, of course, the guidon, were to be fifers, drummers and trumpeters, together with a horse covered in black cloth, adorned and garnished with plumes and escutcheons of the same heraldic design as the standard, banner or guidon it accompanied. Each horse was to be led by, in the case of the four standards, an equerry in close mourning, with a groom in a cloak in attendance, and in the case of the guidon and the six banners (the horse accompanying the great banner of Cromwell was also the chief horse of mourning), two equerries and a groom. An unspecified number of equerries and grooms were also to attend the horse of honour. All this is confirmed as having been what actually took place in the Reverend Prestwich's description of Cromwell's funeral cortège.[10]

Even so there may not have been equerries as such in the court of Oliver Cromwell. The description of equerry may have been a purely temporary one given to a group of individuals for the purposes of the protectoral exequies only, in order that the precedent set by King James I's funeral, on which that of Protector Oliver was based, should be as far as possible adhered to.

The remainder of the protectoral stables staff included a keeper of the Hampton Court stables, William Bedborough, and a keeper of the Whitehall mews, Daniel Wynn and, as mentioned earlier, pages, footmen and the protector's coachman and postilion. In 'a list of the persons of Their Highness's private family' designated to receive mourning for the funeral of Protector Oliver there are a coachman, John Rider, his assistant, William Wotton and a postilion, together with four footmen, Thomas Wright, Florence Makmayhaun, Henry Spence and Robert Rudge, plus four grooms at Whitehall, Andrew Fielder, William Noyse, William Kimber and Robert Whitehorne, and a further three grooms at Hampton Court, William Farwell and two others whose Christian names were Leonard and William and whose surnames were probably Farwell too. These particular stables personnel, together with a number of others on the same list, viz. six 'gentlemen', one of whom was Richard Cromwell's secretary, Mr Rosin, five 'gentlewomen', four 'maiden servants', two 'other servants', one being 'groom of the chambers', three 'others at Hursley [Richard's country home which belonged to his father-in-law] about the children' who included 'a nursery maid', a porter, two chairmen, a tailor and a shoemaker, were most likely members of the young protector's and his protectress, Dorothy's, personal household before Richard's accession when he was, as it were, crown prince. The use of such a royal style is not, incidentally, as whimsical as it at first seems. A letter of 7 September 1657 refers to the fact that 'Prince Richard broke his thigh-bone while hunting in the New Forest, that fatal place to the sons of our princes, but he is recovering'. And after Richard had succeeded to his father's throne a member of Parliament referred to him as 'Richard the Fourth'.[11]

As protectoral master of the horse John Claypole qualified for accommodation both at Hampton Court and Whitehall. At Hampton Court his lodgings were those formerly occupied by King Charles I's master of the horse, the duke of Hamilton. These comprised one bedchamber with a dressing room, a withdrawing room, the furniture of which was upholstered in yellow cloth and cased with red baize, and adjoining the withdrawing room a small closet hung with liver-coloured serge. From this closet it was possible to gain entrance to what was probably the family dining room, adjoined to which was a second dining room rather more sumptuously equipped than the first, being, among other things, furnished with six tapestry hangings. Another room with no specified function adjoined the second dining room, and to this was attached a bedroom for the servants who presumably all slept together because there was only one bed. Also included in this suite of rooms were what were defined as 'a closet in the late King's private oratory' and 'a little room adjoining'. It was most likely in these apartments that Bettie Claypole breathed her last, for it was at Hampton Court on 6 August 1658 that she died. In another part of the building John Claypole's man had his own well-appointed chamber, while part of the armoury, 'hanged round with striped stuff', and a room described as 'formerly the Bishop of Canterbury's', hung with a total of fifteen pieces of tapestry and containing furniture covered in sky-coloured taffeta, some of which was 'embroidered with silver and gold after the Indian fashion', were given over to being nurseries for the Claypoles' children.[12]

Duties of a ceremonial nature were always an important part of the office of master of the horse to a king and in this respect the post under the Protectorate was substantially the same. At the first audience given by Oliver to the representatives of the United Provinces, Claypole was a part of the group, which also included members of the Council and the secretary of state, that accompanied the protector as he entered, through a side or 'privy' door, the Banqueting House at Whitehall, where the reception took place. These Commonwealth grandees and state and court functionaries stood either side of the protector as the ambassadors approached with great deference and discoursed with the symbol of England's growing might, who stood in a railed-off carpeted section of the hall beside 'a chair of state very rich'. And at the ceremonial opening of Oliver's first Parliament in September 1654 the lord protector's coach was followed immediately by Master of the Horse

Claypole on horseback leading the horse of state equipped 'with a rich saddle embroidered with gold and pearl'. The second investiture of Oliver as lord protector in June 1657 which, like the first in December 1653, took place at the scene of Charles I's trial, Westminster Hall, saw the protectoral master of the horse standing with Richard Cromwell and the Privy Council, close to the protector's throne. In the procession from Westminster Hall to the palace of Whitehall following the installation ceremony Claypole 'led the horse of honour in rich comparisons'. This duty he performed again at the protector's funeral, having a place in the cortège which marked the dignity of his office, that is at the rear and close to the 'corpse' or effigy, where he led the horse of honour 'ornamented in very rich trappings, embroidered on crimson velvet, and adorned with white, red and yellow plumes'.[13]

The footmen also had a special part to play in Cromwell's obsequies. When, on the night of 20 September 1658, the corpse of the protector was removed, 'in a private manner, being attended by his own servants', from Whitehall to Somerset House for the lying in state, the footmen acted as torch-bearers to light the way. The form would have been that followed at the like event for James I when the royal footmen 'ran all the way about the body, not ranked, but in such manner as they do when the King removes'. On the occasion of Oliver's state funeral the footmen accompanied the bearers of the bannerols, depicting Cromwell's family devices, who walked either side of the hearse. One of the bannerol bearers at the funeral of James I was, incidentally, Protector Oliver's uncle and godfather, Sir Oliver Cromwell. The footmen performed the same function on that occasion as they did for the exequies of Cromwell. Other stables personnel known to have attended Protector Oliver's state funeral were the clerks of the avery and stables and the keeper of the mews, all of whom were, in the cortège, positioned immediately behind the assistant to the keeper of the wardrobe.[14]

John Claypole continued to occupy the office of master of the horse after the accession of the new protector. 'During the short reign of his brother-in-law, Richard', writes Mark Noble of Claypole in his *Memoirs of the Protectoral House of Cromwell*, 'he retained all his places at court and carried the sword of state when his Highness went to open his Parliament [on 27 January 1659]'.[15]

Within three months of Protector Richard opening his first, and last, Parliament the Protectorate was no more and consequently neither was the post of master of the horse. During the interim period between the abdication of Richard Cromwell and the restoration of the Stuart dynasty, responsibility for the stables, which became, in effect, the state's stables once again, devolved upon Charles Rich who had been his Highness's avenor, but who was now known as the keeper of the state coaches. The ex-protectoral stables reverted to the exclusive conveyance of state and foreign dignitaries, having for the past five years or so combined this with attendance on the lord protector. In October 1659, for instance, Rich was paid a total of £179 15s 0d to cover his own attendance and the expenses incurred in providing coaches for the conveyance of foreign ambassadors. Rich also received £29 10s 0d in April 1660 to cover the transportation of the Portuguese ambassador to his leave-taking audience with the Council of State.[16]

Less than four years after the second investiture of Cromwell as lord protector, and a little under two and a half years after the protector's funeral, London was witnessing a ceremony of a different kind, the crowning of the restored Stuart, Charles II. At the rear of the coronation procession close to the monarch, rode George Monck, sometime General commanding the Commonwealth forces in Scotland and a steadfast supporter of Protector Oliver and the Cromwell dynasty in the person of Oliver's son, Richard, and also a participator in the obsequies of the elder protector, now his Grace the duke of Albermarle and master of the horse to the king. *Tempora Mutantur, et Nos Mutamur in Illis* (Times change, and we change with them). One of Monck's first acts in this new capacity was to discharge, for fraudulent dealings, William Bedborough, the stable keeper of Hampton Court, who had been appointed by Cromwell.[17]

But what of John Claypole, sometime master of the horse to the two protectors, who were also his father-in-law and brother-in-law? 'As he had never, during the whole of his relations holding the helm, done any action that could even inconvenience an individual, at the Restoration he found not an enemy, but in everyone a friend. And he had the humanity, as well as courage, to give an asylum to his mother-in-law, the relict of the Protector Oliver, until the time of her death.' So wrote Mark Noble.[18]

Notes

1. *CSPD*, 1649-50, p. 509; 1650, pp. 46, 64, 481, 484.
2. *Perf. Diurn.*, 27 February-6March 1654; *Sev. Proc.*, 2-9 March 1654; 23-30 March 1654; 4-11 May 1654; Sir William Dugdale, *A Short View of the Late Troubles in England* (Oxford, 1681), pp. 418, 423.
3. *Perf. Diurn.*, 3-10 April 1654.
4. *CSPD*, 1654, p. 443; 1655, pp. 553, 556, 567.

5. *Perf. Diurn.*, 6-13 February 1654; *Merc. Pol.*, 25 June-2 July 1657; 18-25 November 1658.
6. *Thurloe State Papers*, Vol. VII, p. 382.
7. *Sev. Proc.*, 2-9 March 1654; 31 August-7 September 1654.
8. *CSPD*, 1654, p. 443; 1655, p. 23; 1657-8, pp. 96, 453.
9. Ibid., 1655, pp. 257, 606; 1655-6, pp. 308, 309; 1656-7, pp. 116, 590.
10. SP 18/183, fos.274, 275, 276, 277; *Burton*, II, VII.
11. *CSPD*, 1658-9, p. 125; 1660-61, p. 37; SP 18/182, fo.226; SP 18/156, fo.134; *Burton*, Vol. III, p. 65.
12. SP 18/203, fos.86, 87, 91.
13. *Sev. Proc.*, 2-9 March 1654; 31 August-7 September 1654; *Merc. Pol.*, 25 June-2 July 1657; *Burton*, II, VII; SP 18/203, fo.277; Dugdale, p. 423.
14. *Merc. Pol.*, 16-23 September 1658; 'PCR of RC', p. 33; *Burton*, II, VII; Nichols, pp. 1038, 1046.
15. Mark Noble, *Memoirs of the Protectoral House of Cromwell*, Vol. II (Birmingham, 1787), p. 378.
16. *CSPD*, 1658-9, p. 383; 1659-60, pp. 256, 588, 599.
17. Ibid., 1660-61, p. 37.
18. Noble, Vol. II, p. 378.

4 THE CHAMBER, OR HOUSEHOLD ABOVE STAIRS

I

We now come to the third (though not, of course, in order of precedence) court department, the chamber, or household above stairs. Just
as the household, with its out of sight staff, looked after the below
stairs activities of the court, which were mainly to do with provision-
ment, so the chamber, with its staff of more personal servants, many of
whom were calculated to give lustre to the ruler's office, encompassed
responsibility for the above stairs aulic arrangements. It has been said
that generally speaking the household provided most of the necessities
of life, while the chamber regulated the routine and ceremony of a
court.[1]

The chief officer of the chamber was the lord chamberlain of the
household, who was also the effective head of the entire court. This
post, which, like most of the higher royal court offices, carried with it
ex officio membership of the king's Privy Council, had usually been
held by an earl. Two men who occupied the position in the reign of
Charles I were Philip Herbert, fourth earl of Pembroke, and Robert
Devereux, third earl of Essex. Of Pembroke, who was lord chamberlain
from 1626 till 1641, it was said 'he was intollerable, choleric and
offensive, and did not refrain, whilst he was Lord Chamberlain, to
break many wiser heads than his own'. Essex, the son of Elizabeth's
favourite executed for high treason in 1601, received the lord chamberlain's staff of office in July 1641 in pursuance of Charles's attempts to
conciliate the Puritans. He was, however, dismissed in 1642 for refusing
to attend the king at York. Both Pembroke and Essex fought against
their former master in the civil war, in the early part of which Essex led
the main Parliamentary field army.[2]

The duties of royal lords chamberlain involved, in the main, the
administration of the chamber and the supervision of its servants, who
will be enumerated later, the distribution of lodgings, the initiation of
warrants for building work and structural alterations carried out within
the court, and, at times of great ceremonial, the entertainment of guests,
including the representatives of foreign governments, the provision of
the right sort and number of servants, such as flunkeys and musicians,
and the placing of the guard. Lords chamberlain were not, however,
required to concern themselves with the detailed administrative work of

their office. They could consign this to their vice-chamberlains, one of whom under Charles I had been Lord Goring (later first earl of Norwich) assisted by the lord chamberlain's secretary, leaving them free to concentrate on the social and ceremonial aspects of their office.

The post of protectoral lord chamberlain of the household was, like the office of comptroller of the protector's household, held by a Commonwealth grandee, in this case Sir Gilbert Pickering. Pickering 'being so finical, spruce and like an old courtier, is made Lord Chamberlain of the Protector's household or court', so an anti-government tract[3] printed in 1658, or what the pamphlet calls 'the fifth year of England's slavery under its new monarchy' tells us, thus illustrating, albeit caustically, that the man was obviously well suited to hold this particular office, the one which possessed the greatest honour and dignity of any at court. And as an already respected member of the government Pickering's political power would have been as great as that of any magnate and royal favourite of former times, even though his social rank may have been somewhat less exalted.

According to a letter, which has already been remarked upon (see Chapter 2), between Andrew Newport and his fellow royalist Sir Richard Leveson, the institution of the office of protectoral lord chamberlain occurred at the same time as the establishment of the posts of comptroller, cofferer and master of the greencloth. 'His Highness hath made lately several officers of his House', reports the letter, which is dated London, 8 December 1657, 'Sir Gilbert Pickering, Chamberlain, Colonel Philip Jones, Mr. Comptroller, Mr. Waterhouse, Master of the Greencloth.' But a semi-official news-letter dated Westminster, 11 August 1655 states quite categorically that 'Friday last [10 August] his Highness made Sir Gilbert Pickering Lord Chamberlain'. Also on 10 August 1655 a petition addressed to the protector was referred to two councillors who were named in two separate instances as John Lambert and the lord chamberlain. Therefore it would appear that the post of protectoral lord chamberlain had existed over two years before Newport's letter. It could well be that the office was established in anticipation of the acceptance by Oliver of a crown and then shelved. The above-mentioned news-letter also refers to the fact that 'a petition is carrying on in several places here for his Highness to assume the title of Emperor or King'. While an earlier news-letter, dated 9 June 1655, states that 'the altering of his [the protector's] title is much spoken of'. Certainly the arms 'to which his Highness gave his approbation' on 6 March 1655 for inclusion on the Great Seal of the Commonwealth, and later used as a badge to be worn by the protectoral watermen (and described in full further on in this chapter), constitute so regal a device as to lend support to the expectation that Cromwell was about to accept the crown. In any event the term lord chamberlain does not seem to have been used again until the period of the Newport correspondence, at which time, as we have seen, purposeful steps were being taken to assimilate further the Protectorate to a monarchy.[4]

A description of the investiture of Cromwell as lord protector in June 1657 by Edmund Prestwich, who was 'an eye and ear witness to all that passed on this glorious occasion', lists among those present 'Chamberlain of his Highness's Household, Gilbert, Lord Pickering' and 'Comptroller of his Highness's Household, Philip, Lord Jones'. But in his account of Cromwell's second inauguration, which must have been written up some time after the event, Prestwich had anticipated Pickering's and Jones's elevation to the Cromwellian Upper House by six months and it must therefore be assumed that he made a similar error in relation to their household offices.[5]

Perhaps the first known instance of what could be interpreted as Pickering functioning as the protectoral lord chamberlain is contained in a Privy Council instruction, dated 9 March 1658, which authorises the lord chamberlain and Mr Comptroller to give orders for the erection of a guard-house, and the appointment of a guard at the door leading out of the orchard at Whitehall into Channel Row, in order to improve the palace's security. This could have been in belated response to the discovery, a year before, of trains of gunpowder and other combustibles to burn it in the chapel at Whitehall, being part of what the official news-sheet *Mercurius Politicus* described as a 'traiterous design for the destruction of his Highness's person'. Something else that could be taken as an instance of Pickering acting in the capacity of lord chamberlain is his involvement, in July 1658, together with the household comptroller, in the question of an abatement in the allowance of Messrs Kinnersley, Ashwell and Mushee, who had acted as steward, clerk of the kitchen and master cook, respectively, at a reception given for the representatives of Louis XIV of France. And in the previous month the lord protector had given his approval to a Privy Council instruction ordering his lord chamberlain to arrange for Somerset House to be fitted out for the entertainment of ambassadors and to see to it that the people who lodged there were accommodated elsewhere by 29 September. By that date, however, Cromwell was dead and Somerset House was where the lying in state was taking place.[6]

It is the death of Cromwell, or rather the events immediately resulting from it, that provides us with the only examples of the protectoral lord chamberlain carrying out the public and ceremonial duties of his office, apart, that is, from the state opening of Protector Richard Cromwell's first and only Parliament.

The report of *Mercurius Politicus* for 3 September 1658 tells us that:

> This night, about eight o'clock, the Lord Chamberlain of his Highness's household, came from the Council to his Highness's lodgings; and notice being given to his Highness, that the Lord Chamberlain was without with a message from the Council, his Lordship was called in, and the subject of the message was to acquaint his Highness that the Council intended forthwith to wait upon his Highness. The Lord Chamberlain being returned, after a little space, the Noble Lords of the Council, with the Lord President in the head of them, came to the said lodgings, and being admitted to his Highness's presence the Lord President made a speech to deliver the sense of the Council, which was to this effect: In the first place, to let his Highness know how deeply the Council is affected with grief for the death of his princely father, and that they could not but very much condole with his Highness for so great a loss: and withal to acquaint him that his late Highness, his dear father, having in his life-time according to the humble petition and advice, declared and appointed him to succeed him in the government of these nations, the Council had taken the matter into consideration, and thereupon resolved accordingly.

The ensuing proclamation of Richard as lord protector was read the next day at Whitehall, Temple Bar, Cheapside, the end of Wood Street and the Royal Exchange, by Norroy, King of Arms, who was accompanied by 'the Heralds, or Officers at Arms in their formalities [i.e. tabards, etc.]', a number of trumpeters, three serjeants-at-arms and some horse and foot soldiers and also state and military dignitaries, his Highness's life guard and the gentlemen of the household. The document was undersigned by members of the Privy Council, including Lord Chamberlain Pickering, Comptroller of the Household Jones, Captain of the Household Guard Walter Strickland, plus the protectoral master of the ceremonies and a number of other dignitaries. Subjoined were the words 'God Save his Highness Richard, Lord Protector'.[7]

At Protector Oliver's state funeral on 23 November 1658 Pickering's position in the cortège was, like that of the lord chamberlain at the obsequies of King James I, directly in front of the bier. Carrying his staff of office and dressed in close mourning, 'his train borne', Pickering was immediately preceded by the kings of arms and heralds.[8]

The extent of Pickering's involvement in the actual organisation of Cromwell's obsequies was, however, considerably less than that of a royal lord chamberlain in the organisation of the funeral of a king. But then there was no protectoral vice-chamberlain and chamber secretariat upon which the bulk of the work could devolve as in royal courts. The staff of Pickering as lord chamberlain was, as far as is known, confined to a clerk or secretary, a post said to have been held for a time by a cousin of Pickering, the poet John Dryden (see Chapter 7).

Responsibility for the ceremonial and other arrangements of Oliver's funeral was in fact given to a committee of six formed by members of the Privy Council (now, of course, that of Protector Richard), namely the lord chamberlain, Mr Comptroller, Lord Disbrowe, Viscount Lisle, Lord Montague and Secretary of State John Thurloe, who had become a privy councillor in his own right in July 1657. The terms of reference of this committee, for which the quorum was two, were 'to consider what is fit to be done about the funeral and interment of the body of the late Lord Protector . . . and to report to the Council'.[9]

After consulting the master of the protectoral wardrobe, Clement Kinnersley, who had been instructed 'to find out some precedent by which they [the members of the committee] might govern themselves in this affair', Pickering reported to the Council on behalf of the committee in respect of 'the opinion of the heralds as touching the mourning and going in gowns', while Comptroller of the Household Philip Jones acted as spokesman on the subjects of funebrial furnishings for Whitehall and the scene of the lying in state, Somerset House, which was referred back to Kinnersley for action, and 'preparations for removing his Highness's body from Whitehall to Somerset House'. All of this would normally have come under the immediate jurisdiction of the lord chamberlain and his department.[10]

Unlike Philip Jones, Pickering threw in his lot with the military junta when the Protectorate collapsed, and like Jones he took his seat in the restored Rump of the Long Parliament. Similar politic action at the Restoration was, however, impossible because Pickering had been one of the commissioners of the High Court of Justice which tried Charles I. For some reason though he only sat for two days and neither gave judgement against the king nor signed his death warrant. For this omission he escaped the severer punishments meted out to most of those of the king's judges who were still alive at the Restoration. But the fact that he had sat in judgement upon the king at all meant that he was excepted from the general pardon and consequently, so Mark Noble tells us, he was 'subject to the pains and forfeitures as should be inflicted by an act made for that purpose', before dying in 1668.[11]

II

The magnificent public ceremony that was the lord protector's state funeral was preceded by one two months earlier in which more or less only members of the protectoral court were involved. *Mercurius Politicus* reports the event thus:

> This night, September 20, the corps of his Highness was removed hence in a private manner, being attended only by his own servants, viz. The Lord Chamberlain and the Comptroller of his Highness's household, the Gentlemen of his Bed Chamber, the Gentlemen of the Household, the Gentlemen of the Life Guard, the guard of Halberdiers, and many other officers and servants of his Highness. Two Heralds or Officers of Arms went next before the body, which being placed in a hearse drawn by six horses, was conveyed to Somerset House, where it rests for some days more private, but afterwards will be exposed in state to public view.*

This event was also reported by the Venetian resident in England, Francesco Giavarina, in a letter to his masters, the Doge and the Senate, in Venice:

> Somerset House has been prepared for the lying in state of the late Protector, where he will remain until the day of the funeral, which is not yet fixed. The body was brought from Whitehall privately the other night accompanied only by his Highness's servants. There it lies in extraordinary pomp.[13]

*The actual corpse was not exposed to public view. This remained in the coffin which was 'covered without with purple velvet, the handles, nails and all other ironwork about it . . . richly hatched with gold' and was placed 'in a frame of board, like a large bed'.[12] Upon this was placed a life-size effigy of the lord protector and it was onto and around this representation of the dead Cromwell that all the symbolism and ceremony of the lying in state and the state funeral was attached and revolved. The use of a waxen image to represent the remains of a deceased monarch at his own obsequies had been the custom in England since about the time of Henry III in the thirteenth century. Previous to that the body of a dead sovereign had been carried dressed in royal robes, uncoffined, upon a bier, presumably as positive evidence that the king had actually died.

It had already been decided 'that such as his Highness's servants as shall be thought convenient be removed from Whitehall to Somerset House to attend the corps. That particular rooms in mourning be prepared at Somerset House for this purpose', and that 'diet' should 'be kept at Somerset House for those that attend his late Highness's body after it shall be reposed there'.[14]

All those protectoral servants enumerated in the *Mercurius Politicus* account of the small private ceremony that marked the removal of Cromwell's corpse from Whitehall to Somerset House, except the comptroller of his Highness's household, could be described as members of the protector's chamber or household above stairs.

First there are the gentlemen of the bedchamber. The staff of a royal bedchamber had included gentlemen and grooms, there being attached to the bedchamber of Charles I between two and four gentlemen and between five and seven grooms. The office of gentleman of the bedchamber in a royal court, which was usually held by a peer, carried with it considerable prestige. The post of groom was also occupied by men of high birth and, like that of the more elevated gentleman, it afforded the occupant unrestricted access to the monarch. The principal duties of both groups were to dress the monarch and to see to his immediate personal needs. This involved dressing the king at the beginning of the day in accordance with an elaborately prescribed, and singularly tedious, ritual, and to serve him on bended knee when he dined in public – a practice which, seemingly, lasted well into the eighteenth century.

That Oliver would have submitted himself to such a regime is extremely improbable. What is more likely is that the protector's bedchamber staff merely performed the normal functions expected of a body-servant or valet. Their ceremonial duties were, in all probability, confined to introducing men into the protector's presence in his closet, as was the case sixty years later during the reign of George I who had a strong aversion to formal etiquette, although the more ceremonious practices were still being observed at the Prince of Wales's court. The functions of the protectoral gentlemen of the bedchamber were therefore really those of a royal groom of the bedchamber, the personal service of a gentleman of a royal bedchamber being limited to the formal dressing ceremony in the morning and at meals only when the monarch dined in public. Certainly, in spite of their title being frequently given as that of gentlemen of the bedchamber, the position of two of them, Charles Harvey and a Mr Underwood, in the protector's funeral procession corresponds with that occupied by the grooms of the bedchamber in the cortège of James I. Also there is in existence a twenty-two page tract, published in June 1659, attributed to Charles Harvey, the title of which concludes with the words *Written by one that was then Groom of his Bedchamber*. The pamphlet, the full title of which is *A Collection of Several Passages concerning his late Highnesse Oliver Cromwell, In the time of his Sickness; wherein Is Related many of his Expressions upon his Death-Bed. Together with his Prayer within two or three dayes before his death. Written by one that was then Groom of his Bedchamber*, is, in effect, a panegyric upon the late lord protector and makes no mention of the duties expected of a groom of the protectoral bedchamber. As to the private Cromwell that such a man must have known so well, Harvey concerns himself solely with the pious and not at all with the practical aspects of this. He tells of the protector's 'readiness to promote by his authority and influence good works . . . as well as by his own example, for which the souls of thousands have blessed him, even beyond the seas. And this . . . not only in a public way, but also in his family, and especially in his secret retirements. And indeed prayer (as one calls it) was his daily exercise, which he never neglected, notwithstanding all his weighty affairs, yea, the more weighty and urgent they were, the more he buckled to it.'[15]

There were in all four gentlemen of the bedchamber to the lord protector. Their appointment was announced in that semi-official newssheet, dated 11 August 1655, which also reported the designation of a protectoral lord chamberlain. 'Friday last [i.e. 10 August]', goes the message, 'his Highness made Sir Gilbert Pickering Lord Chamberlain and appointed Sir Thomas Billingsley, Mr Rolt, Mr Barrington and Mr Harvey to be Gentlemen of his Bedchamber.'[16]

Sometime between August 1655 and August 1658 Sir Thomas Billingsley was replaced by Mr Underwood. And it was Underwood, together with Charles Harvey, who were in constant attendance on their master during his last hours. Because of this Underwood was despatched to Ireland to give Lord Deputy Henry Cromwell a first hand report of his father's final illness. Underwood carried with him a letter, dated 7 September 1658, from Secretary of State John Thurloe advising Henry Cromwell, who was, of course, already cognisant of his father's death, that: 'This bearer, Mr. Underwood, is a very sober gentleman. [He] was of the bedchamber to his late Highness and attended him in all his sickness, and can give your excellency a full account of all that past on this sad occasion. To which purpose his Highness [Protector Richard] hath sent him over to your excellency, that you might fully understand the particulars of God's dealings with his Highness, your father, through his whole visitation.' The letter goes on: 'It hath pleased God hitherto to give his Highness, your brother a very easy and peaceable entrance upon his government. There is not a dog that wags his tongue so great a calm are we in. The Lord continue it and give him [Richard] a just and understanding heart, that he may know how to go out and in before this great people, whose peace and liberty he is entrusted with.' Thurloe ends with a foreboding: 'But I must needs acquaint your excellency that there are some secret murmurings in the army, because his Highness was not general of the army as his father was, and would look upon him and the army as divided . . . But I am not able to say what this will come to.' Underwood stayed only a few days in Dublin before returning to London aboard the *Basing* in company with Dr Joseph Waterhouse, brother of Nathaniel, by way of Beaumaris.[17]

But it is unlikely that Underwood returned in time to assist with the preparation of the protector's effigy for its lying in state. For this the likeness of his Highness was dressed in shirt, neckband and cuffs of fine linen richly decorated with lace, a doublet and breeches, 'of the Spanish fashion', made of uncut grey velvet, with silk stockings and matching shoestrings and garters, fastened with gold lace. The shoes were of black Spanish leather and had gold buttons. On top of this initial apparel there was placed a surcoat of purple velvet which came down to the knee and was secured with gold lace. Over this there was a royal robe of purple velvet, four yards long and lined with ermine tied with gold lace and having rich cords and bosses of purple and gold. What was described as 'a fair gilt sword' was girt about the figure. To complete the ensemble, in which the funebrial effigy of this one-time Puritan squire was attired, there was 'a rich crown . . . beset with many colours', together with an orb and sceptre.[18]

Gentlemen of the household, or his Highness's gentlemen (they could also be described as gentlemen of the household in waiting) were, it would appear, generic terms intended to cover various above stairs functionaries. Some of these can be seen performing the role of royal gentlemen of the privy chamber. 'The duties of the Gentlemen of the Privy Chamber were', we are informed, 'of a particularly honourable and confidential nature; and that these Gentlemen were very far from being only nominal characters. Strict personal attendance was required in the Privy Chamber to execute the commands of their Sovereigns, to convey their directions to the Ministers and State officers and others.' The duties of royal gentlemen of the privy chamber also involved them 'in accompanying their Princes either in their private interviews, or public progresses through their Dominions. But more especially were they regarded for that high distinction of bearing the King's commands on the faith and credentials of their appointment, without a written or sealed commission. They likewise attended all public ceremonies and solemnities of the Crown and State, coronations, public entries of foreign ambassadors and royal Funerals.'[19]

An example of some of his Highness's gentlemen acting as gentlemen of the privy chamber is provided by the following report, dated 20 April 1654, from the news-sheet *Several Proceedings of State Affairs:*

A declaration and petition from the Corporation of Guildford was (on Tuesday last, April 18, in the afternoon) brought by the Mayor and four of the Aldermen, the Steward and the Bailiff of that town to Whitehall, where they shewed it to one of the Lord Protector's gentlemen, and intreated his assistance to bring them where they might present it to his Highness; which gentlemen courteously brought them to the gallery where the chair is fixed, and desired them to have a little patience till his Highness was risen from Council and they should then have admittance to him. They observed his direction and, after some time of necessary waiting, they were called into the next chamber, which is between the two galleries, and there received by another gentleman of very great and exceeding becoming civility who conducted them where his Highness stood, and some of his heroes, and divers other gentlemen of quality attending on him, in an handsome and somewhat awful posture fairly pointing towards that which of necessity, for the honour of the English nation, must be shewed to him who is their Protector. And Mr. Mayor of Guildford, and his company, by what they then observed, and by what some of them had observed heretofore, do declare and say that they are confident that his Highness is pleased with those phylacteries and fringes of state (if pleased with them at all) because he must. And that his Highness knows that there is no more in harmless ceremonies of state only than common and weak eyes discern, or have any wise cause to be offended at.

Previously, apart from the monarch's personal servants, officers of state and men of 'quality', no one would have had direct access to the ruler in this way.

As to the attendance of his Highness's gentlemen at public and ceremonial events, apropos one of the functions of the royal gentlemen of the privy chamber, there is ample evidence. When, on 17 September 1656, Oliver went to Westminster Abbey, prior to the opening of the second Protectorate Parliament, he was attended by, among others, the

gentlemen of the household. 'It was', we are again informed, 'one of the
most usual duties of the Gentlemen of the Privy Chamber to attend the
King in his going to chapel, or any other public place, upon all occasions
of devotions, solemnities, or recreation, and there to have convenient
places appointed for them at a nearer distance to his royal person than
any other, except great lords and Privy Councillors.' Nine months later
at the lord protector's second investiture 'first went his Highness's
Gentlemen, two and two' in the procession as it proceeded to
Westminster Hall where the ceremony was to be held.[20]

At one of the first diplomatic receptions given by the protector
after his second installation the Portuguese ambassador was 'conducted
by Sir Oliver Fleming [master of the ceremonies] and divers of his
Highness's Gentlemen and other persons of honour and quality, by
water from Greenwich, landed at the Tower, where, being received in
his Highness's coach, and attended by a great train of coaches of the
nobility and other persons of honour, he was with all respect and
honour brought through London to Westminster, to be entertained
there at the usual place in the Palace Yard, at the charge of his Highness'. Similarly, exactly twenty years before, in September 1637, the
then master of the ceremonies to Charles I, Sir John Finet, was sent
down to Gravesend to conduct the ambassador from the king of
Morocco to London. 'The embassy was met at Greenwich by the King's
barge with the Lord Kenwell and twelve Gentlemen of the Privy
Chamber, who were appointed to go thither, to bring them to the
Tower wharf . . . in state as was fitting and honourable.'[21]

The protectoral gentlemen of the household, so *The Commonwealth
Mercury* for 4 September 1658, its title-page edged in black, tells us,
also formed a part of the body of dignitaries and others who accompanied Norroy, King of Arms, at the proclamation of Richard Cromwell
as lord protector. While, as one would expect, the role of these gentlemen at the state funeral of Protector Oliver was, like that of the gentlemen of the bedchamber, a prominent one. 'This being the day appointed for the solemn funeral of the most serene and renowned Oliver,
Lord Protector; and all things being ready prepared', reported *Mercurius
Politicus* for 23 November 1658, 'the effigy of his Highness standing
under a rich cloth of state, having been beheld by those persons of
honour and quality which came to attend it, was afterward removed
and placed on a hearse, richly adorned and set forth with escutcheons
and other ornaments, the effigy itself being vested with royal robes, a
sceptre in one hand, a globe in the other, and a crown on the head.
After it had been a while thus placed in the middle of the room, when

the time came that it was to be removed into the carriage, it was carried on the hearse by ten of the Gentlemen of his Highness forth into the court, where a canopy of state, very rich, was borne over it by six other Gentlemen of his Highness, till it was brought and placed on the carriage; at each end whereof was a seat, wherein sat two of the Gentlemen of his Highness's Bedchamber, the one at the head the other at the feet of the effigy.' And when the procession reached the west door of Westminster Abbey 'the hearse, with the effigy thereon, was taken off the carriage by those ten Gentlemen, who removed it before, who, passing on to enter the church, the canopy of state was by the same persons borne over it again; and in this magnificent manner they carried it up to the east end of the Abbey, and placed it in that noble structure, which was raised there on purpose to receive it, where it is to remain for some time exposed to public view'. The report concludes with the words: 'This is the last ceremony of honour, and less could not be performed to the memory of him, to whom posterity will pay (when envy is laid asleep by time) more honour than we are able to express.'

Thus the closeness to the person of the protector which the gentlemen of the bedchamber and the gentlemen of the household had enjoyed was, when their master had passed beyond the furthest boundary of mortality, expressed symbolically by its transference to the funeral effigy. In this the gentlemen of the household, or rather some of them, were continuing the traditional function of royal gentlemen of the privy chamber, as it would appear that 'the last public appearance of the Gentlemen of the Privy Chamber is . . . on a demise of the King or Queen when, at the funeral, they bear the canopy over the royal corpse . . . The duty, however, of these Gentlemen until nearly the close of the seventeenth century went still further, for they had not only the honour of supporting the canopy, but some of them had the office of carrying the body, in quality of under-bearers.' In the official memoranda concerning the protector's funeral it was stipulated 'that twelve persons of honour [as opposed to the six reported by *Mercurius Politicus*, although the memoranda does stipulate that there should be six earls as assistants to the pall] be appointed to carry the canopy over the effigy at Westminster Abbey Church door. Usually they were Gentlemen of the Privy Chamber who bore the canopy, being persons of quality.' Also 'that certain Gentlemen be appointed out of the number of Gentlemen Waiters to carry the effigy out of the hall at Somerset House to the carriage or chariot and they attend at Westminster Abbey Church door to do the like'.[22]

In Protector Oliver's funeral procession as it moved from Somerset
House to the Abbey at Westminster there were, apart from the six or
twelve who bore the canopy over the effigy, and the ten gentlemen
waiters who carried the effigy itself, twenty-nine other of his Highness's
gentlemen, thirteen of whom were lieutenant-colonels and the remainder
majors. Apart from the absolute necessity of being high born, 'great and
splendid achievement in naval or military warfare, or having been engaged in useful and perilous service', were among the qualifications
looked for in a royal gentleman of the privy chamber. But it could well
be that in spite of their senior military rank the aulic duties of these
twenty-nine gentlemen did not include acting in the capacity of royal
gentlemen of the privy chamber, which was probably confined to the
select band of gentlemen who bore the pall, but were of a somewhat
less exalted nature like the gentlemen waiters who manhandled the
effigy. The position which these twenty-nine occupied as a group in
Cromwell's funeral procession would confirm this, while at the same
time suggesting what some of their duties may have been. Their place
roughly corresponds with that of the squires of the body, carvers, cup-
bearers, sewers, daily waiters and grooms of the privy chamber in the
cortège of James I.[23]

Also in this group of royal servants, and having precedence over the
grooms of the privy chamber but not the rest, were the gentlemen
ushers whose chief concern was to see to it that only the right sort of
people, in the correct garb, gained access to the privy chambers. Two
other gentlemen ushers flanked Clarencieux, King of Arms, who preceded the lord chamberlain and the royal hearse, while two more
flanked Garter, Principal King of Arms, who followed immediately
behind the hearse upon which a gentleman usher rode at the feet of
the king's corpse and a gentleman of the robes at the head.[24]

Likewise in the funeral procession of Protector Oliver the two kings
of arms mentioned above were flanked by gentlemen ushers. This was
in accordance with the memoranda concerning the protector's funeral
which ordained 'that four Gentlemen Ushers be nominated and appointed to go bareheaded, two before the hearse and two after the hearse'.
These four may not necessarily have held the post of gentlemen ushers
in the protectoral court. They could have been simply gentlemen of the
household 'nominated and appointed' to be ushers for the purpose of
the funeral ceremony only. The funeral memoranda also ordained that
'a Gentleman of the Robes [is] to ride at the head of the effigy in the
chariot' and 'a Gentleman Usher [is] to ride in the chariot at the foot',
the two men concerned being Messrs Barrington and Rolf. Both of

these individuals were, in fact, gentlemen of the protectoral bedchamber as is evidenced by the *Mercurius Politicus* account of the funeral which reports that riding on the chariot were 'two of the Gentlemen of his Highness's Bedchamber, the one at the head and the other at the feet of the effigy'. So this is in all probability another instance of individuals being 'nominated and appointed' for the purposes of the funeral ceremony, in this instance two members of the protectoral bedchamber staff being temporarily designated as gentleman of the robes and gentleman usher.[25]

The guard of halberdiers which attended Cromwell's corpse on its journey between Whitehall and Somerset House for the lying in state was the protectoral version of the king's bodyguard of the yeomen of the guard which was both a protection for the monarch's person and 'a state and ornament to the crown'. In fact on one occasion at least during the Protectorate the designation yeoman of his Highness's guard appears in reference to one of Cromwell's household guards. And twice in the post-Protectorate Commonwealth period the term yeomen of the guard was used in official records to describe what were by then ex-members of the defunct protectoral bodyguard. Also, the official newssheet *The Public Intelligencer* tells us that in the procession which accompanied Protector Richard Cromwell to the state opening of his Parliament was 'the captain of his Highness's yeomen of the guard'. Whether or not Oliver's yeomen of the guard were, like their royal equivalents, 'the tallest and stoutest men that could be found in all England, being carefully selected for the service', is not known for sure, but it is extremely likely that they were.[26]

The guard of halberdiers was formed within a few months of the Protectorate being established. At the banquet given by the lord protector for the ambassadors of the United Provinces on 27 April 1654, 'twenty gentlemen were', according to one account of the proceedings, 'taken into his Highness's life guard of foot (the whole number is to be three score) who carried up the meat'. By the end of May the guard had been increased to forty at which strength it appears to have remained throughout the Protectorate in spite of the above projected figure of 'three score'. Even at three score the protectoral guard would have been much smaller than that of Charles I whose yeomen numbered two hundred, fifty of whom were on duty at a time. As their name suggests, the halberdiers were armed with a halberd or halbert, which is a combined spear and battle axe. They were dressed in velvet collared coats of grey cloth welted with velvet, and silver and black silk lace, as were his Highness's footmen, this being the protector's livery.[27]

The post of captain of the guard was occupied by Privy Councillor Walter Strickland. This represented the first instance of a member of the Protectorate government holding a court post. The reason for the appointment was probably not so much that Strickland was politically powerful and close to the protector, but that because of his diplomatic experience, as a Parliament agent to the Netherlands during the civil war and as a co-ambassador there during the early Commonwealth period, he would have gained some knowledge of the sort of ceremonial being practised in a polity not too dissimilar to that existing in England. 'Having so greatly profited by attending the Hogan Mogan [the States General] and become so expert in the ceremony postures, and thereby so apt like an ape with . . . Gilbert [Pickering] . . . to imitate or act the part of an old courtier in the new court, [Strickland] was made Captain of the Protector's magpie, or grey-coated foot-guard.' So another member of the protector's court, besides the lord chamberlain, fell victim to the caustic comments of that anti-government pamphlet 'printed in the fifth year of England's slavery under its new monarchy, 1658'.[28]

Like all the major court posts the captaincy of the guard was, in a royal court, held by a great magnate and a favourite of the monarch, such as Henry Rich, first earl of Holland, who was captain of the guard to Charles I. The post did not, however, give the occupant *ex officio* membership of the king's Privy Council.

The occasions on which the protectoral bodyguard extended their usual duty of providing the protector with bodily protection by occupying the guard or outer chamber, to attending the protector out of doors, were, as one might expect, the same sort of state and public occasions that had, in the past, witnessed the attendance of the king's bodyguard of the yeomen of the guard upon the monarch.

When Oliver rode in procession from Whitehall to the palace of Westminster to open the first Protectorate Parliament on 4 September 1654, 'the gentlemen of his Highness's footguard, and the Wardens of the Tower, all in his Highness's livery, went along about his Highness's coach and the other coaches, and about them, all bareheaded', the foot-guard 'having new halberts'. Walter Strickland 'Captain of his Highness's guard of foot' walked on one side of the protector's coach while opposite him on the other side walked Charles Howard 'Captain of the life guard of horse'. All this was repeated when Oliver returned to Whitehall from his second inauguration in 1657, the journey to the ceremony being accomplished by barge. At the occasion of the opening of the second Protectorate Parliament, on 17 September 1656, the protectoral bodyguard also attended Oliver in Westminster Abbey where he went to hear a sermon by Dr John Owen before declaring the new Parliament open.[29]

As is to be expected the guard of halberdiers, dressed in the mourning allocated to them for the occasion, had a position of honour in 'the solemn funeral of the most serene and renowned Oliver, Lord Protector'. They marched in twos at the rear of the procession between the horse of honour, led by the master of the horse, attended by equerries and grooms, and the gentlemen porters and wardens of the Tower.[30]

To the honour of protecting the protector and providing his office with an adornment was added, so it might appear, a degree of impunity. In May 1656 'one of his Highness's guard' named Newman was arrested by Humphrey Smith and a bailiff named George Watson, probably for debt. But the protectoral Privy Council considered that 'it was done with manifestation of an intended indignity to his Highness', and so Smith and Watson were ordered to be apprehended and brought before the Council 'for procuring the arrest of one of his Highness's guard without leave', the upshot of the matter being that Smith was incarcerated for fourteen days. During the same period William Selsby 'Yeoman of his Highness's guard' complained to the Council that he had been 'unduly arrested' in the Court of Conscience by 'John Lee, citizen and saddler of London' and a sergeant-at-arms, Edward Stafford, most likely for the same reason that Selsby's fellow guard, Newman, was apprehended. The Council responded by ordering Lee and Stafford to 'attend Lord Strickland, Captain of his Highness's guard' to give an account of themselves.[31]

If this does not suggest some sort of immunity then at least it could be said to indicate that in order to prosecute members of the protectoral household guard it was necessary to follow a special procedure. There may even have been something in the nature of a palace court operating during the Protectorate.

Such a court had existed in royal times and it was known as the Court of the Verge, or the Knight Marshall's Court. It was held before the lord steward and knight marshall of the king's household, the knight marshall being responsible, under the master of the household, for policing the court, and had taken cognisance of cases which arose within the verge, that is within a space of twelve miles round the king's court wherever in the kingdom the monarch happened to be. But James I gave the court a fixed and permanent jurisdiction over the twelve miles surrounding his palace at Whitehall only, which covered the cities of London and Westminster, and the court usually sat at Southwark as the Marshalsea Court. The competence of this *curia palitii* was, however, confined to actions of debt or covenant where both parties were members of the king's household, and of trespass where one party was of the household. Parliament had, presumably sometime before the execution of Charles I, voted for the dissolution of the Court of the Marshalsea following complaints from the recorder of the City of London, representing the lord mayor and aldermen, that considerable confusion and disorder was being caused by the existence of this court and one held by the City, also in Southwark.[32]

But in March 1654, the fourth month of the Protectorate, the inhabitants of Southwark, acting on the intelligence 'that some lawyers for private lucre' had petitioned Parliament for the restoration of the Knight Marshall's Court, themselves petitioned Parliament against the court's revival. The supplicants protested that the court had, in the past, proved 'unnecessary, and a grievous oppression to the poor' the residents of Southwark being 'already rendered more miserable than almost any other part of the nation by their multitude and variety of courts'. A special committee designated to investigate the matter advised the Council, there being no Parliament sitting at that time, of the functions of the Court of the Verge or Marshalsea Court, submitting the question of its restoration to the central executive. As far as can be reasonably ascertained there is no extant official decree reviving the court.[33]

With the collapse of the Cromwellian dynasty the protectoral bodyguard was, as one would expect, disbanded. In June 1659 a list of what were described as the late yeomen of the guard was delivered by the commander in chief of the Commonwealth's forces in England and Scotland, Charles Fleetwood, to a committee of officers to consider whom among those of the ex-protectoral bodyguard who had requested it were deserving and fit for employment in the army as ensigns or lieutenants of foot.[34]

The guard commander, Walter Strickland, supported the military when the Protectorate collapsed, as Lord Chamberlain Pickering had done, and resumed his seat, as member for Minehead, in the restored Long Parliament. Being regarded as innocuous he was not molested at the Restoration, after which this 'obscure gentleman' as Clarendon calls him, returned to the shadows, whence he came.

Confusion seems to have arisen in the minds of some historical writers between the life guard of foot, to give them but one of their several titles, who belonged to, and were maintained by the household, and the protector's life guard of horse, who were most generally known as simply his Highness's life guard. The protector's life guard, commanded by Colonel Charles Howard until 1656 and thereafter by Richard Beke, did not belong to the household. It was part of the army establishment and paid for by the Army Committee, at one time by reducing the numbers in each troop of horse in both England and Scotland from 50 to 48 'and the pay of the two applied towards the Life Guard'. The pay of the 'gentlemen of the Life Guard', of which there were 45, besides officers, in 1654 and 1655, 160 troopers, plus four trumpeters, one captain and nine other officers in 1656 and 141 men, four trumpeters and 22 officers at the time of Oliver's death, was considerably higher than the normal rate, being, in 1654, 5s a day as opposed to the usual half-a-crown for ordinary troopers, a differential that was not retained though after the army pay cuts of 1655 when a life guardsman's pay came down to 4s but an ordinary trooper's pay was only reduced to 2s 3d.[35]

Although the life guard was not a part of the household and its commanders were not officers of the court, it did perform what could be considered aulic duties. It accompanied the protector whenever he went riding or when he travelled abroad, say between Whitehall and Hampton Court. And their stables and barracks were situated in the mews well within the confines of the palace of Whitehall. They were also in attendance on state occasions, at which times their commander walked on the opposite side of the protector's coach to the captain of the household guard.

Naturally the men who commanded this esteemed and rather expensive corps (in February 1656 the projected wages bill of the life guard for the year was £14,089, at a time when the pay for the entire 40,000 odd strong army came to just over £1m) were, like the officers of the court, close to Cromwell. Colonel Charles Howard who was captain of the life guard from 1654 to 1656 was to be, in 1657, the recipient of the first of the two hereditary peerages created by Protector Oliver, that of the viscountcy of Morpeth. Howard's successor, Major Richard Beke, was related to Cromwell, being the husband of the protector's niece, Lavinia Whetstone (daughter of Cromwell's sister Catherine Whetstone). Beke was to continue as captain of the protectoral life guard under Richard Cromwell who knighted him at Whitehall on 6 December 1658, making Beke one of the last men to be thus honoured under the house of Cromwell.*[36]

*According to the generally accepted list of Cromwellian knights Beke was the last (see Noble, Vol. I, pp. 447, 448 and Wm. A. Shaw, *The Knights of England*, Vol. II (London, 1906), p. 224). But *Mercurius Politicus* (23-30 December 1658) reports the creation by Protector Richard of another knight, a Colonel Hugh Bethel, on 26 December 1658.

The necessity of selecting for the life guard those who were sympathetic to Cromwell and his regime would have applied not only to the commanders but also to the very last trooper. William Roffe who, about December 1653, petitioned the protector to be one of his Highness's guard, having already served under Cromwell as a trooper, and been faithful through the wars, was, no doubt, a suitable candidate. The same could probably have been said of Captain Thomas Hale who had been promised a place in the life guard by the protector, 'but it did not fall out'.[37]

The intelligence sent to the exiled Charles II early in September 1655 to the effect that Cromwell had for three months been negotiating with the Swiss for a three thousand strong bodyguard because he could not trust his own army is apocryphal. It is true, however, that, as in the rest of the army, certain elements in the life guard were susceptible to radical political and religious notions that were sometimes contrary to those of the government whose chief executive they served. And in the winter of 1655/6 the life guard had to be purged of dissidents, after which it was reconstituted under a new commander, Major Richard Beke. Its strength was also raised from forty odd troopers to 160, excluding trumpeters and officers, because of the growing concern over the protector's personal safety. According to a royalist source Major-General John Lambert, at that time the member of the protectoral government closest to Cromwell, 'made choice of all the new Life Guard, they are absolutely his creatures'. The result was, in the words of the writer of a letter intercepted by Cromwell's secret service, 'the best horse and properest fellows I have seen. I think the world doth not afford better horse and better governed men than the army of this time is.' And another piece of royalist correspondence displays equal enthusiasm for Cromwell's life guard. 'It is a fine troop, all proper men, well armed with back and breast, and [they] have very good horses.' We are also informed that this new and enlarged life guard was 'divided into eight squadrons [which works out at twenty troopers to the squadron, each of which was commanded by a corporal who received a lieutenants pay], two whereof do duty every night watch'.[38]

The reason why two squadrons of the life guard were doing duty every night watch when their real purpose was to provide the protector with an out of doors mounted escort is partially explained in a missive from the Dutch ambassador to England, Nieuport, to his masters in the United Provinces. The letter is dated Westminster, 10 March 1656, which is about the time of the re-organisation of the life guard:

> My lords, a few days since the Life Guard of Horse of the Lord Protector, which formerly consisted of forty persons, most young gentlemen of this nation, was reformed after such a manner that twenty of them are to be employed as ordinary pensioners, who are to wait continually upon the person of his Highness.[39]

This can be interpreted as meaning that one (as opposed to two in the royalist intelligence) squadron of the protectoral life guard at a time took a turn at acting in what had once been the role of the royal band of gentlemen pensioners. Certainly the part played by 'a convenient number' of the life guard at the time of the removal of the protector's body from Whitehall to Somerset House for the lying in state, which, apart from these life guards and two heralds was attended only by members of the household, was identical to that played by the gentlemen pensioners during the corresponding event at the time of James I's obsequies. This was to act as torch-bearers, together with the footmen, to light the way. Also, fourteen of the protectoral life guard were selected to have more expensive mourning for the state funeral than the remainder of their comrades. This suggests some special role possibly that performed by the gentlemen pensioners at James I's state funeral, which was to accompany, again together with the footmen, the bearers of the bannerols, depicting Cromwell's family devices, who walked either side of the hearse.[40]

Royal gentlemen pensioners were, of course, part of the chamber establishment. Under Charles I the band numbered a captain, four other officers and clerks and 50 pensioners, of whom 25 were on duty at a time. The pensioners performed more or less the same day to day functions as the king's bodyguard of the yeomen of the guard, the main difference being that whereas the yeomen stood guard in the outer chamber, which was the first of the public rooms, as well as at the head of the stairs leading to it, the pensioners acted as sentinels in the presence chamber where the king and court society met. Also, as clearly expressed in their respective titles, the gentlemen pensioners were of a higher social class than the yeomen of the guard.[41]

With the abdication of Protector Richard what had been the protectoral life guard of horse was reduced to 120 troopers, plus officers, and given the task of guarding Parliament when it was sitting, and the rest of the time it was to perform the same function for the Council of State. A new rate of pay was also fixed. For the men this was to be three shillings a day, which was a drop of a shilling, but was still ninepence more than an ordinary trooper.[42]

In the new role the life guard would no longer be commanded by Major Richard Beke, but by Colonel Alured. This does not mean that Beke was in disgrace. On the contrary, he seems to have found almost as much favour with the new regime, which gave him a colonelcy, as he did with Protector Oliver and his son Richard. Beke continued in favour after the Restoration and died in 1707 at the age of seventy-eight.[43]

Beke's predecessor as captain of the life guard of horse, Charles Howard, was one of those who contrived at the restoration of the Stuart dynasty following the collapse of the Protectorate, for which he was well rewarded by a grateful Charles II, being created Baron Dacre of Gilleslånd, Viscount Howard of Morpeth and earl of Carlisle. No recognition was made of Howard's, or anyone else's, Cromwellian honours at the Restoration.[44]

Other above stairs servants known to have existed in the Cromwellian court were a master of the music and under him seven gentlemen of his Highness's music, plus 'two lads brought up to music'. These will be discussed in Chapter Six. There was also a group of what had originally been state employees whose salaries were, in April 1655, ordered 'to be taken into his Highness's household and notice given to his steward to supply places with fit offices'. These were three chapel keepers, Hugh Griffith, Theodore Jennings and John Sheriff, the keeper of the privy lodgings, Edward Jolly, the keeper of the gallery and the clock keeper, Henry Shadwell, all at the palace of Whitehall.[45]

Henry Shadwell the clock keeper at Whitehall died sometime in about 1657 and his widow Katherine subsequently petitioned the protector's Privy Council for continuance in her husband's place and the right to draw his salary for the relief of herself and her six children, having made arrangements for someone to keep the clock and ring the bell. The plea was accompanied by a note from one of the protector's two stewards, John Maidstone, to the effect that if the petition was granted he would take care that 'a sufficient person' was provided to carry out the duties of clock keeper. These duties would probably have involved giving some attention to a rather special protectoral acquisition. 'My Lord Protector hath bought a clock for three hundred pounds, invented by Fromanteel, which needs not to be wound up within a month', wrote Samuel Hartlib to the Commonwealth's envoy in Switzerland, John Pell. The clock, acquired by Protector Richard in November 1658, was, in fact, the first example of a pendulum clock to be made in England. This, as those familiar with the history of horologiography will no doubt know, was based on a Dutch design and was therefore only manufactured by the London clockmaker Ahasuerus Fromanteel and not invented by him.[46]

Also taken into his Highness's household together with the above mentioned chamber servants were two porters, Stephen Leews and Thomas Bury, the Whitehall gardener, Anthony Hutton, the keeper of the privy garden, and the keeper of the orchard door, William Spittlehouse. There was also the keeper of St James's Park gates, John Baggot.[47]

The sum of £72 10s a quarter originally allocated for the salaries of these '12 household servants at Whitehall' was raised to £77 10s in December 1657, Anthony Hutton, the gardener, having been given a rise in salary of £20 a year because of an increase in the work required on the Whitehall garden. This allotment of £77 10s was raised again in March 1659 during Richard's rule and on the eve of the demise of the Protectorate, with the addition of the salary (£37 10s a quarter) of another above stairs servent, Captain George Vaux, the housekeeper at Whitehall.[48]

The chapel keepers, the keeper of the privy chamber and the gardener were present in the protector's funeral cortège, being positioned behind the two protectoral falconers, the huntsman, and bird keeper, who were in turn preceded by servants of the 'better sort' belonging to the household below stairs.[49]

As we have witnessed all of the chamber elements described so far in this chapter were in existence within eighteen months or so of the establishment of the Protectorate, while the institution of some like the gentlemen of the household and the guard of halberdiers, was almost coeval with the inception of the Cromwellian regime. But the effective existence of the office of protectoral lord chamberlain dates only from late 1657, which was about nine or ten months before Oliver's demise. Even then Sir Gilbert Pickering operated in a seemingly limited capacity. It would appear that during the period in which there was no lord chamberlain the '12 household servants at Whitehall' came directly under the jurisdiction of the two protectoral stewards, John Maidstone and Nathaniel Waterhouse. The same would not, however, have been true of the bedchamber staff, the gentlemen of the household and the yeomen of the guard, because the status of Maidstone and Waterhouse would not have been sufficiently elevated. The commander of the household guard, for instance, was after all a member of the central executive. It must be presumed, therefore, that at this time each of these chamber elements functioned as independent units recognising no collective head. This arrangement may have continued after the introduction of a lord chamberlain into the protectoral household arrangements because, as already said, Pickering as lord chamberlain appears only to have operated in a limited capacity. From the autumn of 1657 onwards the protectoral court did, however, possess an administrative committee in the board of greencloth, the principal officer of which would have been Comptroller Jones. In royal courts the board had traditionally exercised a degree of supervisory power over above stairs servants, as well as being responsible for paying most of them.

III

An above stairs servant that Protector Oliver possessed and his immediate royal predecessors did not was a personal private secretary. Most of the private correspondence of the previous monarchs had been looked after by the staff of the secretaries of state who were not members of the chamber but government employees. The post of secretary to the protector was occupied by William Malyn, formerly a Draper's Company apprentice of Essex yeoman stock. He had become secretary to the then General Cromwell in 1650 and continued thus until Oliver's death, after which he became secretary to the army for a while before returning to total obscurity. Richard Cromwell had had a secretary of his own before succeeding to his father and he, a Mr Rosin, sometimes spelled Rosine, remained as such after Richard became lord protector.[50]

The functions of this office do not appear on the whole to be very different from those performed by Secretary of State John Thurloe's Privy Council secretariat. There is, for instance, a note addressed to Protector Oliver from Malyn with some documents concerning a matter that, according to Malyn, 'Your Highness commanded me to put your Highness in mind of at the next sitting of the Council'. And the Venetian secretary in England records, in a letter dated 3 January 1654, that when the master of the ceremonies, Sir Oliver Fleming, called to inform him of the change in government Fleming also advised that 'If I had any business I should apply to the secretary of his Highness'. Thus one feels that Malyn, who was accused of obstructing petitions and other approaches made to his master, while at the same time acquiring, through his influence with Oliver, grants for lands in Ireland, much to the annoyance of the lord lieutenant, Henry Cromwell, must, from time to time, have trodden on the toes of the Council secretaries, although it is thought that it would have been difficult for Malyn to have encroached on the preserve of Thurloe himself.[51]

Another extant letter provides an example of the post's more personal and less bureaucratic, or governmental, functions. This is from Dr John Wilkins, warden of Wadham College, Oxford (and husband of Oliver Cromwell's sister, Robina) to Mr Rosin, Protector Richard's secretary. Through Rosin it requests from Richard as chancellor of the University of Oxford, not as lord protector, dispensation for some BAs in attaining their MA degrees and also for one named individual for a licence to practise medicine.[52]

Representing the personal inclinations of the lord protector when they ran contrary to those of his own Parliament seems to have been another role played by Malyn. The well known case of James Naylor illustrates this. Naylor, an extreme Quaker, who had inspired in some of his followers the notion that he could be the Messiah, was tried by the second Protectorate Parliament for 'horrid blasphemies' and found guilty. Cromwell, who seems to have entertained doubts as to the legality of the proceedings, attempted to ease Naylor's circumstances by, among other things, instructing Sir Gilbert Pickering to provide reasonable quarters for his incarceration. And, when Naylor became ill in August 1658, Oliver sent Malyn to enquire of the prisoner's wants. This, described as one of the protector's last public acts, occurred immediately after the death of Bettie Claypole, which left her father prostrate with grief, and during the onset of the illness which was to carry Oliver himself off. So much for the sentiment expressed by one of Naylor's fellow Quakers, Edward Burrough, that Cromwell was too busy with his own schemes of family aggrandisement to care much what persecution fell upon the Quakers.

In the summer of 1659 Malyn, who, it will be remembered, did not continue as the protectoral private secretary with the accession of Protector Richard, was forced to quit his lodgings at Whitehall. These, together with the rooms of Mr Kelway and the lodgings, stable and coach house of Thomas Kirby, who had been respectively described as gentleman and servant to Protector Oliver, were reassigned to men who had found favour with the new regime.[53]

In spite of a testimony, dated June 1659, to the effect that on account of his master's abdication Richard's secretary Mr Rosin was 'quite meloncholy being nothing now', he was nevertheless allowed to continue to occupy his rooms in Whitehall, at least for the time being, and there was a Council of State order to that effect on 9 July 1659.[54]

IV

One category of what had customarily been regarded as above stairs servants, over which it is known that neither the protectoral lord chamberlain nor the board of greencloth exercised jurisdiction, comprised the master of the ceremonies, the protectoral wardrobe and barges departments, and the office of works. Unlike the protectoral gentlemen of the bedchamber and the household, the guard of halberdiers and the musicians, whose offices and departments had been specifically constituted for the exclusive use, glorification, protection and enjoyment of the lord protector, the above stairs elements which belong to this particular category were, like the stables, in being before the Protectorate was established. They had, in fact, existed as departments of state serving the pre-Protectorate Commonwealth in a functional capacity, while, in some instances, at the same time providing some slight ceremonial expression to the corporate existence of the English republic. Like the stables they continued their state functions after the Protectorate had been instituted, even though, in the case of the wardrobe and barges departments and the office of works, the officers were no longer designated as belonging to the state but to his Highness the lord protector, to whom their first duty now lay and whose livery the barges department's officers and complement of watermen now wore. They were not, however, absorbed into the protectoral household as those twelve functionaries at Whitehall, who had also been servants of the Commonwealth, were, but in many respects remained departments of state.

It was the business of a master of the ceremonies, sometimes known as master of ceremonies, to maintain formal links between the government and foreign diplomats in London. He would also greet ambassadors and arrange, as well as stage manage, audiences and entertainments for them. Charles I's master of the ceremonies at the outbreak of the civil war was Sir Charles Cotterell* who, unlike the lord chamberlain of the household, the earl of Essex, inclined towards his master's cause. Parliament, who controlled London, being mindful of the fact that 'there are divers ambassadors and other public ministers from foreign states residing here, and the ordinary way of their introduction and passing of all other public civilities neglected for want of a Master of Ceremonies', decided in November 1643 to appoint one of its own. Sir Oliver Fleming, a cousin of the then relatively obscure Colonel Oliver Cromwell, was subsequently chosen 'to execute the place of Master of Ceremonies, and to receive all profits thereunto belonging'.[55]

---

*He had superseded, in the Summer of 1642, Zeeland born Sir Balthazar Gerbier who had held the post for only a year from the late Sir John Finet, whom *The Dictionary of National Biography* incorrectly gives as Cotterell's immediate predecessor.

Fleming was certainly qualified for this role. He had received diplomatic experience abroad as a representative of Charles I before the war. This was a customary qualification for the mastership of the ceremonies. Also, he had already been made use of in a diplomatic capacity by Parliament. In October 1643, it being known 'that the French ambassador doth want someone to go along with him to shew him what he desires to see of this Kingdom', Fleming was the man appointed to wait upon the ambassador and conduct him 'to such places as he shall have a desire to see'.[56]

Fleming functioned as master of the ceremonies throughout the period of the civil war, nominally for King and Parliament but in reality for Parliament alone. He continued in office after the execution of Charles and the establishment of the Commonwealth, although he complained of being out of pocket, because, under the new regime he was forbidden to accept gratuities, as had previously been the custom, and he asked for an increase in salary lest he be put under 'the temptation to do things dishonourable'. These gratuities from ambassadors had in the time of Charles I pushed the master of ceremonies' income up to £1,000 a year. But with the republican regime regarding the acceptance of such gifts 'as dishonourable to the Commonwealth' Fleming was left with his basic fee of £200 paid out of the exchequer. There was also the absence of the kind of assistance which had previously been afforded to the master of ceremonies in the persons of an assistant master and a marshall. It was, however, resolved that the matter should be looked into.[57]

Problems of another nature beset Fleming during the latter part of the pre-Protectorate Commonwealth period. According to the Venetian secretary in England, who was writing in September 1653:

Though he [Fleming] is visible on business and is the only member of the government to whom access can be obtained easily, yet the constant familiarity remarked between him and the diplomatic agents has awakened some jealousy in the minds of certain leading members of the Council of State and he has received an express order to act with more reserve. Thus facilities for conferring with the one who knows all that passes both at home and abroad are impeded, as he does not show himself so readily as of yore. His Scottish birth exposes him to the present unpopularity of his whole nation, while the Scots complain that the English are not keeping their promises.[58]

One of Fleming's first duties for the pre-Protectorate Common-wealth had been to deliver a message, prepared by the Council of State, concerning the losses of English merchants in the Levant at the hands of French men-of-war, to the French ambassador. And his last, which was also his first under the Protectorate, was to inform the representa-tives of foreign powers of the change in the style of government and that any address made to the new ruler by foreign princes should be directed to 'His Highness Oliver, Lord Protector of the Commonwealth of England, Scotland and Ireland'. The Council directive authorising this is dated 19 December 1653, that is three days after Cromwell's inauguration.[59]

Again the Venetian secretary in England provides us with useful material. On 3 January 1654 he wrote thus to the Venetian ambassador in France:

When about to close this letter I received a visit from Sir [Oliver] Fleming, in greater spirits than usual over the change of government and the honour he enjoys through the confidence reposed in him by the Protector. He told me that by order of his Higness and his Coun-cil he was to go to all the foreign ministers and inform them of this change. He said it had been made for the sake of conducting all busi-ness, both at home and abroad, in a more satisfactory manner and more promptly. If I had any business I should apply to the secretary of his Highness. Henceforward all communications must be addressed to His Highness the Lord Protector of the Commonwealth of England, Scotland and Ireland. I thanked him and said the most serene republic would be pleased to hear of these fresh honours. Fleming expressed his goodwill and so we parted. It is supposed that in a few weeks all the foreign ministers will go and pay their respects to the Protector, in which case I shall consider it my duty to follow their example.[60]

The following months saw Fleming well occupied as the Protector began receiving, with princely pomp and considerable ceremony, the representatives of foreign states. The procedure, an ancient one, for these audiences/receptions was more or less the same for each ambassa-dor. He would be brought from his residence to Tower Wharf from whence, attended by Sir Oliver Fleming, he was conveyed 'in great state' to Sir Abraham Williams's house in the palace yard at Westminster to be entertained before his audience with the lord protector in the Banqueting House at Whitehall.

As already said, the master of ceremonies was traditionally also responsible for managing these affairs. This included seeing to it that a sufficient number of the right sort of servants were in attendance. He also arranged for the payment of such persons and other related expenses. On 2 December 1654 the Council gave their assent to a paper signed by Fleming for the payment of £123 10s 'from the Council's contingencies' for coaches, horses and coachmen used at the reception of the Dutch, French and Portuguese ambassadors the previous March, and a further £148 3s 6d for the footmen, coachmen and trumpeters who attended the representatives from Genoa.[61]

During their brief stay at Sir Abraham Williams' house the ambassadors usually received seven meals with 50 'dishes' for the first and second courses and between 20 and 30 'dishes' of fruit and sweetmeats at each meal. They also received 'a convenient allowance' for their attendants. The diet and plate were provided by Nicholas Bond for which service he received the sum of £30.

It was during these first few months of Oliver's rule that a rather unfortunate incident occurred which must have demanded of Fleming the most consumate skill in diplomacy. On 29 December 1653, the very day on which the Portuguese ambassador received his first audience with Cromwell to congratulate him as England's new ruler, the ambassador's brother Don Pantaleon Sa was committed to the Tower for his part in a brawl in which a man was killed. Don Pantaleon Sa was subsequently 'tried by a Jury of six denizens and six aliens', convicted and, midst a diplomatic flurry which included the French and Spanish ambassadors interceding, at the earnest request of the Portuguese ambassador, with the lord protector to spare the wretched man's life, he was executed on 10 July 1654 on Tower Hill. Also on 10 July 'articles of peace were signed by the Portugal ambassador, who thereupon went out of town'.[62]

Throughout more or less the whole of the Protectorate Fleming received his orders from the Council by way of one of their number, Walter Strickland. Thus it was Strickland whom the councillors nominated 'to direct the entertainment' of the various ambassadors 'and to take order with Fleming to prepare Sir Abraham Williams's house' for them. This should have been the role of the lord chamberlain as head of the household above stairs to which, in a royal court, the master of ceremonies had belonged. But as we know, the office of protectoral lord chamberlain did not come into existence until the end of the Protectorate and the only extant example of Lord Chamberlain Pickering acting in anything like this capacity is the already quoted order from the Council, dated less than three months before Oliver's death, that he arrange for the new venue for the entertainment of ambassadors, Somerset House, to be fitted out for that purpose and the residents there accommodated elsewhere. So the extent of Pickering's jurisdiction, if any, over Fleming, who was after all never a part of the Protector's household establishment, being paid directly out of the exchequer, is impossible to determine. But then the authority of the lord chamberlain over the master of the ceremonies had, even in a royal court, been more theoretical than practical, as the post was more that of a civil servant working for the diplomatic service than that of a domestic and personal servant of the monarch.

Apart from conveying the Council's wishes to Fleming, Strickland was also usually among those councillors and other state dignitaries, who, of course, included Fleming, designated to receive ambassadors and conduct them to their lodgings. Strickland's service abroad was obviously being made good use of. Because of this he would have acquired, as Fleming had, some skill in handling foreigners. Then there was Strickland's knowledge of aulic practices, which was probably one of the reasons why he was made captain of the household guard, not to mention the complex and often touchy subject of diplomatic ceremonial, procedures and precedence.

Just how the breaking, or supposed breaking, of the rules governing such things can manifest itself is exemplified by three incidents, one of which took place at the beginning, one in about the middle, and another at the end of Oliver's rule. In March 1654 during one diplomatic occasion 'there was', so a contemporary news-sheet tells us, 'a mistake at their taking coach between some gentlemen of the lord ambassador of the King of France, and gentlemen of the lord ambassador of the King of Portugal, about precedency of their coaches; some of the French gentlemen thinking that their lord ambassador's second coach should have gone before the Portugal ambassador's first coach, which did occasion drawing of swords, and some small harm; but the soldiers stepping in, disarmed those that drew on both sides, and the mistake being understood, they were reconciled, and in friendly kindness passed along in the order aforesaid'.[63]

Bulstrode Whitelocke provides us with the second illustration:

> The Swedish ambassador had been at Whitehall and was much discontented because he waited above an hour before the Protector came to him, which brought the ambassador to such impatience that he rose from his seat and was going home again without speaking to

the Protector, and said that he durst not for his head admit of such dishonour to his master, by making him so long to attend for his audience.

But Sir Oliver Fleming, the Master of the Ceremonies, did earnestly interpose with his persuasions, and prevailed with the ambassador to stay a little longer, and went himself to the Protector and plainly told him how unfit it was, and how ill taken to put the ambassador to such attendance, and brought him to the ambassador.

[Later] the Protector sent to the Swedish ambassador to excuse his long stay before he had his audience and to assure him that there was not the least intention of reflecting upon the King's honour, or of any disrespect to him, but only the omission of the Protector's servants in their duty. Wherein care should be taken for the future, and that it should be amended. And that his Highness had a very great affection for the ambassador's person, and as great a respect for the King his master, as for any prince in Christendom.[64]

Oliver's excuse and the sentiments he expressed concerning the ambassador and the king of Sweden were undoubtedly genuine for it had been said that 'Cromwell is exceeding intimate with the Swedish ambassador, a person of great estimation. They dine, sup, hunt and play bowls together. Cromwell never caressed any man so much as the King of Sweden.'[65]

Less dramatic than the first mentioned incident, but in its way as diplomatically embarrassing as both this and the second episode, was a letter addressed 'To our much honoured friend Sir Oliver Fleming, Master of Ceremonies', from George Fleetwood and H. Von Tischendorf, Swedish commissioners. The letter refers to the mourning they had been sent and the places they had been given for the Protector's funeral. In this they complained that they had been given the same status as representatives of towns like Danzig. Although they were loath to enter into a dispute on their own account, because of the respect they had for the memory of the late lord protector, from whom they had received so many 'signal civilities', they were, nevertheless, compelled as the public ministers of the king of Sweden 'either to propose our being placed next to ambassadors or a dispensation (to avoid all offence) from our attendance on this solemnity'. The piqued plenipotentiaries also complained that the Commonwealth's envoy to Denmark and Sweden, although of the same standing as themselves, was treated by the king of Sweden 'after a higher rate' than they were. The letter concludes with, 'we depend upon your friendship and discretion for the management hereof'.[66]

But the eventual accommodation of the Swedish representatives resulted in even greater problems, as the Venetian resident in England shows in his report of the funeral to the Doge and the Senate in Venice:

> The Protector did not take part in the function, to which all the foreign ministers were invited, except Brandenberg and Courland. The ambassadors of France, Holland and Portugal were present, with the two ministers of Sweden, and those of Genoa, Holstein, Hamburg, Danzig and Bremen. Denmark, Florence and Venice were not present as they did not have a place assigned to them suitable to the dignity of their princes. It was claimed that the Swedish ministers, who do not bear a much higher character than the Dane or your Serenity's, should go with the ambassadors, and that the rest should all go together among more than 200 persons, who walked after the ambassadors, and among the titled persons of the Country. This has never been done before, as in the memoirs of Finet, a former master of the ceremonies, they went before the barons, while now they want them to give way to all. Having heard of this beforehand and of the great distinction shown to the Swedes, Denmark decided not to go, and I also thought it best not to take part, to avoid creating an injurious precedent. I hope that my decision will not be condemned by the Senate. At the moment when the ambassadors were starting, the minister of the Most Christian objected to the ministers of Sweden going with them, threatening to withdraw, as they were not even residents, but only envoys. So to avoid confusion it was necessary to make an alteration on the spot, and this was done by getting the master of the ceremonies to walk between the ambassadors and the Swedes. He went with four other persons of the palace, all bareheaded, completely separating the two parties, but taking the place from all the titled persons of the realm. Genoa, Holstein and the others mentioned took a very low place, after all the titled persons, and it was observed that Genoa took a lower place than Holstein, although he has a much higher character, and that both gave way to Danzig, Bremen and Hamburg.[67]

Earlier it had fallen to Fleming to acquaint these and other representatives of foreign governments of the death of Protector Oliver and the succession of his son Richard, on the document proclaiming which event Fleming's name appears. 'It was ordered that Sir Oliver Fleming,

Knight, Master of the Ceremonies', reported *Mercurius Politicus* for 6 September 1658, 'do forthwith give notice, in the name of his Highness's Council, to all ambassadors and public ministers of foreign states here residing, that it hath pleased God to take out of this world the most serene and renowned Oliver, late Protector of the Commonwealth; and that the said office of Lord Protector is now devolved upon the Lord Richard, eldest son of his said late Highness, who by his said father in his life time [was] appointed and declared to succeed him in the government of these nations.' This was, of course, merely a matter of officially confirming what must have already been known. It was, as it happens, not until fourteen days after Oliver's death that Fleming got round to formally advising the repsentatives of foreign governments of the fact. In a letter dated 20 September 1658 the Dutch ambassador Nieuport writes:

Tuesday last, the 17th., Sir Oliver Fleming, Master of Ceremonies, came in a coach and six horses, with some lackeys of my Lord Protector, to see me. And, being entered into the hall of the house of the high mightiness with a gentleman and page of the Lord Protector, he told me that he had order from the Council to tell me that it pleased God to take out of this world Oliver the late Lord Protector, and that the Lord Richard, his eldest son, succeeded him in the office of Protector, according to the petition and advice of the last Parliament.[68]

Similarly we hear from the Venetian resident in England in a note, also dated 20 September, to Venice that:

After the Proclamation of the new Protector, Richard on Saturday morning . . . it was . . . ordered that this day should be set apart for fasting and humiliation on the late Protector's death and to implore the blessing of God upon the present government, and this has been observed at Whitehall by all the Court. They also decided to inform all the foreign ministers of the late Protector's death and the accession of the new one. This was done on Tuesday by Sir [Oliver] Fleming, master of the ceremonies, who visited each embassy, asking the ministers to inform their monarchs. I made a suitable response, expressing grief at Oliver's death, and pleasure at the accession of Richard, enlarging on the sincere predilection of the Senate for this government and nation.

In conversation with Fleming I learned that none of the foreign
ministers will be admitted to audience of the new Protector or have
power to negotiate unless they receive new letters of credence from
their masters directed to him. It will be better for your Excellencies
to send these by way of Flanders, which is much shorter than that
of France. For this reason no one will be able to offer official condo-
lences or congratulations, as they will have to wait for these letters;
and France will be the first because he is nearer and can get his
letters quickest.[69]

For Fleming this must have been a far less pleasant duty than the one
performed fifteen months earlier on 26 June 1657, when he was instructed to 'go to the several foreign ambassadors and public ministers
of state that reside here to invite them to be present at the solemnity of
the investiture of his Highness the Lord Protector this day'.[70]

According to what appears to be the order of procession drawn up
before the ceremony Fleming's position in the cortège at Cromwell's
state funeral is listed as being immediately behind the protectoral
gentlemen of the bedchamber, an arrangement that, as we have seen,
had to be changed at the last minute because of a diplomatic incident.
He was, naturally, dressed in the mourning that had been allocated to
him.[71]

At this particular point in time only eighteen months or so were left
to Fleming as master of the ceremonies because at the Restoration he
was superseded by Sir Charles Cotterell who had held the post under
Charles I and was to continue in it until 1686. To the royalists, of
course, Cotterell had been master of the ceremonies continuously since
his appointment in 1642, Fleming being a usurper and the servant of
'unlawful' regimes.

The second element in this category of protectoral above stairs
departments, the wardrobe, has been made the subject of a separate
chapter. It was from about the middle of 1654 that the third element,
what had hitherto been known as the state barges department, and its
staff of state watermen, became known as his Highness's barges and his
Highness's watermen. And in July 1657 the Council decreed that new
coats should be provided for his Highness's watermen, and a livery for
the masters of the barges, of grey cloth (the colour worn by the protectoral footmen and bodyguard), with his Highness's arms for a badge,
thus providing yet another example of the increasing pomp which
began to surround Cromwell after his refusal of a crown in May 1657
and his subsequent second investiture in the following month.[72]

The arms referred to were those which first appeared on the Great Seal of the Commonwealth in 1655, having been approved on 6 March of that year. The device was a singularly regal one comprising as it did the heraldic supporters of the Tudor monarchs which were, for England, a lion guardant imperially crowned, and representing ancient Britain or Wales a dragon in profile with wings raised. The shield was prince-like fashioned as a royal breast-plate over which was set the six-barred helmet of monarchy surmounted by a kingly crown, and on top of this the royal crest of Great Britain (originally the crest of the Plantagenets), that is a lion passant guardant crowned with an imperial crown. All this, including the mantling, was very much the symbolism of royalty. One break with tradition was represented by the use of the cross of St George for England and that of St Andrew for Scotland as quarterings. A harp continued to represent Ireland as it always had. A small shield at the centre of the quarterings bore Cromwell's own arms of a lion rampant. This followed the European custom by which elected sovereigns placed their hereditary arms in an escutcheon over all those of their dominions. This next occurred in England at the end of the seventeenth century when William III, an elected monarch, placed his own paternal arms of Nassau upon the royal arms. The motto on the Protectorate arms, *PAX QUAERITUR BELLO*, translates as Peace is Sought through War.[73]

In addition to the badge were the letters 'O' and 'P', for Oliver Protector, one of which letters was positioned on the left and the other on the right side of the upper half of the arms, just as the letters 'C' and 'R' had appeared with the royal arms on the coats of Charles I's watermen. Presumably one badge was worn on the breast and another on the back of the watermen's coats, as in former times, because in March 1658 a warrant was made out for the payment of £347 6s 5d for 58 such badges and the gilding and colouring of 116 letters ('O's and 'P's) for his Highness's watermen, who at that time numbered 29, including the master of the barges and his assistant. The badges were supplied by Edward Backwell the London financier and goldsmith who also furnished, at a cost of £650 13s 6d, the sceptre used by Cromwell at his second investiture. Although the Privy Council was the source from whence the initial instruction for the supply of new badges and coats emanated, and the cost was borne by the Council's contingencies fund, responsibility for placing the orders for these items rested with the admiralty commissioners, as it had done in the pre-Protectorate Commonwealth period. There is no record as to who provided the cloth for these particular garments nor is there a warrant extant for the payment of the cost, which was £46 11s 3d. But in April 1654 Richard Hampden, who later described himself as his Highness's draper, was paid £36 12s 6d by Gualter Frost, treasurer for Council contingencies, for supplying cloth for what were then called the state's watermen, and it is therefore very likely that he also furnished this later consignment.[74]

Once more the ceremonial barges of state were manned by watermen wearing the livery of the nation's ruler, recalling the days of the master of the king's barge and the royal watermen. A warrant for the arrest of the last master of the king's barges, a Mr Warren, was issued by Parliament in the Summer of 1648. This was the time of the invasion of England by a Scots army which, together with a few small risings by royalists in the west of England, Kent and Essex, constituted what became known as the second civil war. Warren too had risen in support of the defeated and encarcerated Charles I by promoting disaffection among seamen about the Kent side of the River Thames. He was also joined by the Thames watermen who rowed goods and passengers about the capital's main transport artery. They were either the employees of private individuals, or they plied for hire, at a time when water transport provided a more comfortable, and in some respects safer, means of travelling than springless carriages on indifferent road surfaces, with the possibility of receiving attention from footpads. Together, Warren, seamen and watermen, planned to arm themselves and advance on the Thames in pinnaces and long boats to the Parliament building itself and force the government to comply with their demands. The upshot of the affair was that some watermen were arrested in the process of trying to seize and make off with the king's privy barge. A hole was afterwards ordered to be made in the barge and its leader to prevent them from being carried off.[75]

On 31 August, 1649, seven months after the execution of the king and the establishment of the Commonwealth, the Council of State ordered that a committee be set up to consider how many of the late king's barges should be reserved for the use of the state, and how many watermen should be employed to row them, and the likely cost. The committee was also to discover in what way the royal arms could be replaced by those of the Commonwealth on the reserved barge cloths. Already, in the previous May, a warrant had been served on Warren, described in this instance as keeper of the great barge, instructing him to deliver up to the care of the state's wardrobe keeper, Clement Kinnersley, rich cloth belonging to the great barge.[76]

The Council's move was in response to the suggestion made by the new republic's master of ceremonies, Sir Oliver Fleming, in April 1649, that there should be some outward and visible signs that would make foreign princes aware of the Commonwealth's prosperity. One of his recommendations was that there should be a barge of state, richly decorated with arms and other ornaments, and a second barge for more ordinary occasions. Fleming also advised that the bargemasters and the watermen should wear livery. And so on 4 September 1649 it was decreed that Richard Nutt and 21 others were to be watermen to the Council of State and that they should wear the badge of the arms of the Commonwealth, which they received three months later. As master of the Commonwealth barges Nutt was to be allowed £60 a year, as his predecessors, the masters of the royal barges, had been. The ordinary watermen were to receive £4 apiece a year. In January 1650 one of their number, Thomas Washbourne, was elevated to the post of assistant to the master of the barges at a salary of £20 which, like the salaries of Nutt and the rest of his staff, was to be paid in quarterly instalments. In addition to their regular wages the watermen, including Nutt and Washbourne, received a turning out fee. The sum of £27 1s 6d was expended on putting the barges acquisitioned for the state's service in good repair. Consideration was given to what cushions and carpets were fit for the state's barges and Mr Carter, surveyor, was instructed to proceed with the building of a new barge house and to sell the old one to the best advantage.[77]

The conveyance of ambassadors to receptions at Whitehall in impressive splendour, for which it was primarily constituted, was not the only use to which the state barges department was put. In fact one of its first recorded acts was to lend Robert Meredith, master of the lord mayor of London's barge, one of the state vessels to transport the lord mayor and his company to Westminster to take the oath. There was also the conveyance of state dignitaries. On 4 April 1650 Nutt was ordered to have the two state's barges ready to attend the Speaker. The following March the state or public barges were put at the disposal of the English ambassadors to Holland to transport them to their ship. And in May 1653 Admiral Blake was carried to Gravesend and Lee Road in a ten oar barge. A ten oar barge was also used to take General Monck to his ship, the *Hope*, in November 1653. For turning out on these last two mentioned occasions Nutt received the sum of £12 and £4 10s which included his own fee and those of the attendant watermen. Admiral Richard Deane was also the recipient of Nutt's services, or rather his corpse was. In June 1653 the Admiral's body was brought up the Thames to Westminster for burial. This part of the funeral at least must have been rather an impressive affair because Nutt was instructed to take up other barges and to impress up to 350 from among the Thames watermen for the purpose. Similar steps were no doubt taken in 1652 when Nutt carried 500 foot soldiers from Whitehall to the fleet at Gravesend.[78]

The performance of these government or state functions was continued after the Protectorate had been inaugurated, when the primary occupation of the watermen, whose numbers, including Nutt and Washbourne, had increased to 27 by early 1655 and 29 by September 1657, was 'to attend his Highness's barge'. The establishment of the royal barges department under King Charles I was, incidentally, about 45 including the master, half as many men again as those employed in the barges department of Protector Oliver.[79]

In 1654 Nutt received £49 5s 6d for the conveyance of the Dutch ambassadors, and during 1655 and 1656 he received further payments for transporting the Genoese, Spanish, Venetian and other ambassadors from Gravesend to Tower Wharf, from where they travelled to Whitehall for audiences and receptions in carriages which were, like the barges, furnished by the protector. Payments were also made to Nutt, in 1656, for 'attending' the Swedish ambassador on a fluvial journey from London to Gravesend and back and from Dorset House to Whitehall and back, as well as for carrying, in the ten oar barge, Admiral Blake to his ship the *Hope* at Gravesend, and Councillor Edward Montague to Lambeth. While *Mercurius Politicus* reported that on 15 June 1658 'The Duke of Crequi, first gentleman of the bedchamber to the King of France and Monsieur Mancini, nephew of the most eminent Cardinal Mazarin, accompanied by divers of the nobility of France and many gentlemen of quality, arrived at Greenwich, Sir Oliver Fleming, Master of the Ceremonies, with divers lords and gentlemen of quality, received them there, and conducting them thence by water in his Highness's barge, many other barges attending to carry their retinue, they, betwixt five and six o'clock in the evening, landed at the Tower, where entering his Highness's coach, and other coaches being prepared for their company, they passed through the City. And, being followed by a large train of coaches with six horses and many others, they were very honourably conducted to Brook House in Holborn, the place appointed to lodge them, where they were entertained at the charge of his Highness'.[80]

In the pre-Protectorate Commonwealth days the initial instruction for the execution of these duties came from the Council of State out of whose contingencies Nutt's expenses, and his and the other watermen's turning out fees, were paid. This practice was continued by the protectoral Privy Council after the establishment of the Protectorate. The Admiralty Committee, through the navy commissioners, remained as intermediary between the Council and Nutt as it had been before the Protectorate. The Admiralty Committee, through the navy commissioners, was also responsible for the rigging out of a pleasure boat being prepared for the Protector in the early Summer of 1658.[81]

The cost of the wages for the protectoral master of the barges, his assistant and his Highness's watermen was met out of the moneys allocated to Oliver for the expenses of government. In this respect they were in the same category as individuals like the secretary of state, the Latin secretary, the clerk of the records in the Tower, the clerks to the Council (one of whom, William Jessop, was also, from 1655, among other things, treasurer for the lord protector's contingencies, which was an enhanced version of the royal keeper of the privy purse) and also the Council's inferior servants, such as messengers, office clerks, serjeants-at-arms and their deputies, ushers and their assistants, the fire maker for the clerks of the Council and the keeper of the back door of the Council chamber. Nutt now received £80 a year, twenty pounds more than he did in the pre-Protectorate Commonwealth days. The salaries of Washbourne and the ordinary watermen remained the same.[82]

One of the first recorded instances of Oliver's use of the protectoral barge was in September 1654 when, after opening the first Parliament of his rule with princely pomp, 'his Highness went back to Whitehall privately in his barge by water'. Four months later, on 22 January 1655, Cromwell travelled the half mile between Whitehall and the palace of Westminster by barge again, in order to dissolve this same Parliament. The choice of river transport on this last occasion may have been prompted by one of two considerations, or even both. There was the possibility of assassination, which would have been much easier to effect in the narrow congested streets of the metropolis than on the River Thames. Earlier in the month 'a new conspiracy was detected against his Highness and the present government'. Then there was the solemnity of the occasion, Parliament being dissolved much against its will. The need to overawe Parliament would, one imagines, have been accomplished more readily by Oliver's stately arrival at Westminster by ceremonial barge than in a coach.[83]

The protector also travelled from Whitehall to Westminster by barge for his second inauguration in June 1657, returning, after the ceremony, by coach. And, originally, it was proposed that Oliver's effigy should be carried from Whitehall to Somerset House by water, a distance of just under half a mile, for the lying in state, but this was abandoned in favour of land transportation.[84]

Like other of the court servants the staff of the barges department
received, at the death of their master, mourning, Nutt being allocated
seven yards and his assistant, Washbourne, and the then twenty-seven
other of his Highness's watermen four yards apiece. Apart from one
man who died in late 1655 or early 1656 all those who were originally
taken on as state's watermen in 1649 appear on the list of his Highness's watermen at the time of the protector's demise. In the funeral
procession the position occupied by Nutt and his staff was almost at
the front among the lowest servants of the household kitchen, as was
the case with the royal watermen at the funeral of James I. Nutt's
principal duty on the day of Cromwell's state funeral, was to arrange
for three barges 'to attend at Whitehall stairs . . . at eight of the clock,
to carry the lords of his Highness's Council and their attendants to
Somerset House', these same barges also being made available to 'attend
at evening at Westminster, to carry them back to Whitehall'.[85]

One aspect of Nutt's post which was completely outside the aulic
sphere was the impressment of seamen and Thames watermen for the
state's ships. In the Summer of 1657 Nutt, who, incidentally, was a
master of the Watermen's Company, and two other press masters,
crimped 375 such unfortunates, for which service they received a total
amount of £108 15s 8d, representing press and conduct money at the
rate of 4s a man for those taken at Chatham and 3s 6d for those from
Gravesend, and including £13 12s 8d for their own travelling charges,
boat hire, the beating of drums and other incidental expenses. This
naturally unpopular means by which Thames watermen and seamen
were coerced into the service of the state already had a long history. In
1635 for instance it was reported that the most 'sufficient' men flee at
the prospect of such a fate or protect themselves by entering into the
service of noblemen and gentlemen.[86]

The first, and, as it turned out, the last state occasion on which the
protectoral watermen were put to use during the rule of Richard
Cromwell was at the opening of the new protector's Parliament on 27
January 1659. 'This being the day appointed for the meeting of the
Parliament', reports *The Public Intelligencer*, 'his Highness attended by
his Privy Council and the high officers of state and of his household,
with officers of his army and the gentlemen of his household, passed by
water in a stately new-built galley and landed at the Parliament stairs.'
The return journey from Westminster to Whitehall was made in like
manner.[87]

Like the protectoral stables the barges department reverted to being a complete department of state after the abdication of Protector Richard. And at the end of January 1660 Richard Nutt was replaced as master of the barges by Edward Leaman, and Thomas Washbourne's position as assistant was restated. The reason for Nutt's removal was not specified. He may, of course, have died.[88]

The last of those above stairs elements that remained outside the protectoral household establishment to be discussed is the office of works. Traditionally the office of works had been responsible for the care and maintenance of the royal palaces as well as carrying out structural alterations and new building work. Warrants for such undertakings were initiated by the lord chamberlain, the office of works in a royal court being a sub-department of the chamber. At the apex of the office of works' hierarchy stood the surveyor of the works, the last man to hold that post in the reign of Charles I being the illustrious Inigo Jones. Under Jones the department possessed its own comptroller, a paymaster and a clerk, plus a master mason, a serjeant plumber, a master carpenter, a purveyor, between ten and fourteen other artificers and craftsmen and a number of labourers on temporary hire.[89]

With the abolition of the monarchy in 1649 ownership of the ex-royal residences devolved upon the government of the republic and the king's office of works became a department of state. The return of some of the late king's palaces to the role of residence for a monarch, that is Protector Oliver, has already been dealt with in Chapter One, as has the part played by John Embree, who succeeded Edward Carter as the state's surveyor of works (he was also known as surveyor of the works and surveyor-general of works) in April 1653, in preparing the ex-royal properties for the use of England's new ruler. Also mentioned in Chapter One was the transference, in November 1655, of the cost of repairs to Whitehall, the mews and Hampton Court, from the public charge to the revenue settled on Oliver to cover his household expenses. Henceforth no work was to be carried out by Embree on these properties without his Highness's special warrant. The remainder of the ex-royal palaces and all other government buildings continued to be the state's responsibility and orders to Embree to carry out repairs and other work on these emanated throughout Oliver's rule from the central executive, as they had done in the pre-Protectorate Commonwealth days. Thus in the final year of Oliver's Protectorate, for example, there are instances of Embree and his department being concerned with repairs to the state-run tapestry works at Mortlake and, upon recommendations approved by Cromwell personally, repairs to Westminster Hall and adjacent buildings, and the erection of a place in Westminster

Hall to accommodate the new High Court of Justice, set up in the late Spring of 1658 to try a number of conspirators for treason. All this work was undertaken on behalf of the government who footed the bill. During the same period the office of works was also employed on work in Cromwell's own residence which was paid for out of the protector's household expenses. There were, for instance, early in 1658, repairs to be carried out about the guard at Whitehall for which the comptroller of the household was given an estimate of £30 15s 0d for carpenters' and bricklayers' work. Also of a purely aulic nature was the preparation by Embree of what were described as the rooms over his Highness's guard in the gallery near the Council chamber, for some of his Highness's gentlemen.[90]

When Embree submitted the list of members of his department to the committee for mourning at the death of Protector Oliver he did so as his Highness's surveyor of works, and the members of Embree's department enumerated on the roll were regarded as being employed by the lord protector. The list reveals that the protectoral office of works was almost identical in size to that of Charles I. And, as in previous times, labourers were hired on a temporary basis only. In February 1658 Embree reported that £5,000 was due to such dismissed workmen 'whose importunities raise continual clamour'. Under Embree there was his Highness's architect, Edward Dallon, a merchant of timber to his Highness, an ironmonger, a master carpenter, joiner, and mason, and also a master carver, Mr Phillips, who made the body of Protector Oliver's funeral effigy. There were also twelve other artificers and tradesmen, two bricklayers, a painter, two smiths, a carpenter, two plasterers, a paviour, a glazier, a man responsible for the lashing of ropes, and someone described as a mattlayer, plus three other individuals whose occupations are not given.[91]

According to the order of procession drawn up for the protector's state funeral twelve artificers and tradesmen, or 'servants relating to the surveyors office', walked immediately in front of, which meant that they were junior to, four 'servants of his Highness's wardrobe', and what were described as his Highness's master carpenter, master joiner, master carver and master mason are designated as being positioned behind his Highness's gunsmith, shoemaker, hatter, tailor, upholsterer and three measurers of cloth. In a slightly more senior position are listed two 'clerks of the surveyors office'. These do not appear on Embree's roll of office of works personnel. In a more senior position still was the 'merchant for timber to his Highness' and considerably closer to the corpse, as might be expected, was his Highness's surveyor of works who walked directly in front of (and was therefore junior to) the keeper of his Highness's wardrobe, Clement Kinnersley.[92]

Richard Cromwell having abdicated in May 1659 Embree was, in the month following, ordered by the new regime 'to repair to Hampton Court and to take an account of the goods in the houses there so as there be no embezzlement of them. And likewise to take notice of such servants as there remain. Also to take care of the water courses and rivers. And say what servants are fit to be continued for looking after the house and what is fit to be done therein.' At the other ex-protectoral residence, Whitehall, Embree was instructed to prevent the removal of goods, the defacing of lodgings and the forcing of locks there.[93]

At the Restoration Embree reverted to the post he had held from December 1642 until his promotion to surveyor of works in April 1653, that of sergeant plumber, with a salary of £38 10s 0d per annum. As surveyor of works his annual remuneration had been fixed in November 1655 at £300. But this dramatic decline in status and income was not the end of Embree's misfortune. In June 1661 he was dismissed from his post of sergeant plumber of the works to the newly restored Charles II 'for acting under the usurping powers as surveyor of works, purchasing land belonging to Whitehall and demolishing cloisters, chapels, etc., belonging to Exeter Cathedral'. The 'land belonging to Whitehall' was in fact 'a little ruinous house near Willingford House', or at least that is how Embree described this property when he petitioned Protector Oliver, in August 1658, for a ninety-nine year lease on it at a peppercorn rent. The protectoral Privy Council had ordered that four of their number, including Mr Comptroller of the household, should be responsible for inserting such covenants into the lease as they should think fit.[94]

Like so many others Embree paid a high price for his association with the Cromwellian regime, even though this association was non-political. But there's the rub, it could be said, because in some respects it was those with a political affiliation to the regime, like the comptroller of the protectoral household, who were in the best position to square their past Cromwellian association with the restored Stuart dynasty.

V

Two particular groups of people to be found in a royal chamber department, but which were not strictly speaking members of the protectoral court, comprised those whose concern was the spiritual and physical welfare of the ruler, his personal chaplains and physicians. Although Protector Oliver received the ministrations of such men they were not his personal servants in permanent attendance or readiness, as had been the case in previous royal courts, where at least one of a veritable army of chaplains and physicians would be in waiting every day.

The chaplains who attended Protector Oliver can be divided into two categories, the first of these being represented by the three state chaplains resident at Whitehall, and the second by a number of outside clerics who performed a similar function to the state chaplains but on a less regular basis. Both categories possessed men who were prominent for reasons quite apart from the distinction afforded them on account of their capacity as unofficial chaplains to the lord protector.

The three 'preachers at Whitehall' during the Protectorate were Joseph Caryl, who was replaced by Nicholas Lockyer in June 1655, Peter Sterry and that famous Cornish-born 'returned New Englander' Hugh Peter or Peters. Each received a salary of £200 a year and lodgings in the palace. Peter actually occupied the quarters once held by William Laud and they contained that part of the late archbishop's library which had been given to Peter by Parliament after Laud's execution in 1644. This, plus Peter's closeness to the centre of power and the consequential deference afforded him, occasioned some of his friends to refer to him as the archbishop of Canterbury. The post of Whitehall chaplain came into being in the early days of the pre-Protectorate Commonwealth. Sterry had been the first to be nominated, in July 1649, and Caryl's appointment dated from 23 June 1651, by which time all three chaplains living at Whitehall when the Protectorate was established were holding office. Although he did not officially replace Caryl until June 1655 Lockyer had nevertheless been acting in the capacity of Whitehall chaplain since the beginning of Oliver's rule, probably in Caryl's stead, although Caryl was, during this period, still drawing his £50 a quarter salary. And the Council instruction of 26 June 1655 confirming Lockyer's salary also ordered that this be back dated to 25 December 1653, the arrears to be paid out of Council's contingencies.[95]

Originally the Whitehall chaplains had been required to preach before the Council of State. In fact, one of their designations was preachers to the Council. This they continued to do after December 1653, only now they also preached before the lord protector, the role of chaplain to whom, including his family, they incorporated into their office. 'There is every day of the week twice, *viz.* at ten o'clock in the morning, and at six at night, a meeting of the Lord Protector's family at the chapel of Whitehall, where his Highness's chaplain, Mr. Lockyer, expounds to them', reported a news-sheet in May 1654. In September 1654 Peter Sterry was instructed by the Council to preach every alternate Thursday in the chapel at Whitehall, and in July 1655 it was decreed that he should take the 'Lord's day', or Sunday service, to be held in Whitehall chapel or at Hampton Court depending on where the protector happened to be, while Hugh Peter officiated at the weekday services at Whitehall. Both the chapel at Whitehall and that at Hampton Court were, as one might expect at this time, sparsely furnished. Hampton Court chapel, for instance, contained only a pulpit standing on a deal table and a dozen long forms, while the ante chapel had in it just a plank of cedar wood eight feet square lying on two forms, which presumably served as a repository for hats.[96]

In addition to the regular observances there were special days set apart by order of his Highness and Council 'for their seeking God' and, when the occasion warranted it, like the service held at Whitehall, early in 1657, 'to return praises to God for His mercy in the preservation of his Highness's person' which followed the discovery of a plot to assassinate the lord protector, at which Peter Sterry, assisted by two other clerics, officiated. Not to mention the special events connected with Cromwell's rule, such as his first investiture, after which 'his Highness the Lord Protector, being returned to Whitehall, . . . went with his attendants to the Banqueting House, where they heard an exhortation made by Mr. Lockyer, chaplain to his Highness'.[97]

The presence of two other ministers besides a resident Whitehall preacher at the thanksgiving for 'the preservation of his Highness's person' would not have been unusual. Outside clerics frequently assisted the Whitehall trio. They also often officiated at the regular daily services, on occasions such as the one mentioned above, and at public and ceremonial events. Thus it was Dr Thomas Goodwin, president of Magdalen College, Oxford, who preached before the protector, his Council and members of Parliament, who had assembled in Westminster Abbey prior to the opening of Oliver's first Parliament in September 1654. At the opening of the second Protectorate Parliament two years later Dr John Owen, vice-chancellor of Oxford University, performed this service. And at Cromwell's second investiture it was Thomas Manton who, 'by prayer, recommended his Highness, the Parliament, the Council, his Highness's forces by sea and land, the whole government and people of these three nations, to the blessing and protection of God Almighty'. Nine months earlier, on 3 September 1656, *Mercurius Politicus* reported that:

A solemn day was observed by his Highness and the Council in thankful remembrance of those two most wonderful victories which the Lord was pleased to give unto the forces of this Commonwealth; the one upon this day of the month against the Scots at Dunbar, the other at Worcester. Mr. Manton preached before them.'

Prescience of what would, within the space of two years, add particular poignancy to that momentous of dates would have been denied this assembly, including even Mr Manton.[98]

The after-world being of special interest to clerics their presence when Oliver had finally reached the terminus of mortality would have been much in evidence. An interesting anecdote concerning Thomas Goodwin and Peter Sterry immediately prior to, and after, Cromwell's death was allegedly related to Gilbert Burnet, bishop of Salisbury, by John Tillotson, a post-Restoration archbishop of Canterbury. It seems that a week after the protector's death Tillotson happened by chance to be at Whitehall and, hearing that a fast-day was being observed by the protectoral household, he went along out of curiosity to the presence chamber where it was being held. Present at the proceedings was the Cromwell family, headed by the new protector, Richard, and six preachers, including Peter Sterry, Joseph Caryl, John Owen and Thomas Goodwin. 'There', Burnet continues, Tillotson

heard a great deal of strange stuff, enough to disgust a man for ever of that enthusiastic boldness. God was as it were reproached with Cromwell's services and challenged for taking him away so soon. Goodwin, who had pretended to assure them in a prayer that he was not to die, which was but a very few minutes before he expired, had now the impudence to say to God, 'thou hast deceived us, and we are deceived'. Sterry, praying for Richard, used those indecent words, next to blasphemy, 'make him the brightness of his father's glory and the express image of his person'.[99]

Goodwin's assurance that the protector would survive what proved to be a fatal illness was also recorded by Robert Baillie, the vociferous principal of Glasgow College and rabid Presbyterian, in a letter dated January 1662. The unsubtle and jaundiced Edmund Ludlow, who described Goodwin as Cromwell's 'creature and trencher-chaplain', also reported on this incident in his memoirs which are thought to have been written sometime between 1663 and 1673. 'Lord, we beg not for his [Cromwell's] recovery, for that Thou hast already granted and assured us of, but for his speedy recovery', were the words which Goodwin addressed to God according to Ludlow. The story appears yet again in Sir Philip Warwick's *Memoirs*. Needless to say all of those who recorded this affair were antipathetic towards Cromwell's regime.[100] In contrast to Goodwin's railings against the Almighty, Sterry described in one contemporary pamphlet opposed to the Cromwellian regime as 'that cringing court chaplain that also[like Goodwin] bows to whatever is uppermost', is said to have desired those assembled to pray for Cromwell in Whitehall chapel not to be troubled,

> for this is good news; because if he was of great use to the people of God when he was amongst us, now he will be much more so, being ascended to heaven to sit at the right hand of Jesus Christ, there to intercede for us, and to be mindful of us on all occasions.[101]

Hugh Peter's contribution to the sentiment of the hour was contained in the sermon he delivered in the chapel at Whitehall on the Sunday following that fateful September 3. For a text he chose Joshua 1:2, 'My servant Moses is dead'. Comparisons between Cromwell and Moses were not uncommon. In a work published in 1659 and dedicated to Protector Richard Cromwell the author, H. Dawbeny, describes Oliver as 'our second Moses' and goes on to draw what he calls thirty 'lively parallels' between Oliver and the first Moses.[102]

In the protector's funeral procession the three resident Whitehall preachers, Peter Sterry, Joseph Lockyer and Hugh Peter, walked together. In their group were also three others, Dr Jeremiah White, who was yet another cleric described as 'Oliver's chaplain', in this instance by Mark Noble in his *Memoirs of the Protectoral House of Cromwell*, and Messrs Hooke and Howe. Only Sterry, Lockyer and Peter, however, were allocated mourning for the occasion.[103]

Time servers these clerics may or may not have been. What is certain is that, as already said, some had achieved eminence for reasons not connected with their protectoral chaplaincy. There was, for instance, the Platonist Peter Sterry. 'That cringing court chaplain' is what Cromwell's enemies called Sterry. But here was a man whose published works, although now largely neglected, have nevertheless received critical acclaim. He was, according to a twentieth century biographer, 'a writer of an imaginative prose comparable only with that of the greatest masters of that great age of prose poetry'. And others claim that his works are worthy of comparison with those of John Milton. An anti-Presbyterian who nevertheless stayed aloof from the polemical spirit of his times, Sterry was keenly alive to the influences of poetry, music and art, praising as he did the works of Virgil and Van Dyke and also Titian, examples of whose genius adorned the protectoral palaces. It is surely significant that such an individual should form a close attachment to Cromwell who, it is said, was in turn attracted to Sterry because of the man's strong mystical qualities.[104]

Doctors Thomas Goodwin and John Owen, and Messrs Joseph Caryl and Thomas Manton, who had prayed with Cromwell in the morning of the day of the protector's death, together with Philip Nye, who had also preached from time to time at Whitehall during the Protectorate, were positioned in the protectoral cortège among sixteen other ministers, who were all commissioners for approbation of public preachers, one of the many government committees on which all of these clerics, and the Whitehall preachers, sat.[105]

The five men who could be described as the protectoral physicians were Doctors George Bate, or Bates (according to Anthony Wood 'a most noted physician of his time'), Lawrence Wright and Thomas Trapham,* all three of whom were also in the government's employ as state's physicians, Bate being the state's chief physician, together with John Bathurst and Jonathan Goddard.

James Moleyns also treated the protector. He was called in by Bate, Wright, Bathurst and Goddard to attend to Oliver's gall-stone when their own efforts had proved ineffective. The leading lithotomist of his day and the holder of the special office of 'surgeon of the stone' to the royal hospitals of St Bartholomew and St Thomas, Moleyns is said to have felt unable to accept any reward for the successful treatment of his patient because he was a confessed royalist, which moved the protector to beg him to accept the fee of £1,000 in the name of King Charles.[106]

Among the five protectoral physicians were two who not only gave Cromwell the benefit of their medical expertise but who could also be numbered among his political supporters as well. They were Jonathan Goddard and John Bathurst. Goddard sat as member of Parliament for the University of Oxford in the Barebones Parliament called by the then Captain-General Cromwell in the Summer of 1653. He was also a councillor of state during the last six weeks or so of the pre-Protectorate Commonwealth, being sworn in on 3 November 1653 and serving, sometimes with Cromwell himself, on a number of committees which included one for the care of lunatics, another for the Mint, and some

---

*In August 1655 the Council ordered that Trapham should continue as his Highness's surgeon and have 8s a day allowed him and his mates who were to be added to the establishment.

touching on foreign affairs. Thus Goddard was an important element in that government which surrendered its power to Cromwell as lord protector in December 1653. Bathurst represented Richmond in his native Yorkshire in Protector Oliver's second Parliament, summoned in September 1656, and also Protector Richard's Parliament. Like the officers of the household such as the lord chamberlain, the comptroller, the captain of the household guard, the master of the horse, the cofferer and the master of the greencloth, who were also political figures, Bathurst would have been a member of what may be called the court party within Parliament.[107]

On 4 September 1658, the day after Oliver's death, *Mercurius Politicus* announced that 'this afternoon the physicians and surgeons, appointed by order of Council to embowel and embalm the body of his late Highness and fill the same with sweet odours, performed their duty'. No extant official records tell us who these surgeons and physicians were. They are not named in the Council register of the new protector, Richard, the first entries in which are dated 3 September 1658, neither for that matter is there any reference to the Council instruction cited by *Mercurius Politicus*. In fact the only mention relating to the treatment of the late protector's body is contained in an entry dated 14 September 1658, commanding 'that his Highness's corpse being embalmed with all due rites appertaining thereunto, and being wrapped in lead, there ought to be an inscription on a plate of gold to be fixed upon his breast before he be put into the coffin'.[108]

Certainly Lawrence Wright would not have been among those nominated to embalm Cromwell's corpse. Wright, described as physician in ordinary to the protector, had by that time distinguished himself, not only by expiring on 3 September 1657, a year to the day before his master, but also by dying of a similar ailment.[109]

One physician who probably was nominated is George Bate. He attended Cromwell during his last illness. 'Dr Bates watched with his Highness the night before he died', reports a news-letter. Bate also carried out a post-mortem on the corpse on the day of the protector's demise. After the autopsy there was what would appear to have been a preliminary attempt to encoffin the corpse. This, according to Bate, proved unsuccessful for 'though his [the protector's] bowels were taken out and his body filled with spices, wrapped in a fourfold cerecloth . . . put first into a coffin of lead and then into a wooden one' the matter from the putrefactive spleen 'purged and wrought through all, so that there was a necessity of interring it [the corpse] before the solemnity of the funeral'.[110]

Why should Bate wish to admit to something which clearly was not
to his credit as a physician? The answer probably lies in the nature of
the source, and the implication, of the admission. Its origin is to be
found in a politic indictment of Cromwell by Bate, first published in
Latin at the Restoration and entitled *Elenchus Motuum Nuperorum in
Anglia*, which was written it has been said, with the assistance of the
earl of Clarendon. The inference was that the result of Bate's incompe-
tence was really the manifestation of some essential evil surrounding
Cromwell. In an age when nothing could so readily instil awe into
men's collective reasoning than implicit portentous speculation, Bate's
'revelation' was bound to have an anathematising effect on the memory
of Cromwell. What better means of disassociation from a master whom
he had been only too pleased to serve, and of enhancing his esteem in
the estimation of the restored Stuart dynasty, could there have been for
Bate? Surely it is significant that this physician was able to secure the
appointment of principal physician to the king at the Restoration, a
post that he had also held under Charles I, until that monarch's de-
clining fortunes prompted Bate to leave the royal capital, Oxford, for
London.

Bate's politic and, incidentally, uncorroborated, disclosure in
Elenchus Motuum Nuperorum in Anglia was not, it would appear, to be
his last statement concerning the death of his late master, the lord
protector. Anthony Wood, the celebrated Oxford antiquarian, records
that in the year 1663 on 'June 1 or 2, Dr. [George] Bates died at
London of French pox [i.e. syphilis] and confessed on his death-bed
that he poisoned Oliver Cromwell with the provocation of two that are
now bishops, *viz*. [blank], and his majesty was privy to it'. Delusion is,
it should be pointed out, one of the symptoms of the tertiary (which is
also the terminal) stage of this particular venereal disease, at which
point the brain becomes affected.[111]

In the protectoral funeral procession Bate, Bathurst and Goddard
walked together in company with other 'doctors of physic' in the
state's employ, while Trapham occupied a much more junior position
among the state's surgeons who were sandwiched between the apothe-
caries (in front) and their Highnesses' butlers (behind).[112]

VI

Finally, there existed a group of individuals who were not part of the
court, but who did perform some sort of service for the protector,
albeit more often than not nominally. These were the printers, the
draper and the jeweller who, although their services were employed in
the name of his Highness the lord protector, were in reality engaged by

and for the government.

Into this category of employment can be placed the printing, in December 1653, of copies, in pamphlet form, of the new constitution by which the Protectorate was established. Although this document was described as being 'published by His Highness's special commandment' and printed by William du Gard and Henry Hills 'printers to His Highness the Lord Protector', its publication would in fact have been for and on behalf of the central executive and not the protector personally. His Highness's printers were also responsible for the publication of the revised constitution of June 1657, the Humble Petition and Advice, and all other ordinances and proclamations throughout the period of the Protectorate.[113]

The protectoral Privy Seal became the instrument by which his Highness's printers received remuneration. By his letters of Privy Seal dated 22 March 1659, for example, Protector Richard directed that £2,783 7s 10d should be paid to Henry Hills and John Field, who had replaced William du Gard sometime in 1654, printers to his late and present Highness, out of moneys payable for fine, forfeitures, seizures or compositions for uncustomed, prohibited or contraband goods.[114]

As printers to the lord protector Hills and Field, together with the master and wardens of the Stationers Company, were, because of their own diligence in this matter, required to see to it that others did not contravene the four acts passed between June 1643 and January 1653 against the publishing of what were defined as unlicensed, scandalous and seditious books, the execution of these acts being deemed necessary in the interest of public peace. The request, dated 22 June 1658, that Hills and Field carry out this role emanated from the protector himself using the royal 'We'.[115]

The only extant record during the Protectorate period of payment being made for material furnished by Richard Hampden, who styled himself his Highness's draper, is dated April 1654 and is for cloth supplied for the coats of what were still called the state's watermen. The sum was for £36 12s 6d and was paid by Gualter Frost, treasurer for council contingencies. The material would have been supplied to the admiralty commissioners under whose jurisdiction the outfitting of the watermen lay.[116]

The admiralty commissioners were also responsible for the funeral arrangements of Admiral Blake in August 1657. And Hampden petitioned the commissioners requesting that he be the one appointed to furnish them with the necessary cloth and baize for the occasion as, being his Highness's draper, he had always been made use of at such times in this way, like, for instance, on the occasion of the obsequies of Admiral Deane in June 1653.[117]

When the officers of the greencloth were ordered by the Council to see to the supply of funebrial furnishings for Protector Oliver's obsequies, it was at the same time 'recommended to them to make use of Mr Robert Walton and Mr Hampden, drapers, for furnishing the cloth and baize'. It may have been as a result of this that Richard Hampden, together with three others, petitioned the newly restored Charles II in October 1660 for confirmation of their grant of certain goods of Oliver Cromwell, worth £400, to be recovered by them towards satisfaction of a debt of £6,000.[118]

The man styled jeweller to the protector was Christopher Roshe, a German Protestant refugee of the Thirty Years War who had settled in England in the sixteen-forties. Early on in the Protectorate Roshe had requested of Oliver that he be made a free denizen of England, which was a pre-condition to the inheritance of part of their grandfather's estate by Roshe's children by his English wife. In April 1654 the Council decided that the matter should be left to his Highness's pleasure and in course of time Roshe's plea was referred to the first Protectorate Parliament which was dissolved before it could deal with the matter. Whether or not Roshe, who in anticipation of his naturalisation had changed his name to Riddell, obtained his denizenship is not known. Nor, alas, is there any record of work carried out by this would-be Englishman in the name of the lord protector. In fact the only knowledge we have of his existence is contained in the material relating to his naturalisation.[119]

It is possible that Riddell carried out work for, or supplied materials to, Thomas Simon, whose post as the sole maker, to his Highness and the public service, of medals and their chains, and also the office of chief engraver at the mint, were officially confirmed by the Council on 16 March 1655. The manufacture of 'a fair jewel with his Highness's picture' which the Swedish ambassador, Peter Coyett, received at the hands of the protector, simultaneous with a 'rich gold chain' and a knighthood, in May 1656, was something that Riddell could conceivably have been involved in through Simon. For the jewel Simon was paid £863 18s 0d out of a consignment of cocoa from the West Indies, contracted for by Martin Noell, the London merchant and financier.[120]

It was customary for such men as Hills, Field, Hampden and Riddell to take part in ceremonial processions. At the opening of the first Protectorate Parliament in September 1654 Oliver's retinue included 'some well affected citizens, *viz*. his [Cromwell's] draper and other

tradesmen, in rank, three and three (on foot) bare-headed'. These
walked with the protector's 'domestic officers' before the 'rich coach,
drawn by six horses, in the hinder end whereof he [Cromwell] himself
sat'. And in the protector's funeral cortège printers to his Highness,
Henry Hills and John Field, who had been allocated mourning for the
occasion, were placed between the Privy Council's cash-keeper and the
gentlemen who waited at the comptroller's table.[121]

Notes

1. Aylmer, *KS*, p. 29.
2. *The Complete Peerage of England, Scotland, Ireland and the United
   Kingdom*, ed. G.E. Cokayne, revised edn, by Vicary Gibbs and others,
   Vol. V (London, 1926), p. 143; Vol. X (1945), p. 416.
3. *A second Narrative, &c.*, in *Harleian Miscellany*, Vol. III, p. 455.
4. HMC *Fifth Report*, App., p. 152; *The Clarke Papers*, ed. C.H. Firth, Vol.
   III (London, 1899), pp. 43, 47, 48; SP 25/75, pp. 683, 713; SP 25/76,
   p. 230.
5. *Respublica*, pp. 5, 6.
6. *CSPD*, 1656-7, p. 243; 1657-8, p. 321; 1658-9, pp. 57, 99; *Merc. Pol.*, 15-22
   January 1657.
7. *Merc. Pol.*, 2-9 September 1658; *The Commonwealth Mercury*, 2-9
   September 1658; *Proclamation of Richard Cromwell as Lord Protector*
   (London, 1658).
8. *Burton*, II, VII.
9. 'PCR of RC', p. 15.
10. Ludlow, Vol. II, p. 47; 'PCR of RC', pp. 19, 32, 113.
11. Noble, Vol. I, p. 380.
12. 'PCR of RC', pp. 32, 33.
13. *CSP Ven.*, p. 248.
14. 'PCR of RC', pp. 32, 33.
15. Aylmer, *KS*, p. 473; Beattie, pp. 53-63; *Burton*, II, VII; Nichols, p. 1045.
16. *Clarke Papers*, Vol. III, p. 47.
17. *Thurloe State Papers*, Vol. VII, p. 374; *CSPD*, 1658-9, p. 449.
18. *Respublica*, p. 188.
19. Nicholas Carlisle, *An enquiry into the place and quality of the gentlemen of
    His Majesty's most Honourable Privy Chamber* (London, 1829), pp. 288,
    289.
20. *Merc. Pol.*, 11-18 September 1656; 25 June-2 July 1657; Nicholas Carlisle,
    p. 111; *Respublica*, p. 4.
21. *Merc. Pol.*, 27 August-3 September 1657; Nicholas Carlisle, p. 330.
22. Samuel Pegge, *Curialia: or an Historical Account of some Branches of the
    Royal Household*, Vol. I, part I (London, 1791), p. 44; SP 18/183, fos.272,
    274.
23. *Burton*, II, VII; Nichols, p. 1044.
24. Nichols, p. 1044.
25. *Burton*, II, VII; SP 18/183, fos.272, 274, 277; *Merc. Pol.*, 18-25 November
    1658.
26. SP 25/77, p. 174; SP 25/127, pp. 22-3; SP 25/128, p. 20; *Pub. Int.*, 24-31
    January 1659; Pegge, *Curialia*, Vol.I, part III, pp. 2, 31.

27. *Sev. Proc.*, 27 April-4 May 1654; 25 May-1 June, 1654; Aylmer, *KS*, p. 473; James Heath, *Flagellum: or the Life and Death, Birth and Burial of O. Cromwell* (London, 1672 edn), p. 158; Dugdale, pp. 418, 423.
28. *A second Narrative, &c.*, in *Harleian Miscellany*, Vol. III, p. 455.
29. *Sev. Proc.*, 31 August-7 September 1654; Dugdale, p. 423; *Merc. Pol.*, 25 June-2 July 1657; 11-18 September 1656.
30. 'PCR of RC', p. 51; *Merc. Pol.*, 18-25 November 1658; *Burton*, II, VII.
31. *CSPD*, 1655-6, pp. 317, 337, 370, 582.
32. Sir William Holdsworth, *A History of English Law*, Vol. I, 6th edn, Revised (London, 1938), pp. 208-9; *CSPD*, 1654, pp. 46-7.
33. *CSPD*, 1654, pp. 46-7.
34. Ibid., 1658-9, pp. 383-4, 395.
35. Ibid., 1654, pp. 290, 378; 1655, p. 261; 1655-6, pp. 92, 192, 203, 249, 326; 1656-7, p. 214; SP 18/182, fo.281; C.H. Firth, *Cromwell's Army* (London, 1962 edn), Chap. VIII.
36. *CSPD*, 1655-6, p. 192; Firth, *Cromwell's Army*, Chap.VIII.
37. *CSPD*, 1653-4, p. 327; 1654, p. 593.
38. *CSPD*, 1655, pp. 316, 375, 384; 1655-6, p. 236; *A Collection of Original Letters and Papers, concerning the Affairs of England, from the Year 1641 to 1660. Found Among the Duke of Ormonde's Papers*, ed. Thomas Carte, Vol.II (London, 1739), pp. 81, 89; *Thurloe State Papers* Vol. IV, p. 675.
39. *Thurloe State Papers*, Vol. IV, p. 567.
40. *Merc. Pol.*, 16-23 September 1658; 'PCR of RC', pp. 33, 50; Nichols, pp. 1038, 1046.
41. Pegge, *Curialia*, Vol. I, part II, p. 74; Aylmer, *KS*, p. 473.
42. *CSPD*, 1658-9, p. 382.
43. Ibid., Noble, Vol.II, p. 212.
44. *The Complete Peerage*, Vol.III (1913), p. 34, Vol.IV (1916), pp. 614-15.
45. *CSPD*, 1655, p. 128, 1657-8, p.65; SP 18/182, fo.230.
46. *CSPD*, 1657-8, p. 65; *The Protectorate of Oliver Cromwell*, ed. Robert Vaughan, Vol. II, p. 478.
47. *CSPD*, 1653-4, pp. 73, 460; 1655, p. 128; SP 18/82, fo.230.
48. *CSPD*, 1655, pp. 602, 604, 608; 1657-8, pp. 89, 555, 556, 557; 1658-9, pp. 585, 590.
49. *Burton*, II, VII.
50. Aylmer, *KS*, p. 16; Aylmer, *SS*, pp. 264, 265.
51. SP 18/130; *CSP Ven.*, 1653-4, p. 166; Aylmer, *SS*, pp. 136, 344; *Thurloe State Papers*, Vol. VII, p. 39.
52. *CSPD*, 1658-9, p. 352.
53. Ibid., 1659-60, pp. 30, 32, 35, 226, 315, 566, 567.
54. Ibid., 1658-9, p. 367; 1659-60, p.15.
55. *The Humble Narrative of Oliver Fleming, Knight*, in *Somers Tracts*, 3rd Collection, Vol.II (London, 1751), pp. 232-240; *CJ*, Vol.III, p. 299.
56. *LJ*, Vol.VI, p. 252.
57. *CSPD*, 1651-2, p. 334.
58. *CSP Ven.*, 1653-4, pp. 126-7.
59. *CSPD*, 1649-50, p. 24; 1653-4, p. 299.
60. *CSP Ven.*, 1653-4, p. 166.
61. *CSPD*, 1654, p. 402; 1655, pp. 601, 606.
62. *Sev. Proc.*, 29 December 1653-5 January 1654; *Perf. Diurn.*, 3-10 July 1654; Whitelocke, *Memorials*, pp. 575, 577.
63. *Sev. Proc.*, 23-30 March 1654.
64. Whitelocke, *Memorials*, p. 624.
65. *CSPD*, 1655, p. 316.
66. SP 18/183, fos.283, 284.

67. *CSP Ven.*, 1657-9, p. 269.
68. *Proclamation of Richard Cromwell as Lord Protector; Thurloe State Papers*, Vol.VII, p. 382.
69. *CSP Ven.*, 1657-9, p. 242.
70. *Merc. Pol.*, 25 June-2 July 1657.
71. *Burton*, II, VII; *CSP Ven.*, 1657-9, p. 269; SP 18/182, fo.229.
72. SP 25/78, pp. 29-30.
73. SP 25/75, pp. 683, 713; SP 25/78, pp. 29-30; SP 18/156, fo.153; Sir Anthony Wagner, *Historic Heraldry of Britain*, 2nd Impr. reprint (London, 1972), pp. 74, 75; C.W. Scott-Giles, *The Romance of Heraldry* (London, 1929), pp. 189, 190; John Woodward and George Burnett, *A Treatise on Heraldry* (David & Charles Reprints, Newton Abbot, 1969), pp. 486, 487; *Boutells Heraldry*, revised by J.P. Brooke-Little (London, 1973 edn.), p. 215.
74. *CSPD*, 1654, p. 445; 1655, pp. 126, 607; 1655-6, p. 341; 1657-8, pp. 45, 206, 321, 558; SP 25/78, p. 139; SP 18/172, fo.49.
75. *CSPD*, 1648-9, pp. 181, 189-91, 270, 275.
76. Ibid., 1649-50, pp. 154, 189.
77. Ibid., 1649-50, pp. 113, 117, 311, 426, 440, 474, 481; 1650, pp. 95, 382; 1652-3, p. 391; SP 25/2.
78. *CSPD*, 1649-50, p. 549; 1650, p. 83; 1651, p. 72; 1652-3, pp. 9, 139, 391, 479; 1653-4, p. 526.
79. Ibid., 1655, p. 128; 1657-8, p. 87; Aylmer, *KS*, p. 473.
80. Aylmer, *KS*, p. 473; *CSPD*, 1654, p. 452; 1655, pp. 602, 604; 1655-6, pp. 544, 585, 586; 1656-7, pp. 589, 591.
81. *CSPD*, 1658-9, p. 425.
82. Ibid., 1655, p. 128; 1656-7, p. 359; Aylmer, *SS*, p. 236.
83. *Sev. Proc.*, 31 August-7 September 1654; *Merc. Pol.*, 4-11 January 1655; 18-25 January 1655.
84. *Merc. Pol.*, 25 June-2 July 1657; 'PCR of RC', pp. 32, 34.
85. SP 18/182, fo.229; SP 25/2; *CSPD*, 1655-6, p. 114; *Burton*, II, VII; Nichols, p. 1041; 'PCR of RC', p. 153.
86. *CSPD*, 1635, p. 4: 1657-8, pp. 401, 412.
87. *Pub. Int.*, 24-31 January 1659.
88. *CSPD*, 1659-60, p. 569.
89. Aylmer, *KS*, p. 473.
90. *CSPD*, 1657-8, pp. 109, 210, 286, 294; 1658-9, pp. 17, 584.
91. SP 18/182, fo.301; Aylmer, *KS*, p. 473; *CSPD*, 1657-8, p. 285; SP 18/182, fo.301.
92. *Burton*, II, VII; SP 18/182, fo.301.
93. SP 18/203, fo.82; *CSPD*, 1658-9, p. 383.
94. *CSPD*, 1655-6, pp. 14, 15, 102, 282; 1658-9, p. 111; 1660-61, p. 586; 1661-2, pp. 25, 59.
95. Ibid., 1649-50, p. 239; 1651, p. 263; 1651-2, p. 56; 1655, p. 214; R.P. Stearns, *The Strenuous Puritan: Hugh Peter, 1598-1660* (Urbana, Ill., 1954), p. 366.
96. *Sev. Proc.*, 11-18 May 1654; *CSPD*, 1654, p. 370; 1655, p. 256; SP 18/203, fo.92.
97. *CSPD*, 1656-7, p. 239; *Sev. Proc.*, 15-22 December 1653.
98. *Sev. Proc.*, 31 August-7 September 1654; *Merc. Pol.*, 28 August-4 September 1656; 11-18 September 1656; 25 June-2 July 1657.
99. *Bishop Burnet's History of His Own Time*, Vol. I (Dublin, 1724), p. 47.
100. Ludlow, *Memoirs*, Vol.II, p. 45; *The Letters and Journals of Robert Baillie*, ed. David Laing, Vol.III (Edinburgh, 1842), p. 425; Sir Philip Warwick, *Memoirs of the Reign of King Charles I with a continuation to the Happy*

Restoration of King Charles II (London, 1701), p. 388.
101. Ludlow, *Memoirs*, Vol.II, p.45, f.n.2; *Baillie, Letters and Journals*, Vol.III, p. 425.
102. HMC *Fifth Report*, App. p. 143; H. Dawbeny, *Historie and Policie reviewed, in The Heroick Transactions of his Most Serene Highness, Oliver, Late Lord Protector, from his Cradle to his Tomb* (London, 1659).
103. *Burton*, II, VII; Noble, Vol. I, p. 146; SP 18/182, fo.231.
104. Vivian de Sola Pinto, *Peter Sterry, Platonist and Puritan, 1613-72* (Cambridge, 1934), p.3.
105. *Burton*, II, VII.
106. Anthony Wood, *Athenae Oxonienses*, Vol.III (London, 1817), col. 827; *CSPD*, 1655, p. 279; William Munk, *The Roll of the Royal College of Physicians of London*, Vol. I, 2nd edn. (London, 1878), p. 193; George C. Peachy, 'Thomas Trapham – (Cromwell's Surgeon) – and Others', *Proceedings of the Royal Society of Medicine*, Vol. 24, Pt.II (1931).
107. *CSPD*, 1653-4, pp. 230, 233, 237, 262.
108. 'PCR of RC', p. 32.
109. Munk, Vol. I, pp. 182-3; *DNB*.
110. Karl Pearson and G.M. Morant, 'The Wilkinson Head of Oliver Cromwell', *Biometrika*, Vol.XXVI (1935); George Bate, *Elenchus Motuum Nuperorum in Anglia: or a short Historical Account of the Rise and Progress of the Late Troubles in England* (London, 1685), Part II, p.236.
111. *The Life and Times of Anthony Wood, Antiquary, of Oxford, 1632-1695, described by Himself.* Collected from his diaries and papers by Andrew Clark, Vol. I (Oxford Historical Society, 1891), p. 475.
112. *Burton*, II, VII.
113. *The Government of the Commonwealth of England* [&c.] . . . *as it was publickly declared at Westminster the 16th day of December, 1653.*
114. *CSPD*, 1658-9, p. 323.
115. Ibid., 1658-9, p. 71.
116. Ibid., 1654, p. 445.
117. Ibid., 1657-8, p. 68.
118. 'PCR of RC', pp. 19-21; *CSPD*, 1660-1, p. 338.
119. *CSPD*, 1654, p. 134; 1655, pp. 206, 283, 284.
120. Ibid., 1655, p. 83; Whitelocke, *Memorials*, p. 633; *CSPD*, 1656-7, pp. 95, 115, 589.
121. Dugdale, p. 423; *Burton*, II, VII; SP 18/182, fo.230.

5 THE WARDROBE

The wardrobe represents one of the two departments of the royal court (the other was the office of works) which survived to be of service to Protector Oliver. It did not, however, maintain its old form. In former times there had been a great wardrobe, an autonomous offshoot of the chamber, with a master of the wardrobe, who was usually a government office-holding peer, as its titular head, the mastership being in reality a sinecure, and the real work being done by a deputy and his staff. Until April 1643, when he died of wounds received in the king's service, William Fielding, first earl of Denbigh, was the royal wardrobe master, a post that he had held since 1622.

The great wardrobe was principally responsible for buying in all furniture and fittings for the state apartments and maintaining and storing them when they were not in current employment. When such household stuff was moved out of the great wardrobe it became the responsibility of the yeoman of the removing wardrobe and his assistants while in transit, and once installed it came into the care of a keeper of the standing wardrobe, of which there was one at each of the royal palaces. Unlike the great wardrobe the removing wardrobe and the keepers of the standing wardrobes came directly under the jurisdiction of the king's lord chamberlain.

At the outbreak of civil war in 1642 all wardrobe activity was concentrated under the jurisdiction of the king's yeoman of the removing wardrobe, Clement Kinnersley, the keeper of the great wardrobe having joined the king at Oxford. In September 1643, for example, the House of Commons at Westminster ordered 'that fifty pounds shall be forthwith advanced, out of the king's revenue, to Mr. Clement Kinnersley, chief officer of the king's removing wardrobe, for the fitting of Somerset House for the French ambassador'.[1]

Upon the death of the king and the establishment of the English republic in 1649 Kinnersley became keeper of the state's wardrobe. Most of the standing wardrobes were, at this time, abolished. The quarters occupied by Mr Pidgeon 'late keeper of the standing wardrobe' at the Tower of London, for instance, were re-allocated to Edward Ansley, 'storekeeper and master workman of the Armoury Office'. And Clement Kinnersley was, in June 1649, ordered 'to receive all wardrobe stuff from the various officers at Whitehall, St. James's and other places', the wardrobe at York being transferred to Whitehall to furnish the accommodation there of Councillor of State Sir William Masham.[2]

The two standing wardrobes which remained were at Windsor Castle and Hampton Court, under their respective keepers William Thomas and William Smithsby who was a distant relation to Oliver Cromwell. But although these standing wardrobes were not immediately abolished in 1649 their demise was not too far away. A Council order was issued to William Thomas in August 1654 (during the first year of the Protectorate) instructing him to deliver up all the hangings and other wardrobe stuff in his charge, and in this and other similar warrants he is described as keeper of the late standing wardrobe at Windsor, or late keeper of the wardrobe, Windsor. Also in August 1654 the Council commanded that William Smithsby remove himself, his family and his goods from Hampton Court within a month. Cromwell's kinsman had, it seems, claimed the keepership of the privy lodgings and the standing wardrobe at Hampton Court by virtue of a patent dating from the fourth year of Charles I's reign, but this had been disallowed.[3]

Although the concentration of wardrobe activity under the jurisdiction of the king's yeoman of the removing wardrobe had been more or less automatic and supported 'by several orders of Parliament', Kinnersley had nonetheless to fight off a rival claimant to his newly constituted office of keeper of the state's wardrobe. The challenge came from William Legg who had been keeper of the king's standing wardrobe at Whitehall. The earliest extant mention of the dispute is dated March 1650. And from mid-1651 until the end of the same year both men were working in double harness as keepers of the state's wardrobe furnishing Greenwich House with hangings, chairs and other furniture for the use of ambassadors and members of Parliament, as well as furnishing the Parliament House and the Inner Court of Wards in preparation for the reception of ambassadors there.[4]

But in December 1651 the Council of State decided that the office of keeper of the state's wardrobe should be exercised by Legg, and Kinnersley was instructed to deliver up to Legg all the carpets and other wardrobe stuff in his possession, together with the list of goods reserved for the Commonwealth and details as to where they might be located. Also a decision was to be made concerning Legg's salary as keeper of the state's wardrobe and the sum to be paid to Kinnersley for his former services, a situation which must have brought, in equal proportion, joy to Legg and mortification to Kinnersley.[5]

Kinnersley, however, continued to press his claim to the office of keeper of the state's wardrobe, now occupied by Legg, and in the winter of 1652/3 a committee of councillors of state was convened to investigate the matter. The committee included an ex-member of the household of Charles I, Sir Henry Mildmay, who had been master of the jewels and plate, and two future office holders in the household of Oliver Cromwell, Sir Gilbert Pickering and Walter Strickland, who were to become respectively protectoral lord chamberlain and captain of the protector's household guard. In furtherance of his cause Kinnersley laid certain information before the relevant authority concerning Legg's past activities as one who had actively aided the late king in his struggle with Parliament. According to Kinnersley it was the weapons first committed to Legg's custody, when he was keeper of the king's wardrobe at Whitehall, which armed 'that rabble of roaring boys' who were taken into the palace of Whitehall to guard the late king and attended him when he went to the House of Commons on that fateful day in January 1642, in order to arrest the five members. Legg had afterwards, again according to Kinnersley, retained these arms in his keeping until the following July when he secretly delivered them up for transportation to the king who was then at York. Kinnersley also mentioned 'columnies' that had been directed at *him* from which he wished the opportunity to clear himself. Consequently the investigating committee's terms of reference were not only to consider Legg's and Kinnersley's respective claims to the office of state's wardrobe keeper, but also to examine the charges that had been laid against the two men.[6]

The upshot of the matter was that in February 1654, some two months after the establishment of the Protectorate, Kinnersley emerges acting as wardrobe keeper to the protector, and on the 21st and 23rd of that month he was instructed by the protectoral Council to furnish the apartments in Whitehall that had been set aside for the use of the lord protector, according to the instructions of her Highness the Lady Cromwell. The furnishings to be used were those deemed suitable from among the wardrobe stuff belonging to the state. To this end such individuals as William Thomas, keeper of the now defunct standing wardrobe at Windsor and, significantly, William Legg, were ordered to deliver up to Clement Kinnersley all the rich hangings and other wardrobe stuff still in their possession.[7]

Nevertheless the Kinnersley/Legg controversy was apparently not yet resolved because later in 1654 Kinnersley complained in a petition to the protector that the original committee of investigation had referred the matter elsewhere, and so judgement was still pending. This was in spite of the fact that Kinnersley was *de facto* his Highness's wardrobe keeper, which was the state's wardrobe keeper redesignated.

In the meantime Legg's continued 'scandalous assertions' were making it difficult for Kinnersley to function efficiently as wardrobe keeper because they encouraged obstructiveness in those who considered that the office rightly belonged to Legg. What is more Legg was still receiving the £300 a year settled on him by the pre-Protectorate Commonwealth Council of State as keeper of the state's wardrobe, while Kinnersley had not yet had his office as his Highness's wardrobe keeper officially confirmed, neither was he in possession of suitable accommodation, nor in receipt of diet. So desperate was Kinnersley to put a period to this unsatisfactory state of affairs that at one point he offered to 'render up' his post if Legg's claim was the better and assist Legg as his servant. But Kinnersley's direct appeal to Cromwell brought forth a more positive reaction than hitherto and in January 1655 the protectoral Council advised that Kinnersley should be confirmed as wardrobe keeper with whatever salary his Highness may think fit.* It was further recommended that Kinnersley should receive the sum of £5,486 10s 10d for salary and expenses which were due to him for the period 1642 to 1652. As for accommodation, Kinnersley was to have Legg's lodgings in Whitehall which Legg had occupied since his days as keeper of the king's Whitehall standing wardrobe, and which he had now been given two weeks to vacate. Kinnersley had lost the lodgings he would have occupied in Whitehall as yeoman of the king's removing wardrobe and he was forced to operate from, and presumably live in, a part of the Banqueting House which, so a disgruntled Kinnersley complained in December 1654 'is not fitting, especially at this season'.[8]

We next hear of William Legg in a petition, dated January 1656, in which the 70 year old ex-wardrobe keeper, who according to the document quit his Whitehall lodgings on 16 February 1655, requested the arrears in salary and expenses due to him for his previous service, plus a pension. Thirteen months later, in March 1657, a warrant was issued for the payment of £53 15s 10d to 'William Legg, late keeper of the wardrobe'. This sum represented the balance of the moneys owed to Legg for expenses incurred in the state's service. And the following month four protectoral privy councillors were designated to consider Legg's demand for the payment of arrears in his salary. The outcome is not known but the chances are the matter was never resolved. Legg did not have much longer to live at this time anyhow.[9]

*For the discharge of his office at Hampton Court the Council recommended on Christmas Day 1655 that Kinnersley be issued with a patent under the Great Seal by the protector for a salary of £600 per annum, which included £100 in lieu of diet, back dated to 21 February 1654 when Kinnersley was appointed.

As with the two protectoral stewards the first few months or so of the Protectorate were busy ones for Keeper of his Highness's Wardrobe Kinnersley, whose time was taken up with the accumulation of what remained of the late king's wardrobe stuff for the use of the lord protector. (This has already been dealt with in Chapter 1:II).

As well as furnishing the protector with wardrobe stuff Kinnersley continued to provide, at the government's expense, a similar service for the departments of state, government dignitaries, the entertainment of representatives of foreign powers, and England's own ambassadors, who were loaned furniture whenever they went abroad, as he had done as keeper of the state's wardrobe during the pre-Protectorate Commonwealth period, and just as the former royal wardrobe had also done.

Kinnersley, for instance, supplied such hangings, chairs, carpets and the like as were deemed necessary, at the convening of Oliver's Parliaments and of course that of his son Richard, to furnish the palace of Westminster, which in the case of the reconstituted Upper House necessitated the purchase of new furnishings including woolpacks (stuffed cushions). In conjunction with the surveyor of works, John Embree, Kinnersley also arranged for seats to be installed in Westminster Abbey for the protector and his Privy Council to hear the pre-opening of Parliament sermon. Similar arrangements were made in the Upper House where Kinnersley and Embree provided chairs for the Privy Council and a throne for the protector placed upon a railed-off dais from which Oliver, standing under a cloth of state, addressed his Parliament. The members of the House of Commons were summoned to his Highness's presence by the usher of the black rod and they were seated upon forms, again furnished by Kinnersley with the co-operation of Surveyor of Works Embree. While Parliament sat all this wardrobe stuff was in the custody of the senior sergeant-at-arms who surrendered it up to Kinnersley upon each dissolution.[10]

There was, too, the provision of furnishings for the new High Court of Justice set up in the late Spring of 1658 to try a number of conspirators for treason. To this end Kinnersley was instructed to hang the place in Westminster Hall where the court was to sit with what was simply described as red stuff.[11]

Of the officers of state supplied with furnishings there was, in 1655, the secretary to the protectoral Privy Council, for whom Kinnersley was ordered to prepare rooms at Somerset House, and the lord deputy of Ireland, Cromwell's son-in-law Charles Fleetwood, who, upon his recall to London in that year, was allotted quarters at Derby House in the Strand.[12]

As already stated, it was the house of Sir Abraham Williams, situated within the confines of the palace of Westminster, which was used to accommodate foreign ambassadors when they were being entertained by the government of the Protectorate. For these occasions Kinnersley would hire suitable furnishings from private individuals, such as the six beds, one with a purple velvet valance and curtains, the counterpoint pillow cases trimmed with gold lace, the quilt of yellow tapestry and other bedroom furniture rented for the receptions of the Dutch and French ambassadors early in 1654.[13]

As for the loaning of wardrobe stuff to England's own ambassadors whenever they went abroad, in February 1657 Kinnersley was instructed by the protector's Privy Council to look out twelve large pieces of old but well-lined, clean and repaired tapestry from the hangings that belonged to the state for the use in France of England's ambassador to the court of Louis XIV, the one-time royalist Sir William Lockhart. These tapestries were to be put into the custody of Lady Lockhart (née Robina Sewster, Lockhart's second wife and niece to Oliver Cromwell). Also handed over to Lady Lockhart for Sir William's use in France were sixteen dishes, thirty-six trencher plates and six trencher salt-cellars, all of silver, which Kinnersley was instructed to look out from among the plate left in his charge for the provision of ambassadors, and to have the dents knocked out of them before being boiled and burnished. Both the tapestries and the plate that had been handed over to Lady Lockhart were ordered to be returned to Kinnersley on the termination of Sir William's appointment. But when at the Restoration Charles II's master of the jewel house demanded of Lockhart the return of the plate 'marked with the arms of the state', it had already been disposed of in France 'by order of the usurped powers', as had the hangings 'bearing Cromwell's arms', with the return of which Lockhart was also charged.[14]

So we have Wardrobe Keeper Kinnersley incorporating into his office some of the functions of the jewel office in a royal court. Like the royal great wardrobe, but infinitely smaller, this was an autonomous sub-department of the chamber department, the mastership of which, again like that of the great wardrobe, was held by a member of the government or favourite of the monarch. Charles I suffered the unedifying spectacle of seeing his master of the jewels and plate, Sir Henry Mildmay, sitting as one of the judges at his trial, although Mildmay's name does not appear on the death warrant. As a member of the English republic's Council of State, Mildmay served on the committee which considered what goods of the late king should be reserved for the use of the Council. And for his part in disposing of the crown jewels his royalist enemies were to dub him 'Knave of Diamonds'.[15]

In spite of the inclusion of some of what had been jewel office activity in the post of his Highness's wardrobe keeper the demands upon Kinnersley and his staff would have been considerably less than those made upon the former royal wardrobe. To begin with the protectoral wardrobe did not incorporate every function of that of its royal predecessors. The provision of livery and other items of clothing for members of the household, which had been the responsibility of the king's great wardrobe, did not come under Kinnersley's jurisdiction. Many of what had been household servants in royal times had, as we have seen, in any case gone out of court as it were, even though under the Protectorate they still performed aulic duties. Cases in point are provided by the wardrobe itself and by the protectoral barges department. The provision of new coats for his Highness's watermen, and livery of grey cloth for the master of the barges and his assistant, together with his Highness's arms for a badge, was, for instance, the responsibility of the admiralty commissioners acting on direct instructions from the protector's Privy Council. There was also the fact that although considerable pains were taken, and much expense incurred, in surrounding Oliver with the customary appliances of sovereignty, the protectoral court was, nevertheless, a rather modest affair when compared with that of the late king. And the government was of an altogether different kind than hitherto. So there would have been far less wardrobe stuff to be handled, there being a much smaller number of dignitaries entitled to be loaned such things and only two protectoral residences to be equipped.[16]

The lack of pressure on Kinnersley could be reflected in his request in 1654 for 'a competency' only for performing the office of keeper of the protectoral wardrobe, instead of the twelve dishes a day, plus a salary of £1,000 a year, that he had received as yeoman of the king's standing wardrobe. This could, however, have just as easily been an attempt to further his case in the dispute with Legg which had at that time not yet been resolved. Certainly Kinnersley had sufficient time at his disposal to act as steward for the entertainment of the Portuguese ambassador in early September 1657, Nicholas Bond, who usually executed this office, being indisposed. For this service Kinnersley received the usual fee of £30. Kinnersley also acted as steward at the entertainment, in the latter half of June 1658, of two French dignitaries, the Duc de Crequi, first gentleman of the bedchamber to Louis XIV of France, and Monsieur Mancini, nephew to Cardinal Mazarin, who were 'accompanied by divers of the nobility of France, and many gentlemen of quality'. The two men had been sent to congratulate the protector on the part his military forces had just played in the successful Anglo-French campaign against Spain in Europe, culminating in the Commonwealth's acquisition of Mardyke and Dunkirk. They also came 'to assure his Highness of the high esteem his Majesty [the king of France] hath of his friendship, and that he shall not be wanting upon any occasion to testify his earnest desire to maintain the amity and good correspondence happily established with his Highness'. For performing the duties of steward on this occasion Kinnersley claimed a fee of £60, which was double the usual remuneration for such a service. Perhaps he considered that the extra work involved in catering for 'divers of the French nobility, and many gentlemen of quality', or the singular auspiciousness of the occasion, warranted the extra money. Certainly the £1,098 15s 9d above the £500 allocated for the reception of this mission during its six-day stay in England was considerably more than the cost normally incurred in entertaining foreign ambassadors over a similar period of time, which rarely exceeded the £300 allotted by much more than about 10 per cent. But during a Privy Council meeting in the following month, at which the protector, now ailing and close to death, was himself present, the disbursements for the entertainment of the French legates were subjected to the scrutiny of those present. The outcome was a recommendation that the lord chamberlain, Mr Comptroller, and a third councillor, William Sydenham, who was also a treasury commissioner, should 'speak with Kinnersley concerning some abatement in the allowance of £60 to himself as steward' at the recent reception.[17]

If the protectoral household was rather less magnificent than its royal predecessors, thus giving Kinnersley the opportunity of playing the role of a veritable court Pooh-Bah, the same could not be said of the protector's chargeable and splendid funeral', as the contemporary philosopher Thomas Hobbes called it, which was every bit as splendid as those of England's rulers who had gone before; in fact Cromwell's obsequies, which *Mercurius Politicus* announced were 'to be performed with all honour and magnificence . . . as becomes the dignity and renown of so great a Prince', are generally regarded as being among the most spectacular, and the most expensive, England has ever seen.[18]

The rabid republican Edmund Ludlow tells us that the Council having resolved that the funeral of what he calls 'the late usurper' should be very magnificent, 'the care of it was referred to a committee of them, who, sending for Mr Kinnersley, Master of the Wardrobe,

desired him to find out some precedent by which they might govern
themselves in this important affair. After examination of his books and
papers, Mr Kinnersley, who was suspected of popery, recommended to
them the solemnities used on the like occasion for Philip the Second,
King of Spain, who had been represented to be in purgatory for about
two months.'[19]

This report is, in part at least, substantially true. The committee of
privy councillors designated 'to consider of what is fit to be done in
reference to his late Highness's funeral' did ask Kinnersley's advice concerning the wardrobe aspect of the forthcoming obsequies, all instructions putting into effect Kinnersley's, and for that matter everyone
else's, side of things having to emanate from the Council. That
Kinnersley was a papist, or even a suspected one is, however, unlikely,
as indeed is the suggestion that he recommended the rites performed at
the funeral in 1598 of that most Catholic of monarchs, Philip II of
Spain. Ludlow, it must be remembered, had come to hate Cromwell
and his regime and the funeral of the protector by its very nature would
have offended the Puritan within him, and certainly the 'folly and pro-
fusion', as he calls it, of the lying in state, and the ritual connected with
it, would, in Ludlow's eyes, have smacked of popery. The exequies in
1665 of Philip IV of Spain, whom Cromwell considered his greatest
enemy, as Elizabeth I had regarded Philip II, were again not unlike
those of Protector Oliver. It was, in fact, the procedure followed for
the exequies of the last king of England (and in this case Scotland too)
to have a state funeral, James I, who was, of course, no papist, that
Kinnersley studied. 'At Whitehall they are now preparing for the funeral
of the late Protector, . . . which will take place . . . with extraordinary
pomp and magnificence. They are consulting ancient books to see what
was done by the kings on such occasions, and say that it will be more
splendid than ever before . . . It was decided to follow the forms observed at the burial of King James, but this will be much greater',
wrote the Venetian resident in England to his masters in Venice.[20]

Having consulted the records Kinnersley submitted his findings to
the funeral committee of privy councillors thus:

According to former times every presence chamber, drawing chamber and privy chamber had cloths of estate, and chairs, stools and
cushions of velvet. If these are wanting, the rooms will lack much
of what many subjects in the like cases have, for every earl may have
a cloth of estate, though with distinction. If enough velvet to make
sufficient cloths of estate is not to be found then two might be of

velvet, one for the hearse and a second for his Highness, and the
others may be of cloth. There should be in Whitehall and Somerset
House no less than seven cloths of estate, whereof five may be of
cloth, though if possible his Highness should have one of velvet.[21]

An indication of the extent of the desire to match in magnificence
this particular aspect of Cromwell's state obsequies with that of the
last monarch to be so buried, and the measure of Kinnersley's success
in achieving this, is exemplified by the following extract from *Mercurius
Politicus* published under the heading 'A particular and exact relation
how Somerset House is prepared for the effigy, or representation, of his
late Highness, by particular order of the Council':

The first room the people enter was formerly the Presence Chamber,
which is hung completely with black, and at the upper end a cloth of
estate, with a chair of estate standing upon the Haut-place under the
state. From thence you pass to a second large room, which was the
Privy Chamber all completely hung with black, and a cloth of estate
at the upper end, having also a chair of estate upon the Haut-place,
under the cloth of estate. The third room is à large withdrawing
chamber, completely hung as the other, with a black cloth, and a
cloth of estate at the upper end, with a chair of estate as in the
other rooms. All these three large rooms are completely furnished
with escutcheons of his Highness's arms, crowned with the imperial
crown, and upon the head of each cloth of estate is fixed a large
majesty escutcheon fairly painted and gilt upon taffety. The fourth
room, where both the body and the effigy do lie [is] completely
hung with black velvet, the roof of the said room ceiled also with
velvet, and a large canopy or cloth of estate of black velvet fringed
over the effigy. The effigy itself [is] apparelled in a rich suit of uncut velvet, being robed first in a kirtle robe of purple velvet, laced
with a rich gold lace, and furred with ermines. Upon the kirtle is the
royal large robe of the like purple velvet, laced and furred with
ermines, with rich strings, and tassels of gold. His kirtle is girt with a
rich embroidered belt, in which is a fair sword richly gilt, and
hatched with gold, hanging by the side of the effigy. In the right
hand is the golden sceptre representing government; in his left hand
is held the globe, representing principality; upon his head, the cap
of regality of purple velvet, furred with ermines. Behind the head is a
rich chair of estate of cloth of gold tissued. Upon the cushion of the
chair stands the imperial crown set with stones. The whole effigy lies

upon a bed covered with a large pall of black velvet, under which is
a fine Holland sheet upon six stools of cloth of gold tissued. By the
sides of the bed of state lies a rich suit of complete armour, representing his command as General. At the feet of the effigy stands his
crest, as is usual in all ancient monuments. This bed of state, upon
which the effigy so lies, is ascended unto by two ascents, covered
with the aforesaid pall of velvet, and the whole work is incompassed
about with rails covered with velvet. At each corner is a square pillar
or upright, covered with velvet. Upon the tops of them are four
beasts, supporters of the imperial arms, bearing banners or streamers
crowned. The pillars are decorated with trophies of military honor,
carved and gilt. The pedestals of the pillars have shields and crowns
gilt, which makes the whole work noble and complete. Within the
rails stand eight great standards or candlesticks of silver, being
almost five feet in height, with great tapers in them of virgin wax,
three foot in length. Next to the candlesticks are set upright in
sockets, the four great standards of his Highness's arms, the guidons,
the great banners, and banrolls, all of taffety, richly gilt and painted.
The cloth of estate hath a Majesty scutcheon fixed at the head, and
upon the velvet hangings on each of the effigies is a Majesty scutcheon, and the whole room [is] fully and completely furnished with
taffety scutcheons.[22]

A contrast indeed to the obsequies of the monarchs immediately preceding and succeeding Cromwell. The funeral of the executed Charles I
in 1649 had been a private affair for which the government had allotted
only £500. Charles II it seems faired little better after his death in 1685.
'The king's body', writes Burnet, 'was very indecently neglected . . . His
funeral was very mean. He did not lie in state. No mournings were given.
And the expense of it was not equal to what an ordinary noble man's
funeral will rise to.'[23]

All the wardrobe activity for the state funeral of Protector Oliver
was, as we have already seen (in Chapter 2), paid for out of the new
protector's household revenue, through the board of greencloth.

As to the instructions regarding preparations for the obsequies, these
Kinnersley received direct from the Council, as he had for everything
else both during the pre-Protectorate Commonwealth period and the
Protectorate itself. In a royal court this would not, however, have been
the case. Such instructions would have come to the master of the wardrobe from the lord chamberlain (see Chapter 4:I). An example of this
is provided by what is described as 'a warrant for a pall of cloth of

tissue for the funeral of King James' issued by the then lord chamberlain, William Herbert, the third earl of Pembroke to 'the right honorable
William, earl of Denbigh, Master of his Majesty's Great Wardrobe'. The
document instructs the royal wardrobe master 'to cause to be provided
and delivered . . . one chair with a back of black velvet with a cushion
for the Master of the Horse and one pall of cloth of tissue . . . lined
with purple satin as hath been formerly accustomed. And likewise to
be delivered unto the sergeant painter two yeards of crimson velvet to
line the great crown and one ell of white taffata for the inside of the
said crown'.[24]

The disposal of the wardrobe stuff acquired for Protector Oliver's
funeral was, as might be expected, also the responsibility of the protectoral Privy Council. Contained in the Privy Council register of Protector Richard, with a marginal note 'Attention Mr. Kinnersley', is the
following order:

That none of the velvet, cloth, baize, or other things appertaining to,
or provided for, his late Highness's funeral at Somerset House, or
elsewhere, shall be disposed of in any other way than as the committee of the Council for the business of the said funeral shall direct.
And that no part thereof shall be demanded, or taken as fees, by any
person without special order of the Council.[25]

One very important role which normally fell to the king's great wardrobe at this time, but in which the protectoral wardrobe had no part,
thus going some way to enable it, in spite of its diminutiveness, to carry
out to the full its other obsequial duties, was the issue of mourning. In
this instance the provision of mourning to those entitled to it, which
appears to have been everyone from great officers of state to the workmen employed about the protectoral palaces, and also parish officials,
the poor, and the civic dignitaries of the cities of London and
Westminster, and many others besides, was executed by a special
committee set up for this express purpose.[26]

It is the list submitted to this committee by Kinnersley, for its authori-
sation of mourning for members of his department, that provides us with
the only evidence we have as to the number of people employed in the
service of what is described as 'the office of the wardrobe'. The total
involved was only fourteen, a figure that represents only a fraction of
the number employed in the wardrobe departments of the two preceding monarchs. Apart from the 'master of the office', Clement Kinnserley,

there is John Kinnersley, Clement's son and assistant, Richard Marriott who was responsible for the wardrobe at Hampton Court, Mr Hornlock, a tailor, who in the funebrial cortège of the protector walked with his Highness's gunsmith, shoemaker, hatter, upholsterer and three measurers of cloth, plus ten others whose individual functions are not known, of whom only four received mourning and took part in the obsequies of the protector, being positioned in the funeral procession immediately behind the artificers and tradesmen employed in the office of works.[27]

It will be noticed that Kinnersley was referred to as 'master of the office' of the wardrobe which is a rather more elevated title than the one he was more usually known by, that of keeper of the wardrobe. This is not the only instance of Kinnersley being thus styled. Edmund Ludlow in describing Kinnersley's role in the protector's funeral arrangements refers to him as master of the wardrobe (see above). While a semi-official news-letter dated May 1658 tells us that 'the two caps of crimson and purple velvet, worn by princes [i.e. caps of estate which are badges of rank worn instead of a crown], are at this moment being made up by order of the Master of the Wardrobe, making the people talk largely of kingship'. Kinnersley's official title, however, most probably remained keeper of his Highness's wardrobe, that of master being in this instance simply a loose term to describe a head of a court department or office, which Kinnersley, of course, was. Certainly in the Reverend Prestwich's description of Cromwell's funeral procession Kinnersley is listed as being keeper of the wardrobe and his son John as assistant to the keeper of the wardrobe, Clement being positioned immediately behind, and therefore slightly senior to, Surveyor of Works John Embree, and John being situated directly in front of the mews-keeper, to whom he was an inferior. Kinnersley's son is also designated as being assistant keeper in an account for 'work bespoke, provided and done' to adorn the framework of 'the standing hearse at Westminster to receive the effigy of his Highness'.[28]

The two caps of state made up, as the above-mentioned news-letter suggests, for Cromwell's impending coronation, did in fact do service at the protectoral lying in state, or rather one of them did. 'In the right hand' of the funeral effigy we are told 'was a sceptre, and in the left a globe. Upon the head was placed a purple-velvet cap furred with ermine suitable to the robes. Behind the head was placed a rich chair of tissued gold, whereon was placed an imperial crown which lay high that the people may behold it . . . When this show had been seen for many weeks together the scene was altered, the effigy being removed into another room it was there set up standing upon an ascent under a cloth of state, being vested as it was lying, only now his purple-velvet cap was changed for a crown.' In January 1654 'two great swords of the late king' were repurchased by the government from a private individual for £50, which was the price he had originally bought them for. These royal accoutrements, like the caps of state, were undoubtedly acquired for the use of the lord protector.[29]

With the collapse of the Protectorate Kinnersley was given the combined post of house and wardrobe keeper at Hampton Court, the new Council of State being anxious that the ex-protectoral palace should be guarded against waste or defacement and the household stuffs and goods therein saved from spoil and embezzlement. To assist him Kinnersley was allowed an under wardrobe keeper and two porters, but only until the furnishings there had been disposed of. Two gardeners were also allocated to him. He continued to be responsible for the state's wardrobe though, being paid £170 19s 0d in October 1659 for furnishing the Parliament House and its adjacent rooms, and also the rooms used by the Council of State and the admiralty commissioners. And in January 1660 he was ordered to furnish the lodgings of General George Monck and to fetch goods from Hampton Court for an unspecified purpose.[30]

At the Restoration hundreds of petitions were addressed to the king for offices in the royal household, including, of course, some for the wardrobe. A John Whynyard petitioned for the reversion of the office of keeper of the standing wardrobe at Hampton Court, which he claimed had been held by his ancestors during the previous three reigns but which William Smithsby had obtained by surprisal. By way of a self commendation Whynyard claimed that he had ever been steadfastly loyal to the royal cause, while his father had lost his entire estate and been imprisoned for seven years for being one of Charles I's admirals. Another petition, this time from someone who already held one post in the royal household, Francis Rogers, page of the bedchamber, was for William Legg's old post. Rogers claimed that at York on 13 August 1642 Charles I had decreed that he was next in line for the office after Legg, who was now dead. One individual, at least, did not wait until the Restoration to solicit for a post in the royal wardrobe department. Acting on the maxim that it is the early bird which catches the worm, Thomas Ross as prematurely as 1656 requested of the then exiled Charles II that he be considered for the office of yeoman of the removing wardrobe in the event of the king being restored to his throne. In order to justify his request Ross cites the loss of his fortune and the ruination of himself and his family because of his faithfulness to the royalist cause during the late rebellion, and contrasts this with the activities of the former occupier of the post of yeoman of the removing wardrobe, Clement Kinnersley, who had, according to Ross, long adhered to the rebels, having been employed by them as a commissioner for the sale of the king's goods and was currently a menial servant to Oliver Cromwell. When the restoration of Charles II finally did take place the office of yeoman of the removing wardrobe was given to someone named Weekes.[31]

Obviously Kinnersley was at somewhat of a disadvantage when it came to securing a post in the wardrobe of Charles II. But this did not prevent him from attempting to do just that. In his petition to the king for his former office of yeoman of the removing wardrobe, Kinnersley endeavoured to match the impressive qualifications of loyalty to the royalist cause of the above suppliants with the claim that he had served the wardrobe continuously since his birth, and that between the collapse of the Protectorate and the Restoration he had, as combined house and wardrobe keeper at Hampton Court, managed to preserve from sale or embezzlement £500,000 worth of his Majesty's goods. There was also the sum of £7,000 owed to him in wages and expenses.[32]

Kinnersley's son, John, ex-assistant keeper of the protectoral wardrobe, also applied to the newly restored monarch for a post in the royal household. In fact he petitioned for no less than three separate offices, the keepership of the standing wardrobe at Theobalds, which he claimed was granted to him by Charles I in reversion after a person now deceased, the office of keeper of the New Lodge Walk in Windsor Park, and the reversion, after the present occupier, of the keepership of the still-house at Hampton Court.[33]

Apparently neither Clement nor John Kinnersley succeeded in their attempts to become reinstated in royal service, thus breaking what was probably an ancient family tradition. But Clement Kinnersley's exit is not without its legacy of interesting speculative material. In 1649, when the estate of the executed Charles I was being disposed of, a silver gilted spoon weighing three ounces, which had been part of the crown jewels, was sold to a Mr Kinnersley for sixteen shillings. It has been intimated that this, and what was described in the Restoration inventory of the crown jewels as the anointing spoon, might conceivably have been one and the same. The chances are that the Mr Kinnersley who bought the spoon in 1649 was Clement Kinnersley. Is it therefore possible, one wonders, that this was returned by its purchaser in an attempt to ingratiate himself, and thus procure employment, with the regime of 1660? Of this, and Kinnersley's eventual fate, we shall probably never be absolutely sure.[34]

Notes

1. *CJ*, Vol.III, p. 252.
2. *CSPD*, 1649-50, p. 535; 1650, pp. 54, 312.
3. Ibid., 1654, pp. 342, 347.
4. Ibid., 1650, p. 57; 1651-2, pp. 32, 33, 35.
5. Ibid., 1651-2, pp. 44, 45, 83, 181, 545.
6. Ibid., 1652-3, pp. 23, 24.
7. Ibid., 1653-4, p. 415; 1654, pp. 395, 483.
8. Ibid., 1654, pp. 394, 410, 411, 449; 1655, pp. 15, 71.
9. Ibid., 1655-6, p. 128; 1656-7, pp. 307, 357, 592.
10. Ibid., 1654, pp. 322, 342, 343, 440; 1655, p. 27; 1656-7, pp. 100, 110; 1657-8, pp. 262, 296, 557; 1658-9, p. 256; *Merc. Pol.*, 4-11 February 1658.
11. *CSPD*, 1658-9, pp. 27, 584.
12. Ibid., 1655, pp. 260, 268.
13. Ibid., 1653-4, p. 414; 1654, pp. 315, 447.
14. Ibid., 1656-7, p. 261; 1660-61, p. 397.
15. Ibid., 1649-50, p. 276.
16. Ibid., 1657-8, p. 39.
17. Ibid., 1654, p. 411; 1657-8, pp. 81, 124, 556; 1658-9, pp. 63, 94, 99, 252.
18. Thomas Hobbes, *Behemoth, or the Long Parliament*, ed. Ferdinand Tönnes (London, 1889); *Merc. Pol.*, 9-16 September 1658.
19. *Ludlow*, Vol.II, p. 47.
20. 'PCR of RC', p. 19; Lady Anne Fanshawe, *Memoirs of Lady Fanshawe* (London, 1905); pp. 202-4; *CSP Ven.*,1657-9, pp. 243, 248.
21. SP 18/182, fo.232.
22. *Merc. Pol.*, 14-21 October 1658.
23. *Bishop Burnet*, Vol.I, p. 337.
24. Nichols, p.1036.
25. 'PCR of RC', p. 129.
26. *CSPD*, 1658-9, pp. 143, 171.
27. SP 18/182, fo.303; SP 18/203, fo.95; *Burton*, II, VII.
28. *Clarke Papers*, Vol.III, p. 150; *Burton*, II, VII; *Republica*, p. 199.
29. *Republica*, pp. 188, 189; *CSPD*, 1653-4, p. 457.
30. *CSPD*, 1658-9, p. 371; 1659-60, pp. 310, 319, 589; SP 18/203, fos.95, 96.
31. *CSPD*, 1656-7, p. 179; 1660-61, p. 27; 1661-2, p. 522.
32. *CSPD*, 1660-61, p. 396.
33. Ibid., pp. 27, 241; 1661-2, p. 223.
34. Martin Holmes and H.D.W. Sitwell, *The English Regalia* (HMSO, London, 1972), p. 5.

6 THE NATURE OF COURT LIFE

Naturally the court of Oliver Cromwell possessed little of the atmosphere of either its Stuart predecessors, those of James I and Charles I, or its sybaritic successor, that of Charles II. It was not the heart of London society, nor was it the haunt of jackanapes and pimps vying with one another for favours and preferments for themselves and others. A description of the protectoral court is handed down to us by one who would have had some knowledge of it, the physician George Bate. The account appears in Bate's politic post-Restoration indictment of the master he had been once only too pleased to serve. And it is contained in a passage, the contents of which, paradoxically, make Bate, who, at the Restoration succeeded in securing his old post of principal physician to the king, an apologist, albeit a reluctant one, of the Cromwellian regime:

> To give the devil [Cromwell] his due, he restored justice, as well distributive as comutative, almost to its ancient dignity and splendour; the judges without covetousness discharging their duties according to law and equity; and the laws (unless some few that particularly concerned Cromwell) having full and free course in all courts without hindrance or delay. Mens manners also, at least outwardly, seemed to be reformed to the better, whether by really subtracting the fuel of luxury, or through fear of the ancient laws, now revived and put in execution. His own court also was regulated according to a severe discipline; here no drunkard, nor whoremonger, nor any guilty of bribery, was to be found, without severe punishment. Trade began again to prosper; and in a word, gentle peace to flourish all over England.[1]

At the same time the picture of the protectoral court as a cultural wilderness, and a singularly dour one at that, is one which may appeal to many an imagination, but which is nonetheless quite untrue.* Even James Heath in his vicious calumniation of Cromwell concedes that Oliver 'was a great lover of music, and entertained the most skilful in

---

*Ernest Law in volume two of his *History of Hampton Court Palace* deals at some length with, what is alleged to be, life at Cromwell's court, as indeed does Antonia Fraser in *Cromwell: Our Chief of Men*.

that science in his pay and family'. But Heath, as was his wont, found it necessary to qualify this by declaring that this manifested itself in Cromwell as it had 'in that like wicked Saul who, when the evil spirit was upon him, thought to lay and still him with those harmonious charms'. Heath continues in the same carping vein:

> . . . but generally he respected, or at least pretended a love to, all ingenious and eximious [i.e. choice] persons in any arts, whom he arranged to be sent or brought to him. But the niggardliness and incompetence of his reward shewed that this man was a personated act of greatness, and that private Cromwell yet governed Prince Oliver.[2]

Leaving aside their qualificatory component these particular observations on Cromwell are confirmed by other evidence. There was, in Oliver's funeral procession, John Hingston who exalted in the title master of music, together with seven other musicians employed by Cromwell, Richard Hudson, Thomas Mallard, John Rodgers, the violinist David or Davis Mell, who had been a member of Charles I's orchestra and was with the king at Oxford during the civil war, William Howes, sometime one of the king's singers in St George's Chapel, Windsor, and two others previously employed by King Charles, William Gregory, who like Mell had also seen service in the court of James I, in whose funeral both had taken part, and Thomas Blagrave, plus 'two lads brought up to music'. In spite of the fact that they had been in Cromwell's service, all of the protectoral musicians except one, Thomas Mallard, gained employment with Charles II, and Thomas Blagrave even served James II. Hingston did not continue in the role of master of the music. Instead he served his new master in the somewhat less exalted position of a musician for the viols and keeper, tuner and repairer of the royal organs and other instruments.[3]

As master of the music, or master of music, to the lord protector, at a salary of £100 a year, Hingston arranged for the 'two lads brought up to music' to sing to Cromwell Latin motets composed by Richard Deering which, it is said, 'Oliver was most taken with'. Hingston was also music teacher to Cromwell's two youngest daughters as well as being organist to the lord protector, the chapel organ at Magdalen College having been transferred to Hampton Court, as we have already seen, for Oliver's delectation, to complement one in the Cockpit at Whitehall which Charles I had converted into a private court theatre.

The removal of the organ out of Magdalen chapel reflects the Puritan attitude to music in places of worship, which was anathema to them. This led to a decline in study and practice of music, such institutions as the choirs of cathedrals 'where the study and practise of the science of music was especially cherished' having been dissolved. This in any case was the contention of John Hingston, together with four other of those musicians in the protector's funeral procession, David, or Davis, Mell, William Howes, Richard Hudson and William Gregory who, describing themselves as 'Gentlemen of his Highness's Musique', petitioned Cromwell in February 1657 for a corporation or college of musicians to be 'erected' in London, 'with reasonable powers to read and practise publicly all sorts of music, and to suppress the singing of obscene, scandalous and defamatory songs and ballads, and to reform the abuses in making all sorts of instruments of music'. The petition would no doubt have been put before seven councillors, 'or any of them', including Pickering and Jones, who, in February 1657, had been nominated to 'be a committee to receive any addresses that shall be made to them, in order to the advancement of music, and to report to the Council as they shall see cause'.[4]

Although the abolition of cathedral choirs had reduced considerably the scope in musical careers there were still some limited openings in the secular field, which was flourishing during the Protectorate – a period that witnessed the performance of the first full-length English opera. Employment could still be had, for instance, in the households of the wealthy and, of course, Oliver made a contribution by employing eight musicians and two boys in training.[5]

One rather interesting anecdote concerning Oliver's love of music, and his patronage of those inspired by its muse and accomplished (more or less) in its art, is provided by the Oxford antiquarian Anthony Wood. Writing in October 1659 Wood tells us:

In this month James Quin, M.A., and one of the senior students [i.e. fellows] of Christ Church, a Middlesex man born, but son of Walter Quin of Dublin, died in a crazed condition in his bedmaker's house in Penyfarthing Street, and was buried in the cathedral of Christ Church. Anthony Wood had some acquaintance with him, and hath several times heard him sing with great admiration. His voice was a bass, and he had a great command of it. Twas very strong and exceeding trolling, but he wanted skill and could scarce sing in consort. He had been turned out of his student's place by the Visitors. But being well acquainted with some great men of those times that loved music, they introduced him into the company of Oliver Cromwell, the

Protector, who loved a good voice and instrumental music well. He heard him sing with very great delight, liquored him with sack, and in conclusion said: 'Mr Quin you have done very well, what shall I do for you?' To which Quin made answer with great compliments, of which he had command with a great grace, that 'his Highness would be pleased to restore him to his student's place'; which he did accordingly, and so kept it to his dying day.[6]

Others, it seems, were permitted to share in Oliver's Euterpean pleasures. *Mercurius Politicus* informs us that on 2 February 1658 'the Parliament observed the day of public thanksgiving at Margaret's Church for the happy deliverance of the person of his Highness, the Lord Protector, from the late dangerous and bloody design of assassination', which was to have been the purpose of yet another royalist plot. 'After the sermons', continues the news-sheet, 'the Speaker and the Members of Parliament repaired to Whitehall to dine with his Highness, who gave them in the Banqueting House a most princely entertainment. After dinner his Highness withdrew to the Cockpit and there entertained them with rare music, both of instruments and voices, till the evening.'[7]

As to poetry, there were, during the protectorate, three major poets in the service of the state as secretaries of the Latin and French tongues, which must represent something of a phenomenon in government service. John Milton had held his post since the inception of the Commonwealth in 1649. John Dryden, the future Stuart poet laureate, came into the picture towards the end of the Protectorate and, so it has been suggested, probably owed his office more to the fact that he was related to two protectoral grandees, Edward Montague and Sir Gilbert Pickering, than to anything else.[8] In fact it has been suggested that Pickering, as lord chamberlain, employed Dryden for a time as his secretary or clerk. This is what the dramatist, and also poet laureate, Thomas Shadwell reveals in a satirical poem directed against Dryden, which was the product of the open feud that developed between the two men in the sixteen eighties. The poem entitled *The Medal of Bayes: a Satire against Folly and Knavery*, published in 1682, refers to Dryden's career at Cambridge where, according to Shadwell, 'you had been expell'd had you not fled', and continues thus:

The next step of advancement you began,
Was being clerk to Noll's Lord Chamberlain,
A sequester and a committee man.

There all your wholesome morals you suck't in,
And got your gentile gaiety and mien.

Your loyalty you learn'd at Cromwell's court,
Where first your muse did make her great effort.

The 'great effort' was Dryden's *Heroique Stanzas to The Glorious Memory of Cromwell*, published in 1659, a sample of which is:

His grandeur he deriv'd from heav'n alone,
For he was great e're fortune made him so;
And war's like mists that rise against the sun
Made him but greater seem, not greater grow.[9]

This was followed soon after by *Astraea Redux. A Poem on the Restoration of Charles the Second* and another work entitled *To His Sacred Majesty. A Panegyric on His Coronation.*

The third member of this remarkable trio was the one-time royalist Andrew Marvell, for whom a post as a government servant followed a period as tutor to Sir Thomas Fairfax's daughter, Mary, and to a ward of Cromwell's, William Dutton, the orphan of a wealthy royalist. Of the three poets in question Marvell was the only one to apply the muse to the glorification of the Cromwellian regime in Oliver's lifetime. His ode on *The First Anniversary of the Government under O.C.*, published early in 1655 when Marvell was still William Dutton's tutor, lauds 'the wondrous order and consent' of Oliver's rule. He wrote a further work commemorating Blake's victory against the Dutch at Teneriff in April 1657. For the wedding of Cromwell's daughter, Mary, Marvell, who was by this time in the state's employ, having become Latin Secretary Milton's assistant in September 1657, wrote his *Two Songs at the Marriage of the Lord Fauconberg and the Lady Mary Cromwell*. And among the many eulogies that the demise of the lord protector inspired was *A Poem upon the death of O.C.* by Marvell, which contained among many others those singularly poignant lines:

Valor, religion, friendship, prudence, death
At once with him, and all that's good beside;
And we death's refuse, nature's dregs, confined
To loathsome life, alas! are left behind.[10]

Thus can Marvell be justifiably regarded as the protectoral poet laureate,

although officially the post did not exist, and at the obsequies of the
lord protector, arrayed in the mourning that had been allotted to him,
Marvell took his place, as Milton and Dryden did, as a state functionary
and not as a poet, laureate or otherwise.[11]

That Andrew Marvell, like John Dryden, flourished after the Restoration is well known. Having purged himself by attempting to have ex-
purgated from all known editions of his work the two great odes he had
written during the Protectorate, together with *An Horatian Ode upon
Cromwell's return from Ireland*, published earlier, he took his place in
the Restoration or Convention Parliament, and later in the first Parliament of Charles II, as one of the members for Kingston-upon-Hull, a
borough that he had first represented as a member of Protector
Richard's Parliament. To Marvell's eternal credit he interceded to some
effect on behalf of his old master John Milton who did not fair as well
as his two assistants of yesteryear.

Special entertainments were laid on at the protectoral court for
particular occasions, the most frequent of these being receptions for
foreign ambassadors. The following is a description of the splendid
entertainment given by the protector for the three representatives of
the United Provinces in April 1654. The words are those of one of the
Dutch envoys, A.L. Jongestall:

The Master of the Ceremonies came to fetch us in two coaches of
his Highness about half an hour past one, and brought us to Whitehall,
where twelve trumpeters were ready, sounding against our coming.
My Lady Nieuport and my wife were brought to his Highness presently . . . who received us with great demonstration of amity. After
we stayed a little we were conducted into another room, where we
found a table ready covered. His Highness sat on one side of it
alone; my lords Beverningh, Nieuport, and myself at the upper end,
the Lord President Lawrence and others next to us. There was in the
same room another table, covered, for other lords of the council
and others. At the table of my Lady Protectrice dined my Lady
Nieuport, my wife, and my lady Lambert, my lord Protector's
daughter, and mine. The music played all the while we were at
dinner. The Lord Protector [then] had us into another room, where
the Lady Protectrice and others came to us, and where we had also
music, and wine, and a psalm sung, which his Highness gave us, and
told us it was yet the best paper that had been exchanged between
us. From thence we were had into a gallery, next the river, where we
walked with his Highness about half an hour, and then took our

leaves, and were conducted back again to our houses, after the same manner as we were brought.[12]

No form of entertainment whatever was associated with the second investiture of Cromwell as lord protector in June 1657. In spite of its relative splendour and elaborate ritual it would have been regarded as too grave an occasion for any such diversions. But weddings were apparently regarded in a different light, and it was the celebration of three nuptials which provided the protectoral court with its most outstanding festive and social events. The first of these took place on 7 February 1656 when Major Richard Beke, soon to be made captain of the protectoral life guard, married the protector's niece, Lavinia Whetstone. The ceremony, Noble tells us, 'was performed at Whitehall in a very pompous and magnificent manner, the protector and several nobles gracing it with their presence'. The attendance of 'the quality' at Oliver's court was by this time a fairly regular feature. As early as May 1655, for instance, it was reported that: 'The Marquis de Lede, Lord Ambassador from the King of Spain, had audience by his Highness in the Banqueting House in Whitehall, where were the greatest assembly of English nobility and gentry present that have been these many years'.[13]

The old nobility enjoyed much greater prominence at the other two protectoral weddings than at that of Oliver's niece. This has been interpreted by some as a purposeful attempt on the part of Cromwell to solicit support from this quarter for the new regime. But it could equally well be that it was the nobility, or rather certain members of it, who were courting Cromwell. After all, Protector Oliver was in fact a monarch of sorts and even though he refused a crown there is sufficient evidence to suppose that the possibility of acceptance at some later date still remained. And by the revised constitution of 1657 the protectorship ceased to be elective and Cromwell was permitted to name his successor who was, in the course of time, accepted as being Oliver's eldest surviving son. Thus Cromwell could have been regarded, by those of the nobility who were inclined to think of themselves as lions under a new throne, as the founder of a fresh dynasty and therefore a substitute fount of honour and the embodiment of the hereditary principle, as the usurper Henry Tudor had been one hundred and seventy years before. Charles Howard, one time captain of the protector's life guard and the grandson of a peer 'hath also tasted with the first of that sweet fountain of new honour, being made a viscount'. Thus was the comment in a contemporary tract upon the subject of Howard's elevation to the

peerage by Cromwell as baron of Gilsland and Viscount Howard of
Morpeth, which took place on 20 July 1657. A further example of
Oliver's assumption of the rights of kingship in this respect is provided
by the conferment of a barony by the protector on one of his cousins,
Edmund Dunch, who became Baron Burnell of East Wittenham. The
letters patent for this barony, issued by Cromwell on 26 April 1658
and addressed 'To all and singular dukes, marquesses, earls, viscounts,
barons, knights, provosts, freemen, and all our officers, ministers, and
subjects whatsoever to whom these our letters shall come greeting',
declare that 'Amongst other [of] the prerogatives which adorn the
imperial crown of these nations none is of greater excellency or doth
more amplify our favours than to be the fountain of honour'. These
were the only hereditary peerages conferred by Cromwell, although in
August 1658, just before his death, Oliver did sign a bill for a patent to
make Bulstrode Whitelocke a viscount, 'but Whitelocke did not think it
convenient for him'. As already stated elsewhere, at the Restoration
no recognition was made of these or any other Cromwellian honour.[14]

It is certainly conceivable that the second earl of Warwick regarded
Cromwell as the originator of a new dynasty. The earl had retired into
private life after the execution of the king and the abolition of the
monarchy, both of which acts he deplored in spite of his parliamen-
tarian sympathies, only to effect a partial re-emergence when the Protectorate was established, becoming an admirer of Cromwell's and
playing a leading role in the second inauguration of the lord protector
as the bearer, before his Highness, of the sword of state, and assisting in
the investment of Oliver in 'a robe of purple velvet, lined with ermine,
being the habit anciently used at the solemn investiture of princes'.
On this same 'glorious occasion' the lord protector's train 'was borne up
by several noble persons', including Lord Sherard, whom *Mercurius
Politicus* styled, incorrectly, as 'the Lord Sherwood', and Lord
Warwick's grandson, Robert Rich.[15]

It was this same grandson and namesake whom the earl of Warwick
was anxious should marry Oliver's youngest daughter Frances. And, in
spite of the fact that the protector was as much opposed to this match,
because of the suitor's past dissipation, as he was supposed to have
been to the proposed union between Frances and Charles II, Warwick's
desire was, after a settlement concluded by Privy Councillors Philip
Jones, John Desborough and Secretary of State John Thurloe, fulfilled
on 11 November 1657. On this day, so *Mercurius Politicus* tells us, 'the
most illustrious Lady, the Lady Frances Cromwell, youngest daughter
of his Highness the Lord Protector, was married to the most noble

gentleman, Mr. Robert Rich, son of the Lord Rich, grandchild of the Earl of Warwick and the Countess Dowager of Devonshire, in the presence of their Highnesses, and of his grandfather, and father, and the said Countess, with many other persons of high honor and quality'.[16]

On the following day, according to the royalist Sir William Dugdale, 'was the wedding feast kept at Whitehall, where they had 48 violins, 50 trumpets and much mirth with frolics, besides mixed dancing (a thing heretofore accounted profane) till 5 of the clock' the following morning. Amongst the dancers there was the earl of Newport 'who danced with her Highness'.[17] And from another contemporary source we learn that:

> The discourse of the town has been much filled up with the great marriage at Whitehall, which was solemnized there three or four days last week, with music, dancing and great feasting, and now it begins for two or three days at the Earl of Warwick's.[18]

Some of the members of the nobility present at these nuptials were actually royalists, and quite notable ones at that. Included among these were the earl of Newport, who, as we have seen, danced with the protectress, and the bridegroom's grandmother, the dowager countess of Devonshire who, according to Dugdale, presented the bride with £2,000 worth of plate and whose son, Sir Charles Cavendish, had been killed fighting for the king in the late wars.[19]

The union between Frances Cromwell and Robert Rich, although it was short lived (within three months of his marriage the twenty-three year old bridegroom had succumbed to consumption) and produced no issue, is interesting because of its historical echoes, calling to mind that the fortunes of the house of Rich really originated from another time of great change when Richard Rich hitched his wagon to a rising star in the person of another Cromwell, Thomas, during the 1530s, and then eventually found it politic to give evidence against his benefactor when he fell from royal favour in 1540.

In contrast to his attitude towards Frances's choice of bridegroom, Oliver gave his unconditional support to the alliance between Viscount Fauconberg, or as he was also known, Falconbridge, and his second youngest daughter Mary (whose £15,000 dowry was paid by the protector through Nathaniel Waterhouse), for whom, it is said, there had previously been thoughts of a possible marriage with two royalist nobles, the second duke of Buckingham or the earl of Chesterfield, which would have undoubtedly resulted in the successful suitor being fully restored to his sequestrated estates.

As in the case of her sister's wedding a few days earlier, the event of Mary's nuptials was reported in *Mercurius Politicus*: 'Yesterday afternoon', reports the issue for 19 November 1657, 'his Highness went to Hampton Court, and this day the most illustrious Lady, the Lady Mary Cromwell, third daughter of his Highness the Lord Protector, was there married to the most noble Lord, the Lord Falconbridge, in the presence of their Highnesses and many noble persons.'

Mary's Hampton Court wedding is generally regarded as being a rather more sedate affair than her younger sister's at Whitehall. The boisterousness of the previous week's affair gave way to the enactment of *Two Songs at the Marriage of the Lord Fauconberg and the Lady Mary Cromwell* by Andrew Marvell, in which it has been suggested the protector may possibly have played a part. Thus Protector Oliver's court witnessed the revival, albeit in an extremely shadowy form, of those magnificent masques which had helped to make the courts of the first two Stuarts among the most extravagant in Europe and which, in the Caroline court, invariably featured a gloriously bedizened Charles I, whose belief in the divine right of kings these ephemeral and ostentatious extravaganzas were, in symbolic terms, designed to express. The day following Mary's marriage the protector and protectress, together with the bride and groom, went back to Whitehall.

The actual wedding ceremonies of the two protectoral 'princesses' were performed in accordance with the 1653 marriage act, which means that they were essentially civil affairs executed by a justice of the peace before two or more witnesses. 'No other marriage whatsoever within the Commonwealth of England, after the 29th September, in the year one thousand six hundred and fifty-three, shall be held or accompted a marriage according to the laws of England', stipulated this act. In Frances's case, 'Mr Henry Scobell, as Justice of the Peace, tied the knot, after a goodly prayer made by one of his Highness's divines'.[20]

Clarendon, however, says of these nuptials (both of which he states, incorrectly, 'were celebrated at Whitehall with all imaginable pomp and lustre') that 'it was observed that though the marriages were performed in public view according to the rites and ceremonies then in use, they were presently afterwards in private married by ministers ordained by bishops [Dr John Hewett the Anglican divine executed for treason in 1658 is said to have officiated at Mary's 'second' marriage], and according to the form in the Book of Common Prayer; and this with the privity of Cromwell, who pretended to yield to it in compliance with the importunity and folly of his daughters'.[21]

A word should be said at this juncture about the office of master of the revels and the curious circumstances surrounding its suggested existence during the protectorate. The post of master of the revels came into existence in the reign of Henry VIII for the purpose of producing, and providing the necessary equipment and costumes for, masques and other entertainments at court. By the 1580s the powers of the master of the revels had extended beyond the control of entertainments at court to jurisdiction over the dramatic amusements of London audiences, through the assumed right of holders of the office to license all plays intended for performance before the public. And it was through this arrogation that the lord chamberlain, in whose department the master of the revels resided, came to exercise his control over theatres and the licensing of plays, which was legally defined by the Licensing Act of 1737.

At the Restoration Charles II appointed two masters of the revels, Thomas Killigrew and Sir William Davenant. The grant of these offices was contested by Sir Henry Herbert on the grounds that he alone had the right to the post of master of the revels, having, 'by virtue of several grants under the Great Seal of England . . . executed the said office as Master of the Revels, for about 40 years, in the times of King James and of King Charles, both of blessed memory, with exception only to the time of the late horrid rebellion'. And Herbert particularly deplored the fact that he should have been, in the words of one of his petitions, 'ousted of his just possession, rights and profits by Sir William Davenant, a person who exercised the office of Master of the Revels to Oliver the Tyrant and wrote the first and second part of *Peru*, acted at the Cockpit in Oliver's time, and solely in his favour, wherein he set the justice of Oliver's actings by comparison with the Spaniards, and endeavoured thereby to make Oliver's cruelties appear mercies in respect of the Spanish cruelties'. Herbert concludes with two other pieces of what he considered to be damning evidence: 'that the said Davenant published a poem in vindication and justification of Oliver's actions and government and an epithalamium in praise of Oliver's daughter Mrs. Rich'.[22]

It is perfectly true that Sir William Davenant, the alleged, both by himself and others, natural son of William Shakespeare, did write a play entitled *The Cruelty of the Spaniards in Peru*, which he produced at the Cockpit in Drury Lane in 1658. It is also true that it was something of an exercise in propaganda, which would have been essential to circumvent the government with its objections to the public theatre. This too was the reason why Davenant put the production to music and

called it an opera. There is, however, no reason to suppose that
Davenant did not believe in the message he was attempting to propa-
gate, even though he had been imprisoned for over two years for royalist
activities, being released in October 1652. But as to Davenant having
'exercised the office of Master of the Revels to Oliver', there is no real
evidence. No mention has ever been made of his involvement in entertainments at the protectoral court. Neither does he appear to have
been a licenser of plays. He was, it would appear, what Herbert said he
was in his first protest against the proposed grant of office to Killigrew
and Davenant, simply a man 'who obtained leave of Oliver and Richard
Cromwell to vent his operas'.

There is, coincidentally, one other reference to Davenant and the
mastership of the revels besides that of Herbert's. This was made by the
anonymous author of a satirical ballad directed against Davenant and
published in 1656. The two relevant stanzas are:

> At the months end they will come again,
>   Molesting him like Devils,
> Well now Ile pay ye all, quoth he,
>   I must be master o' th' Revels.
>
> The State hath promis'd this to me,
>   As the Clerk of the Parliament saith,
> And I hope that you will do as I do,
>   Believe the PVBLIQUE FAITH.[23]

The first three lines quoted refer to the creditors who seemed, up to the
date of the poem, always to be hounding Davenant whose debts were
responsible for his imprisonment for several months in 1654. The
reference to the mastership of the revels and the vision of this as a
panacea for Davenant's pecuniary liabilities could well be an exercise
in paradoxical speculation, the chances of the current regime ever
resurrecting this particular office being as unlikely as Davenant seemingly
was of clearing his debts.

Little is known of the day to day life of the protectoral court or the
more personal social and domestic habits of the protector and his
family. A report in a news-sheet[24] dated March 1654 to the effect that
'The Privy Lodgings for his Highness the Lord Protector in Whitehall
are now in readiness, as also the lodgings for his Lady Protectress; and
likewise the privy kitchen, and other kitchens, butteries, and offices:
and it is conceived the whole family will be settled there before Easter',

did include the following under the heading 'The tables for diet prepared are these':

A table for his Highness.	A table for the Gentlemen.
A table for the Protectress.	A table for coachmen, grooms and
A table for Chaplains and	other domestic servants.
Strangers.	A table for Inferiors, or sub-servants
A table for the Steward and	
Gentlemen.	

Other intelligence comprises the fact that Oliver entertained officers
of the army once a week at Whitehall, and 'at his private table very
rarely, or never, were our French *quelque choses* suffered by him, or
any such modern gustos', his diet being 'spare not curious': this being
one of the few reliable contemporary comments.[25]

There does exist a post-Restoration publication entitled *The Court
and Kitchen of Elizabeth commonly called Joan Cromwell, the Wife of
the Late Usurper, Truly Described and Represented and Now Made
Public for General Satisfaction* (seemingly the only thing which could
be said against the protectress was that in all her life she never did anything except keep house, and not very imaginatively either), but this
can tell us nothing as it is a purely satirical work published, according
to its introduction, as a retribution for what the author regards as
'those many libels, blasphemous pamphlets and pasquinades, broached
and set on foot, chiefly by the late usurper, against the blessed memory
and honour of our two late sovereigns: more especially those vile and
impious pieces called "The Court and Character of King James" and
"The Nonesuch Charles" '.

Notes

1. Bate, *Elenchus*, Pt.II, pp. 190, 191.
2. Heath, *Flagellum*, p. 160.
3. *Burton*, II, VII; *The King's Musick; A Transcript of Records Relating to
   Music and Musicians (1460-1700)*, ed. Henry Carte de Lafontaine (London,
   1909).
4. SP 18/153, fo.254; SP 25/77, p. 730.
5. Percy A. Scholes, *The Puritans and Music in England and New England*
   (Oxford, 1934).
6. *Life & Times of Anthony Wood*, Vol.I, p. 287.
7. *Merc. Pol.*, 19-26 February 1658.
8. Charles E. Ward, *The Life of John Dryden* (Chapel Hill, NC., 1961).
9. *The Works of John Dryden*, general eds. E.N. Hooker and H.T. Swedenberg,

Jr., Vol. I (Berkeley, Calif., 1956).
10. P. Legouis, *Andrew Marvell, Poet, Puritan, Patriot*, 2nd edn (Oxford, 1971); *The Poems and Letters of Andrew Marvell*, ed H.M. Margoliouth, 2 Vols., 3rd edn. revised by P. Legouis with the collaboration of E.E. Duncan-Jones (London, 1952).
11. *Burton*, II, VII; SP 18/182, fo.229.
12. *Thurloe State Papers*, Vol. II, p. 257.
13. Noble, Vol. II, pp. 210-11; *Perf. Proc.*, 3-10 May 1655.
14. *Harleian Miscellany*, Vol. III, p. 459; *The Complete Peerage*, Vol. II (1912), p. 436, Vol. III, p. 34, Vol. IV, pp. 614-15; Noble, Vol. II; Whitelocke, *Memorials*, p. 675.
15. *Merc. Pol.*, 25 June-2 July 1657; *Respublica*, p. 4.
16. *Thurloe State Papers*, Vol. VI, p. 477; *Merc. Pol.*, 5-12 November 1657.
17. HMC *Fifth Report*, App. p. 177.
18. Ibid., p. 183.
19. Ibid., p. 177.
20. *Acts and Ordinances of the Interregnum*, Vol. II, p. 716; HMC *Fifth Report*, App., p. 177.
21. Edward, Earl of Clarendon, *The History of the Rebellion and Civil Wars in England*, ed. W. Dunn Macray (Oxford, 1888), Book XV, 51.
22. *The Dramatic Records of Sir Henry Herbert, the Master of the Revels, 1623-1673*, ed. Joseph Quincy Adams (Yale UP, 1917), pp. 85, 122, 123.
23. Leslie Hotson, *The Commonwealth and Restoration Stage* (Cambridge, Mass., 1928), p. 142.
24. *Weekly Intelligencer*, 14-21 March 1654.
25. Fletcher, *Perfect Politician*, p. 210.

7 CONCLUSION

Although so much material on the subject of the protectoral court is wanting, no doubt because of a desire on the part of those directly involved to cover the traces of the past, there is, as witnessed by the foregoing chapters, a sufficient body of evidence to give us some idea of its essential form and structure. In achieving this the comparison between what we know of Cromwell's court and the vastly more documented Stuart courts has proved invaluable.*

From this the first and strongest impression gained is of the difference in size and complexity between the protectoral court and the royal courts which preceded and succeeded it. The numbers involved in the maintenance of the protectoral court, whether high office holders or the lowest menial servants, probably represented only a fraction of those employed in a similar capacity by preceding and succeeding monarchs. The complex and fragmentary wardrobe arrangement of Charles I, with its total staff of about eighty, for instance, gave way to a simplistic and integral protectoral wardrobe of only fourteen servants. And while the royal wardrobe had been headed by a great magnate occupying the post of master of the wardrobe, which was largely a sinecure, the principal of the protector's wardrobe, who was certainly no sinecurist, received the somewhat less exalted title of keeper of the wardrobe and retained the relatively lowly status that he had as yeoman of the removing wardrobe under Charles I.

This question of the variation in the nature of court posts and the individuals who occupied them under the lord protector *vis à vis* a royal regime can be applied to other aspects of the protectoral household arrangements. For example there was, during the Protectorate, no movement from court office, especially those of the first rank, to a high position in the administration, as was the custom in royal courts. Quite the reverse, in fact, because the offices of the first rank in the protectoral court, such as the lord chamberlain and the comptroller, were

---

*Of particular usefulness here have been G.P.V. Akrigg's *Jacobean Pageant, or The Court of King James I* (London, 1962), *The King's Servants: The Civil Service of Charles I, 1625-1642* by G.E. Aylmer, and John M. Beattie's *The English Court in the Reign of George I*. As Beattie himself tells us: 'The structure of the household of George I's reign had been well established by the late fifteenth century and perhaps earlier.'

occupied by, and were a means of conferring further dignity upon, men who were already politically powerful, so that these posts could be said to have been filled from above rather than from below. Furthermore, although these principal officers of the protectoral household were, with the exception of Master of the Horse John Claypole, Commonwealth grandees, they were not magnates in the way that their royal predecessors had been, but men who had become prominent because of the civil war or its immediate aftermath. They were not members of the nobility and there was no attempt to make them so even though Protector Oliver did create hereditary peerages. In fact the names of these 'officers of honour both to his [Cromwell's] person, and his wife's',[1] as James Heath called them, are noticeably missing from the lists of those whose social status was elevated by the protector. Not even a Cromwellian baronetcy nor a knighthood was conferred upon one of their number. (Lord Chamberlain Sir Gilbert Pickering's baronetcy was, incidentally, a Stuart creation.) While the designation lord which Pickering, Comptroller of the Household Philip Jones, Master of the Horse John Claypole and Captain of the Household Guard Walter Strickland received when they became members of the Cromwellian Upper House was simply a notation to denote membership, which was conferred on all those nominated to sit in this assembly who did not hold a hereditary peerage.

One striking innovation in the financial arrangements of the protector's household was, as we have seen, the allocation of funds specifically for its maintenance. This was not continued at the Restoration and so the old device whereby monarchs were expected to meet both aulic and governmental expenses out of a single revenue was reconstituted. The idea of a genuine civil list, exclusive of the cost of maintaining every department of government, did not re-emerge until the reign of George III.

Although financially there existed a clear division between government and the household during the Protectorate, functionally there was no such clear division. Certain elements which would have been part of a royal household were, under the Protectorate, governmental departments, and financed as such, even though they carried out aulic as well as state duties and were nominally personal servants of the protector. Into this category can be placed the barges department with its master, assistant master and complement of twenty-seven of his Highness's watermen, all of whom wore the protector's arms for a badge, the master of the barges and his assistant also being arrayed in his Highness's grey livery. Then there were the wardrobe department and the

office of works headed, respectively, by his Highness's wardrobe keeper
and his Highness's surveyor of works, both of which, like the barges,
were government financed departments of state performing household
as well as state duties. Also to be included in this category are the
'ordinary pensioners', who were the protectoral equivalent of the royal
band of gentlemen pensioners, the functions of which were roughly
similar to those performed by the yeomen of the guard. But, whereas
the royal pensioners were part of the household establishment, the
protector's band comprised one or two squadrons (twenty or forty
men) drawn from his Highness's life guard, which was part of the army
establishment.

Many household posts were dispensed with altogether, especially
from among those which had traditionally been part of the above stairs
or chamber establishment. There were, for instance, no court painters
as such, whereas Charles I had employed two painters as well as two
limners. The three artists commissioned by the Cromwellian regime to
paint the official portraits of the protector, Samuel Cooper, Peter Lely
and Robert Walker, who died in the same year as Oliver, were not retained as members of the protectoral court. The miniaturist Samuel
Cooper, 'commonly stil'd the Vandyck in little', who was, incidentally,
working for Cromwell and his family as early as 1650,* had, however,
been employed at the court of Charles I and was to become king's lim-
ner at the Restoration. Peter Lely was also to find favour with the
restored Stuart dynasty, succeeding to Sir Anthony Van Dyck's post of
principal painter.[2]

The seventeenth century is generally regarded as being a period in
which the conditions for advancement rested to a large extent on a
tripartite axiom, patrimony, purchase and patronage. Partly because of
its novelty and its reliance on 'new' men the Commonwealth regime
would have been less governed by this triarchy than its predecessors,
the overriding criteria for office in the republic being known ability
coupled with a noticeable identification with the regime.

There is, however, evidence of one instance of potential patrimony,
that is son succeeding father in the same office, within the Cromwellian
court. This involves John Kinnersley, assistant to the keeper of his
Highness's wardrobe, Clement Kinnersley, who was also John's father.
It is almost certain that the intention was, as far as the senior Kinnersley

*It was about the year 1650 that the famous unfinished miniature of Cromwell
in the collection of the duke of Buccleuch and Queensbury, upon which Cooper's
reputation as the one and only true capturer of Cromwell is based, was painted.

was concerned at least, that John should eventually succeed his father as wardrobe keeper to the protector, just as Clement would have succeeded his father as yeoman of the king's removing wardrobe. It is significant that this example of potential patrimony occurred in one of the two departments of the Cromwellian court that had direct links with its royal predecessors.

The only true patronage within the Cromwellian household seems to have been the direct patronage of the protector himself, although the suggested appointment, if it occurred at all, of the poet John Dryden to the post of secretary or clerk to the protectoral lord chamberlain, Sir Gilbert Pickering, who was also Dryden's cousin, could, of course, be interpreted as nepotism. Known instances of members of the protectoral court using their influence to advance the causes of other parties are confined to what can be described as little more than character references and professional recommendations, generally speaking for prospective government employees.

One of the earliest examples is dated Whitehall, 23 April 1654, at which time the Protectorate was only four months old. It takes the form of a letter from John Maidstone, at that time one of the two recently appointed protectoral stewards, to the admiralty commissioners, requesting that Philip Mead be given the position of steward on the *Phoenix*. Also in 1654 the other steward of the protector's household, Nathaniel Waterhouse, together with Martin Noell, financier and ship owner, were asked by the admiralty commissioners if they could recommend Captain Thomas Hale as lieutenant of the *Victory*. According to the note the protector had promised Hale a place in the life guard, 'but it did not fall out'.[3]

In June 1655 Noell was again using his influence to further the interests of another, this time in company with John Maidstone. Both men wrote letters of recommendation which Thomas Hamor, a seaman, presented, together with himself, to Robert Blackbourne, secretary to the admiralty commissioners. Maidstone, from Whitehall, writes:

Sir,

The bearer hereof Thomas Hamor is the seaman concerning whom I spake with you. I hope his proficiency in his calling and fair carriage in it hath qualified him for preferment, wherein, if you further him, it will much oblige

Your assured friend and servant,
John Maidstone.[4]

Noell's communication, which was by way of being a covering letter, declares:

> Honoured Friend,
>
> This bearer Thomas Hamor is the seaman in whose behalf I spake to you and for whom Mr. Maidstone writ for some preferment. This young man is son to his Highness's chief cook. But that which most especially doth commend him to the consideration of your commissioners is the qualification of the person himself, which I am confident you will find such as will invite them to prefer him accordingly, and thereby gratify the greatest wish of his Highness's family, who are all his suitors in this particular as well as
>
> > Your affectionate friend,
> > Martin Noell.[5]

Truly, young Thomas Hamor did not lack for friends at court.

In the same month as the Hamor recommendation Maidstone, writing from Hampton Court, which, it will be remembered, was the protector's country retreat, requested of no less a person than the lord president of the Council, Henry Lawrence, to move the admiralty commissioners to release a waterman who had been pressed into service with the navy, because he was the sole means of maintenance for his mother and grandmother, both of whom were widows.[6]

Whitehall chaplain Hugh Peter seems to have done his share of commending others for a position in the service of the state during the Protectorate. He sent a list of six ships to Robert Blackbourne requesting him to recommend Captain Isaiah Blowfield to the admiralty commissioners as the captain of one of them, Blowfield being, in the estimation of Peter, 'a stout honest man, and one my lord intends some special good'. Peter performed a like service for Mr Hodge, a fellow New Englander, for the command of one of the state's frigates, Hodge 'having been a master twenty years, and being a very worthy man', and for a fellow cleric whom he recommended to Blackbourne for the post of ship's chaplain at a salary of £100 a year.[7]

Another protectoral chaplain, Joseph Caryl, also supported parties in their quest for employment and aid. One case in particular involved Abigail, widow of William Flesher a London fishmonger and the mother of five small children. Abigail's late husband had, at the outbreak of the civil war, lent money, plate and horses to Parliament, in whose service at Gloucester he lost his life. Abigail had since been 'brought into a very sad condition' and was petitioning the lord protector 'to confer some place of employment upon her present husband, either in your royal [*sic*] family, or where your Highness shall think fit, or some present relief as others have had in the like case'. Appended to this petition are the words 'Mr Caryl, minister, spake to his Highness'. It is not known whether or not the petitioner's second husband, whose name was not given, received a place at court. But the Council did order that Abigail's first husband's loan should be repaid out of the fine of a royalist peer. Unfortunately this instruction was soon afterwards rescinded and the moneys originally allotted to the fishmonger's widow were reallocated to clear the arrears in pay of a senior army officer, who naturally would have possessed more pull.[8]

One of the more fundamental differences between a royal and the protectoral court is that whereas a royal court of the seventeenth century was very much a social and cultural institution that of the Protectorate was not. The protectoral court tended to reflect current society rather than set patterns for attitudes, manners and customs for society, or at least sections of it, to imitate as royal courts did. As such it appears to have possessed, to an acceptable degree, both aestheticism and sybaritism, thus proving that contrary to popular belief the epoch in which the court existed was not one in which unrelieved dourness obtained. It was a period in which May Day 'was more observed by people going a-maying than for divers years past, and indeed much sin committed by wicked meetings with fiddlers, drunkenness, ribaldry and the like. Great resort came to Hyde Park, many hundreds of rich coaches and gallants in attire, but most shameful powdered hair, painted men and spotted women. Some men played with a silver ball, and some took other recreation.' This disapprobatory description of events that took place on the first May Day of Oliver's rule, which appeared in a contemporary official news-sheet, ended with an obligatory example of corresponding piety: 'But his Highness the Lord Protector went not thither, nor any of the Lords of the Council, but were busy about the great affairs of the Commonwealth.' Another occurrence, this time during the third year of the protector's rule, was 'a cockney feast of the better sort of citizens born within the walls at Merchant Tailors' Hall. Three thousand dined in one room and 300 in another, at 5s a head, by the care of City cooks and caterers. Such a feast was never seen in the City.'[9]

Yet another difference is contained in the very real fact that the protectoral court, like the Protectorate itself, was the product of political expediency and, again like the Protectorate, it was in some respects a symbol of the failure to establish a wholly acceptable and lasting alternative to a monarchical form of government.

Having accepted this situation, and naturally being desirous to permeate an atmosphere of stability and normalcy, it was incumbent upon the protectoral regime to surround the new ruler with all the trappings of monarchy including, of course, a court. As we have seen this began almost immediately after Oliver's acceptance of the protectorship which, together with other evidence, would suggest that from the very beginning if the protectorship were ever to give way to a 'legitimate' regime it would be one with Cromwell as king.

But the title of king apart Cromwell, even as lord protector, would, as has already been pointed out, have needed to invest himself with a degree of majesty, that is majesty in the sense of external magnificence befitting a sovereign, of which a court is the essential element. Protector Oliver was after all the outward and visible symbol of the nation and the not inconsiderable might that it possessed under him. The accredited representatives of foreign states would have expected, and the innately conservative and precedent-ridden English would have demanded, this visual splendour. But it did not, of course, meet with universal approval. There was, for instance, published in 1656, a condemnatory pamphlet entitled *The Picture of a New Courtier drawn in a Conference between Mr. Timeserver and Mr. Plain-heart. In which is discovered the abominable Practises and horrid Hypocrisies of the Usurper and his timeserving Parasites*. In this dialogue, by quite naturally an anonymous author, Mr Timeserver is, as is to be expected, a protectoral courtier dwelling at Whitehall from which place Mr. Plain-heart had, he explains, been 'banished . . . at the first erecting of the new court, for none of my name . . . could abide there any longer without making shipwreck of faith and a good conscience'. At one point in the discourse Mr Plain-heart addresses himself to Mr Timeserver thus:

> Truly my bowels yearn for the poor soldiers who have run so many hazards and fought so many famous battles, stormed so many towns, waded through so many rivers, with the loss of limbs and blood, besides all the hunger and cold and lodging on the ground, which they have gone through during summer service, and in winter season. And after all this to have the tenth part of their pay taken away and spent in your new court, that the gentlemen Ushers, the gentlemen Waiters, the Grooms of the Stole, gentlemen Sewers, besides the

fiddlers and others that I could name which shine in their silver and gold, and that these might be maintained the poor soldier must pay a penny a day.

While it is certainly true that the pay of the army was reduced in 1655 the reason for this was the necessity of economising, plus the fact that the cost of living had declined considerably since the end of the civil war, rather than the extravagance of the protectoral household.[10]

Even Oliver's most vehement detractors must have found it difficult to see in the aulic magnificence that surrounded the office of lord protector a cloak to mask the absence in Cromwell of majesty as a personal attribute, which has so frequently happened in the case of other sovereigns. Majesty, in this particular sense, is surely a most necessary ingredient of a man's power to influence his times, and no one could possibly doubt the immensity of Oliver Cromwell's influence on *his* times. 'In this I am confident, that however unjustly he might be said to have come to the crown, yet it cannot be said he ever abused it. For by his sword, judgement, great spirit, gratitude and magnanimity, he was beloved, feared and obeyed, and made foreign nations know more of England's strength than any of her king's of the Stuart line.' This was written of Cromwell in the late eighteenth century, at a time when the generality of historiographers were ensuring that the character of the protector should remain in the depths of the calumnious grave into which it had been interred some century and a quarter earlier. The author also testifies to the fact that Oliver Cromwell 'Made my ancestors . . . sorely pay for their loyalty and adherence to their king', but nevertheless describes his forefathers' adversary somewhat fulsomely as 'his Highness the most serene and most illustrious Oliver Cromwell, Supreme Chief or Lord Protector of the Commonwealth of England, Scotland and Ireland and the Dominions, Islands and Territories thereunto belonging'.[11]

Notes

1. Heath, *Flagellum*, p. 158.
2. Aylmer, *KS*, p. 473; J. Douglas Stewart, 'Samuel Cooper: an English Baroque "Man of his Century" ' in Daphne Foskett's *Samuel Cooper and his Contemporaries* (HMSO, London, 1974).
3. *CSPD*, 1654, pp. 482, 593.
4. SP 46/117, fo.72a.
5. Ibid., fo.71.
6. *CSPD*, 1655, p. 492.

7. Ibid., 1655, p. 416; 1655-6, p. 549; 1656-7, p. 394; 1658-9, p. 503.
8. Ibid., 1655, pp. 318, 339, 354, 446, 487; 1656-7, p. 512; SP 18/100, fos.225, 226.
9. *Sev. Proc.*, 27 April-4 May 1654; *CSPD*, 1655-6, p. 396.
10. Firth, *Cromwell's Army*, p. 185.
11. *Respublica*, pp. 23, 208, 245.

APPENDIX A: OLIVER CROMWELL AND REGALITY

In the Autumn of 1657 Cromwell's household adopted a hierarchical structure which contained elements that had existed in the households of Oliver's royal predecessors, but which had hitherto been absent in the household of the protector. It was suggested in the foregoing text that this could be seen as an essential part of a policy designed to assimilate further the Protectorate to the traditional form of a monarchy, that of a crowned head, in order to give the Cromwellian regime stability. It was suggested too that this could also be taken as evidence that although the crown had been refused by Oliver its acceptance by him at some later date nevertheless remained a feasibility. There was certainly a resurgence of rumours to this effect at that time.

A further possible explanation is that even though, under Parliament's Humble Petition and Advice, Cromwell continued to rule, or in the words of the revised constitution 'to hold and exercise the office of chief magistrate of these nations',[1] with the style Lord Protector of the Commonwealth, he had in fact become, or at the very least was about to become, *de jure* King of England, Scotland and Ireland, and of the dominions and territories thereunto belonging.*

The principal evidence for this is contained first in the extent to which the eventually accepted version of the Humble Petition and Advice, ratified on 25 May 1657, after the word protector had been substituted for that of king and the replacement title 'bounded, limited and circumstantiated', and clarified by an Additional and Explanatory Petition on 26 June, represented a compromise settlement, and secondly in the re-investiture of Cromwell on 26 June 1657.[2]

As already intimated the essential differences between the version of the Humble Petition originally submitted to Cromwell and rejected, and that accepted by the protector, are confined solely to an alteration of the title with which Cromwell would rule, and to that title's circumscription. This is because Cromwell's objections to the revised constitution were also confined solely to his assumption of the title king. These objections did not, however, extend to the restoration of the office of

---

*For a contrary view see R.C.H. Catterall's 'The Failure of the Humble Petition and Advice' in the *American Historical Review*, Vol.IX, No.1 (1903).

king. This is quite explicit in the statement, 'I think the Act of Government [the Humble Petition and Advice] doth consist of very excellent parts, in all but that one thing, the title, as to me . . . I cannot undertake this Government with that title of King', which the protector made in his declinatory speech on 8 May 1657. There are also the protracted deliberations on the subject of Cromwell and the crown. In these the protector demurred in respect of the restoration of the title, not the office, of king. The gist of Cromwell's argument had been, why should the person in which the supreme authority resides be any less a king simply because his style is spelled P-r-o-t-e-c-t-o-r? 'Signification goes to the thing, certainly it does, and not to the name', asserted Oliver. In answer to the contention that the style of protector, being a new one, was not known by law (which is why in the revised Humble Petition and Advice it had to be 'bounded, limited and circumstantiated'), whereas the title of king 'is known by the law of England . . . and more conformable to the laws of the nation', Cromwell cited the proposal to alter James I's title from king to one that was also new and not known by the law, that of emperor. This style had, in the summer of 1655, also been suggested as a suitable one for Oliver to adopt if he were to accept the crown.* Thus Cromwell, at least, would have seen nothing paradoxical in ruling as king, but with the title that had originally been bestowed upon him under the Instrument of Government in December 1653. As the Humble Petition and Advice remained, apart from the title, substantially the same as when it contained the style of king, then the process of circumscription must be interpreted as making the office of protector conformable to that of king. Certainly one of the ingredients of the Humble Additional and Explanatory Petition and Advice of 26 June 1657 could be interpreted thus. This requested 'That your Highness will be pleased, according to the usage of former Chief Magistrates [i.e. kings] in these Nations, and for the better satisfaction of the people thereof, to take an Oath in the form ensuing . . . That your Highness Successors do, before they take upon them the Government of these Nations, take an Oath in the form aforesaid'.[4]

*The idea was apparently not entirely new. One of Secretary of State John Thurloe's agents in 'a letter of intelligence' dated 29 September 1654, requested confirmation of 'a common report' circulating in Cologne 'that the Protector went into the Parliament House and there had his peroration for an hour; and that after, the Parliament, with unanimous consent called his Highness Emperor; and his title they have written thus: "Oliver, the first Emperor of Great Britain, and the Isles thereunto belonging, always Caesar".'[3]

'I did always believe this Parliament would make him [Cromwell] king before they parted', wrote Sir Henry Vane in February 1657, and that, it seems, is exactly what the second Protectorate Parliament did. Four months later, therefore, on 13 June 1657, we have Lady Elizabeth Conway communicating to a correspondent in France the veracity that 'Parliament, having settled the government which they proferred under the style of kingship to one as absolutely regal and hereditary, only altering the name to Protector, are prorogued till 23 October'.[5]

A month after the enactment of the revised constitution the lord protector was reinvested in Westminster Hall, following which Cromwell was *ipso facto* truly and legally a king. The kingly office, albeit not the title, had remained enshrined in the Humble Petition and Advice and now, by way of augmentation or amplification, all the essential processes required in the making of a king were to be effected at the re-investiture of the protector on 26 June 1657.

The elaborate re-investiture ceremony was reported in some detail by the official news-sheet *Mercurius Politicus*.*[6] From this we learn that as he entered Westminster Hall, accompanied by an entourage which included the gentlemen of the household, kings of arms, state and civic dignitaries, 'divers of the nobility and other persons of great quality', Oliver was preceded by 'the Earl of Warwick, who bore the Sword of State before his Highness'. This was the custom at a coronation, the sword of state being representative of the monarch's presence.

'His Highness being entered in the place, and standing under a rich cloth of state' he was vested with 'a robe of purple velvet lined with ermine, being the habit anciently used at the investiture of princes', by the Speaker of the House of Commons, assisted by the earl of Warwick, Bulstrode Whitelocke and others.

*This journal has been described as 'The most complete newspaper of the interregnum'. (*Bibliography of British History*, Stuart period, 1603-1714, ed. G. Davies, 2nd edn ed. by M.F. Keeler (Oxford, 1970), p. 440.) For the purposes of comparison between Cromwell's second investiture and a coronation ceremony *Mercurius Politicus* has been used in conjunction with: *A Collection out of a book called* Liber Regalis (London, 1661); L.G. Wickham Legg's *English Coronation Records* (Westminster, 1901); P.E. Schramm's (trans. L.G. Wickham Legg) *A History of the English Coronation* (Oxford, 1937); B. Wilkinson's *The Coronation in History* (Historical Association Pamphlet-General Series No. 23, 1953); Sir Thomas Butler's *The Crown Jewels and Coronation Ritual* (London, 1973).

After this a richly gilt and bossed Bible was presented to Cromwell. He was then girt with a sword by the Speaker. At the crowning of kings the girting is followed almost immediately by the removal of the sword 'which', according to the precepts contained in the order of service for coronations, dating from the fourteenth century, the *Liber Regalis*, 'the chief nobleman there present . . . carrieth naked before the king during the solemnity', having exchanged it for the sword of state. The earl of Warwick performed this function at Oliver's investiture. Also borne unsheathed before a king by three great lords were three more swords of state symbolising Justice to the Spirituality, Justice to Temporality, and Mercy. So it was at Cromwell's inauguration, the swords on this occasion being carried by Philip Sidney, Viscount Lisle (and heir to the earldom of Leicester), Admiral of the Fleet Edward Montague, both of whom were members of the protector's Privy Council, and Bulstrode Whitelocke, who was at that time a treasury commissioner.

Having been girt with a sword the protector was furnished, again by the Speaker, with a sceptre, signifying kingly power and justice. The sceptre, which was of massy gold, weighed 168 ounces 20 grains and cost £650 13s 6d.[7]

The protector then took a form of the tripartite coronation oath, prepared by Parliament, prescribed in the Additional and Explanatory Petition, and administered by the Speaker:

I do in the presence, and by the Name of God Almighty, promise and swear, that to the uttermost of my power I will uphold, and maintain the true Reformed Protestant Christian Religion, in the purity thereof, as it is contained in the Holy Scriptures of the Old and New Testament, to the uttermost of my power and understanding, and encourage the profession, and professors of the same; and that to the uttermost of my power I will endeavour, as Chief Magistrate of these three Nations, the maintenance and preservation of the peace and safety, and of the just rights and privileges, of the people thereof. And shall in all things according to my best knowledge and power, govern the people of these Nations according to the Law.

Then with 'his Highness standing thus adorned in princely state, according to his merit and dignity', Thomas Manton, an Independent cleric, pronounced a dedicatory prayer, after which 'the people giving several great shouts, and the trumpets sounding, his Highness sat down in the Chair of State, holding the sceptre in his hand'. The 'Chair of State' was in fact the Coronation Chair, sometimes called King Edward's Chair, which had been used at the crowning of every English monarch since that of Edward II in 1308.

This last act, the enthronement, represents the moment in a coronation ceremony when the monarch formally takes possession of the kingdom, after which he receives the homage of the princes and peers. In Oliver's case, 'while his Highness thus sat a Herald stood up aloft, giving a signal to a trumpet to sound three times, after which he did by authority and direction of Parliament there publish and proclaim his Highness Lord Protector of the Commonwealth of England, Scotland and Ireland and the dominions and territories thereunto belonging, requiring all persons to yield him due obedience. Hereupon the trumpets sounded and the people made several great acclamations with loud shouts, "God save the Lord Protector".'

The ceremony having come to an end Cromwell descended from the throne, being preceded, as was customary at a coronation, by the four unsheathed swords of state. The train of the protector's 'princely habit' was 'borne up by several noble persons'.

The procession moved out of Westminster Hall into New Palace Yard 'where his Highness entered into his coach of state, being in his robes . . . The coach was attended by his Highness's Life Guard and other guards, with the officers of arms on horseback; the officers of state, judges, Lord Mayor and Aldermen, all waiting on his Highness in their coaches to Whitehall; the whole [which included the master of the horse leading 'the horse of honour in rich comparisons'] being managed with state and magnificence suitable to so high and happy a solemnity.'

Three of the essential elements in the ceremonial making of a king had been adhered to at this the second investiture of Cromwell as lord protector. First there was the coronation oath. Secondly there was the process of election and recognition, both of which embody the concept that kings were chosen by the people as well as being designated by God, there being, as history has shown, no absolute priority of hereditary right. The election of a monarch was traditionally symbolised by his elevation or 'secular' enthronement by prelates and nobles in Westminster Hall prior to the actual coronation. In Cromwell's case his elevation (in the absence of prelates but in the presence of nobles and Puritan divines) could be said to have been combined with the enthronement proper, which represents the third element, the entire investiture ceremony having taken place in Westminster Hall. The recognition of a monarch is contained in the acclamation 'God save the King', and in the case of Cromwell by that of 'God save the Lord Protector'.

The only significant ingredients of a true coronation that were missing at the re-investiture of Oliver were the anointing and the crowning. The anointing of a monarch is regarded as the conferment of divine sanction upon his kingship. But if one takes the view of Archbishop of Canterbury Thomas Cranmer the anointing is not necessarily an essential element in the coronation ritual. The primate expressed his opinion on this subject when counselling the young Edward VI at the time of his coronation in February 1547. 'Kings', asserted Cranmer, 'be God's anointed, not in respect of the oil which the bishop useth, but in consideration of their power, which is ordained, of their sword, which is authorised, of their persons, which are elected by God, and indued with the gifts of the spirit for the better ruling and guiding of his people. The oil, if added, is but a ceremony; if it be wanting, that king is yet a perfect monarch notwithstanding, and God's anointed as well as if he was inoiled.'[8]

It goes without saying that to many, all of those necessary attributes of kingship espoused by Cranmer could be found in Cromwell (to which could be added his undoubted military prowess, which to some implies spiritual strength), the confident assumption, for instance, that Oliver was 'elected by God' being embraced in his style and titles, which described him as protector by the grace of God.

As for the crowning, although this represents the climax of the coronation ceremony it is nevertheless of less importance than the taking of the oath, the election and recognition and, to the Puritan mind, the not strictly essential anointing. The crowning, like the bestowal of the other insignia of office such as the sword and sceptre, which were, of course, accorded to Oliver, merely constitutes the outward assumption of the royal dignity.

Episcopacy having been formally abolished by Parliament in October 1646,* there was, of course, no archbishop of Canterbury to invest Cromwell with his royal robes and all the other ensigns of the kingly state, and to administer the oath. As we have seen this was carried out by the Speaker of the House of Commons, signifying the primacy of Parliament. While the pronouncement of the dedicatory prayer, also by tradition the prerogative of the primate of all England, was made by a cleric of the Independent persuasion, to which the Cromwellian regime adhered. But as Cranmer had also opined in his counsel to Edward VI:

*Article twelve of the Humble Petition and Advice reconfirmed the abolition of episcopacy.

'The Bishops of Canterbury for the most part have crowned your predecessors and anointed them kings of this land: yet it was not in their power to receive or reject them, neither did it give them authority to prescribe them conditions to take or leave their crowns, although the Bishops of Rome would encroach upon your predecessors by his bishops' act and oil, that in the end they might possess those bishops with an interest to dispose of their crowns at their pleasure. But the wiser sort will look to their claws and clip them.'[9]

It would appear then that the objection of the Council of Officers and others to the restoration of the kingly office had to all intents and purposes been circumvented with what can only be described as supreme subtlety. The eventual assumption of the title king, which was rumoured to be imminent throughout the remaining fifteen months of Oliver's life, would therefore have been a mere formality.

The extent to which this was so is illustrated by Cromwell's assumption, immediately after his re-investiture, of one of the most fundamental prerogatives of kingship. On 20 July 1657 the protector created his first hereditary peerage when he conferred the viscountcy of Morpeth and the barony of Gilsland upon the ex-captain of the protectoral life guard, Charles Howard. This was followed in April 1658 by the elevation of a cousin of Cromwell, Edmund Dunch, who became Baron Burnell of East Wittenham.

'Amongst other of the prerogatives which adorn the imperial crown of these nations none is of greater excellency or doth more amplify our favours than to be the fountain of honour', asseverated Oliver royally in his letters patent of ennoblement, which were addressed 'To all and singular dukes, marquesses, earls, viscounts, barons, knights, provosts, freemen, and all our officers, ministers, and subjects whatsoever to whom these letters shall come greeting'.[10]

Cromwell's hereditary peers were expected to take their places in the newly constituted Upper House, allowed for in the revised constitution (as indeed was Oliver's right to name his successor who was ultimately regarded as being his eldest surviving son), together with commoners nominated to sit there by Cromwell, and certain members of the old nobility. Although these representatives of the ancient peerage were somewhat lacking in enthusiasm for the composition of the Cromwellian Upper House, or doubted its legality,* some of them were,

*A news-letter dated 17 November 1657 reported that 'The judges being lately required by his Highness to make the form of writ whereby the intended members of the Upper House might be called to sit in Parliament, their answer was that until his Highness did accept the title of king no legal writs could be made,

as we have seen, nevertheless only too anxious to identify with the
originator of a new dynasty, and consequently a substitute fount of
honour and the embodiment of the hereditary principle. It will be
remembered that the elevation by Cromwell of the one time captain of
his life guard, who was, incidentally, the grandson of a peer, was
commented upon in a contemporary tract thus: 'Charles Howard . . .
hath also tasted with the first of that sweet fountain of new honour,
being made a viscount.'[12]

Included in the further possible proof that Oliver was in fact made a
king in June 1657 is the decree, in July 1657, that the master of the
barges and his assistant should henceforth be apparelled in the protector's grey livery, and that the badges, depicting the original arms of
the Commonwealth, worn by the masters of the barges and his Highness's watermen, should be exchanged for badges depicting the singularly royal device of his Highness. There was also the report, in a semi-
official news-letter dated May 1658, that 'the two caps of crimson and
purple velvet, worn by princes, are at this moment being made up by
order of the Master of the Wardrobe, making people talk largely of
kingship'. It could well be that these caps of estate, which are badges of
rank worn instead of a crown, were being made up in anticipation of
the purely perfunctory adoption by Cromwell of the style of king. It
was one of these, described as a 'cap of regality of purple velvet, furred
with ermines', that adorned Oliver's funeral effigy. Also in May 1658 a
Colonel Humphreys was instructed by the Privy Council to deliver up
to the sword bearer appointed by the High Court of Justice the sword,
formerly that of the late king, which had been purchased for his Highness's use.[13]

But surely most significant of all the evidence suggesting that
Cromwell was indeed made a king in June 1657 was the appearance of
an imperial crown* on the head of the protector's funeral effigy,

---

nor House of Peers constituted'. Writs were, nonetheless, issued on 10 December
1657 and the recipients included nine members of the old peerage (seven English,
one Scots and one Irish) of whom only three (two English and the one Irish peer)
obeyed the summons.[11]

*This crown was possibly made in the Spring of 1657 when the protector was
invited to adopt the title of king. Although it has been suggested that it may have
been one of the items preserved from the old regalia which was subsequently re-
fashioned for Charles II and is in use today as the St Edward's crown.

replacing, at a particular point in the procedure, the 'cap of regality', and in the left hand what is perhaps the most sacred ornament of the coronation regalia, an orb, symbolising the dominion of the Christian religion over the world, although a contemporary description of Oliver's lying in state describes the orb as 'representing principality'. Also, all the rooms used for the lying in state at Somerset House were 'completely furnished with escutcheons of his Highness's arms, crowned with an imperial crown'. While the standards of England and Scotland and the banner of the Union (between England and Scotland), borne in the funeral procession, were also adorned with an imperial crown, the standard of England and the banner of the Union carrying an additional embellishment in the form of the letters 'O' and 'P'.[14]

Thus the reason for strict adherence to the procedure followed at the obsequies of King James I for Oliver's funeral was not simply that those who surrounded Cromwell were interring a head of state, it was because they were burying a king. The reference to Oliver's son and heir as Richard the Fourth by a member of the younger protector's Parliament was therefore a fundamental truth, making the Restoration of 1660 that of the Stuart line and not the monarchy.[15]

But because neither Oliver nor Richard Cromwell assumed the actual title of king, even though they occupied, and exercised the prerogatives of, that office, their position was of necessity not so much defined by constitutional power as by the qualities and defects of their characters. Hence the eventual collapse of the Cromwellian dynasty with the abdication of Richard in the Spring of 1659. The feelings of many on this matter are defined in the argument of one of the committee of tidy-minded constitutionalists nominated to put Parliament's case for the acceptance of the crown before Cromwell: 'There seems to be more certainty and stability and civic sanction in the supreme authority under the title of king than any other.'[16]

Notes

1. *CJ*, Vol. VII, p. 537.
2. Ibid., p. 535.
3. *Thurloe State Papers*, Vol. II, p. 614.
4. Abbott, Vol. IV, pp. 513-14; *Monarchy Asserted to be the Best, most Ancient and Legal Form of Government: In a Conference had at Whitehall with Oliver Cromwell and a Committee of Parliament* (London, 1679); *Clarke Papers*, Vol. III, p. 48; *Acts and Ordinances of the Interregnum*, Vol. II, pp. 1184-5.
5. *Thurloe State Papers*, Vol. VI, p. 15; SP 18/113, fo.220.

6. *Merc. Pol.*, 25 June-2 July 1657.
7. SP 25/78, p. 170.
8. Robert Ware, *Foxes and Firebrands: or, a specimen of the danger and harmony of Popery and Separation*, 2nd edn, 2 pts (Dublin, 1682), Pt. 2, p. 5.
9. Ibid., p. 4.
10. Noble, Vol. II.
11. *Clarke Papers*, Vol. III, p. 127; C.H. Firth, *The House of Lords during the Civil War* (London, 1910), pp. 248-50.
12. *Harleian Miscellany*, Vol. III, p. 459.
13. SP 25/78, pp. 29-30, 139; SP 18/156, fo.153; *Clarke Papers*, Vol. III, p. 150; *Merc. Pol.*, 14-21 October 1658; SP 25/78, p. 623.
14. *Merc. Pol.*, 14-21 October 1658; *Respublica*.
15. *Burton*, Vol. III, p. 65.
16. *Monarchy Asserted to be the Best, Most Ancient and Legal Form of Government*, p. 14.

APPENDIX B: KNOWN MEMBERS OF THE PROTEC-
TORAL COURT OR THOSE WHO PERFORMED AULIC
DUTIES

*Denotes offices and departments of which no mention can be found
in extant official documents. Evidence of their existence is therefore
based on such sources as pamphlets, memoirs and semi-official and
private correspondence.

† Denotes offices and departments that were not part of the household
establishment but which nevertheless performed aulic duties. All had
been in existence, as offices and departments of state, before the
institution of the Protectorate.

Dates in parentheses signify years in which offices or departments came
into being.

Other figures in parentheses signify the numbers employed in each
department.

PC, MP, UH denote, respectively, privy councillor, member of Parliament during the Protectorate, member of the Cromwellian Upper
House.

Household Above Stairs

LORD CHAMBERLAIN OF THE HOUSEHOLD (1655, revived 1657)
   Sir Gilbert Pickering, Bart. (PC, MP, UH)

*LORD CHAMBERLAIN'S CLERK/SECRETARY
Said to be John Dryden

†MASTER OF (THE) CEREMONIES
   Sir Oliver Fleming, Kt. (cousin to Cromwell)

HIS HIGHNESS'S SECRETARY
   William Malyn

GENTLEMEN OF THE HOUSEHOLD (1654)
   Also known as His Highness's Gentlemen.
   Employed as Gentlemen of the Privy Chamber, Gentlemen Waiters,

Gentlemen Ushers, Gentlemen Sewers and Grooms of the Stole, etc.
(Actual number not known)

GENTLEMEN OF THE BED CHAMBER (1655)
Actually employed as Grooms of the Bedchamber
Sir Thomas Billingsley, replaced by Mr Underwood; Mr Rolt; Mr
Barrington; Charles Harvey
*For the purposes of Cromwell's state funeral Barrington and Rolt
assumed the role of Gentleman of the Robes and Gentleman Usher,
respectively.*

HOUSEHOLD GUARD (1654)
Also known as the Life Guard of Foot, Guard of Halberdiers
or Yeomen of the Guard.
(About 40)
CAPTAIN of, Walter Strickland (PC, MP, UH)

†LIFE GUARD
Also known as the Life Guard of Horse or Horse Guard
CAPTAIN of, 1654-6 Colonel Charles Howard
        1656-9 Major Richard Beke (Cromwell's nephew by
        marriage)
*The Life Guard was part of the army establishment. From early 1656
onwards 1 or 2 squadrons (20 or 40 troopers) were employed as
Gentlemen Pensioners (described as *Ordinary Pensioners).*

†CHAPLAINS TO HIS HIGHNESS
PREACHERS AT WHITEHALL
Joseph Caryl, replaced by Nicholas Lockyer in June 1655; Peter
Sterry; Hugh Peter(s)
OTHERS INCLUDED
Thomas Goodwin; John Owen; Jeremiah White; Philip Nye;
Joseph Caryl; Messrs Hooke and Howe; Thomas Manton

†PHYSICIANS AND SURGEONS
George Bate(s); Lawrence Wright; Thomas Trapham; John Bathurst;
Jonathan Goddard
Bate(s) had been employed by Charles I.

*MASTER OF (THE) MUSIC
John Hingston
GENTLEMEN OF HIS HIGHNESS'S MUSIQUE
    Richard Hudson; Thomas Mallard; John Rodgers; David, or Davis
    Mell; William Howes; William Gregory; Thomas Blagrave
    Plus 2 *Lads brought up to music
    (Total 10)
    Mell, Howes, Gregory and Blagrave had been employed by Charles
    I.

† THE WARDROBE
HIS HIGHNESS'S WARDROBE KEEPER *also known as*
    Master of the Wardrobe
    Clement Kinnersley
ASSISTANT WARDROBE KEEPER
    John Kinnersley
KEEPER OF THE WARDROBE AT HAMPTON COURT
    Richard Marriott
TAILOR
    Mr Hornlock
Plus 10 others.
(Total 14)
Clement Kinnersley had been Yeoman of the Removing Wardrobe to
Charles I

† OFFICE OF (THE) WORKS
HIS HIGHNESS'S SURVEYOR OF (THE) WORKS *also known as*
    Surveyor-General of Works.
    John Embree
HIS HIGHNESS'S ARCHITECT
    Edward Dallon
*CLERKS (2)
TIMBER MERCHANT
MASTER CARPENTER
MASTER MASON
IRONMONGER
MASTER JOINER
MASTER CARVER
Plus 15 other artificers and tradesmen, etc.
(Total, excluding clerks, 23)
Labourers were hired on a temporary basis only.

†BARGES
  MASTER OF THE BARGES
    Richard Nutt
  ASSISTANT MASTER
    Thomas Washbourne
  HIS HIGHNESS'S WATERMEN (27 at Cromwell's death)
  (Total 29)

MISCELLANEOUS WHITEHALL SERVANTS (*originally government employees*) 'taken into his Highness's household' in April 1655.
  CHAPEL KEEPERS (3)
  KEEPER OF THE GALLERY
  PORTERS (2)
  KEEPER OF THE PRIVY GARDEN
  KEEPER OF THE PRIVY LODGINGS
  CLOCK KEEPER
  GARDENER
  KEEPER OF THE ORCHARD DOOR
  KEEPER OF ST. JAMES'S PARK GATES
  HOUSEKEEPER AT WHITEHALL (added in March 1659)
    Captain George Vaux

OTHER MISCELLANEOUS ABOVE STAIRS SERVANTS
  HOUSEKEEPER AT HAMPTON COURT
  * FALCONERS (2)
  * HUNTSMAN
  *BIRD KEEPER
  *GUNSMITH
  *SHOEMAKER
  *HATTER
  *TAILOR
  *UPHOLSTERER
  *MEASURERS OF CLOTH (3)

Household Below Stairs
STEWARD OF THE HOUSEHOLD (1654, abolished 1657)
  John Maidstone (MP) and Nathaniel Waterhouse (MP)

BOARD OF GREENCLOTH (constituted 1657)
  COMPTROLLER OF THE HOUSEHOLD (1657)
    Colonel Philip Jones (PC, MP, UH)

COFFERER (*or* MASTER-COFFERER) OF THE HOUSEHOLD (1657)
  John Maidstone (MP)
*MASTER OF THE GREENCLOTH (1657)
  Nathaniel Waterhouse (MP)
  (*In one contemporary document dated post-1657 Waterhouse is referred to as* *Steward of the Lands *and in another simply as* *Steward.)
CLERK OF THE GREENCLOTH (1657, *previous to that* his Highness's Auditor (1654))
  Abraham Barrington (*returned as MP 1659 but election declared void*)
CLERK COMPTROLLER (1657)
  Mr Ewer

The following are taken from a description of the protector's funeral cortège which is obviously based upon the order of procession drawn up before the ceremony. As it is unlikely that the entire household below stairs would have taken part in Cromwell's obsequies the figures quoted probably represent a chosen number designated to represent the whole department.

KNIGHT MARSHALL
  Colonel Biscoe
DEPUTY KNIGHT MARSHALL
  Richard Gerald
MARSHALL'S MEN *or* TIPSTAVES (13)
(Total 15)

PRIVY KITCHEN
  CLERKS (2)
  HIS HIGHNESS'S CHIEF COOK
    Mr Hamor
  OTHER COOKS (?)
  OTHER SERVANTS (7)

HOUSEHOLD KITCHEN
  CLERKS (2?)
  COOKS (3)
  OTHER SERVANTS (8)

  HALL-PLACE (2)

BUTLER TO HIS HIGHNESS

BUTLER TO HER HIGHNESS

DEPUTY SEWER

CATERER

LARDER (6)

PRIVY CELLAR (3)

BAKEHOUSE (6)   PANTRY (3)

BUTTERY (5)   CELLAR (1)

GREAT BEER CELLAR   WINE CELLAR
  ALE BREWERS (?)   PURVEYOR OF WINE
  Plus 2 others   CLERK

COOPER   SPICERY (2 including CLERK)

PASTRY (4)   SCULLERY (4)

SLAUGHTERHOUSE (2)   WOODYARD (2)

SERVANTS TO OFFICERS OF THE HOUSEHOLD
  GENTLEMEN WAITERS AT THE COMPTROLLERS TABLE
  BUTLER TO THE COMPTROLLER
  OTHER WAITERS (3)
  WAITERS AT THE COFFERERS TABLE (4)

Stables

MASTER OF THE HORSE (1654)
  John Claypole (MP, UH and Cromwell's son-in-law)

GENTLEMAN OF THE HORSE (1657)
  Nicholas Baxter

AVENOR (1655)
  Charles Rich

EQUERRIES   PAGES
  (*Possibly a temporary
  designation for the purposes
  of Cromwell's state funeral.*)

CLERK OF THE AVERY   CLERK OF THE STABLES

STABLE KEEPER (Hampton Court) MEWS KEEPER (Whitehall)

COACHMEN   POSTILIONS

FOOTMEN   GROOMS

BIBLIOGRAPHY

A. Manuscript Sources

Marquess of Bath, Longleat House:
  Privy Council Register of Richard Cromwell, September 3rd 1658 -
  January 18th 1659
County of Glamorgan Record Office, Cardiff:
  Fonmon Castle Mss. – Papers of Philip Jones, (Document D/DFF/
  177)
Public Record Office:
  State Papers 18/100, 113, 125, 130, 153, 156, 179, 182, 183, 203
  (Interregnum – Letters and Papers)
  State Papers 25/2, 57 (Interregnum – Council of State Draft Order
  Book)
  State Papers 25/75 to 78, 127, 128 (Interregnum – Council of State
  Fair Order Book)
  State Papers 46/117 (Interregnum – Papers of Commissioners for
  the Admiralty and Navy)

B. Contemporary or Near Contemporary Printed Matter

British Library (Thomason Tracts); Cromwell Museum and Cambridge
  County Library Headquarters, Huntingdon; University Library,
  Cambridge; County of Glamorgan Record Office, Cardiff.
Bate, George, *Elenchus Motuum Nuperorum in Anglia: or a Short
  Historical Account of the Rise and Progress of the Late Troubles in
  England* (London, 1685)
Burnet, Bishop, *History of His Own Time*, Vol. I (Dublin, 1724)
The Commonwealth Mercury
Dawbeny, H., *Historie and Policie reviewed, in The Heroick Transac-
  tions of his Most Serene Highness, Oliver, Late Lord Protector, from
  his Cradle to his Tomb* (London, 1659)
Dugdale, Sir William, *A Short View of the Late Troubles in England*
  (Oxford, 1681)
Fletcher, Henry, *The Perfect Politician: or a full view of the Life and
  Actions (Military and Civil) of O. Cromwell*, 2nd edn (London,
  1680)
*The Government of the Commonwealth of England Scotland and
  Ireland, and the Dominions thereunto belonging; as it was publickly
  declared at Westminster the 16th day of December, 1653. Published*

by His Highness the Lord Protector's special commandment.
(London, 1653)

Harvey, Charles, *A Collection of Several Passages concerning his late Highnesse Oliver Cromwell, In the time of his Sickness; wherein Is Related many of his Expressions upon his Death-Bed. Together with his Prayer within two or three dayes before his death. Written by one that was then Groom of his Bedchamber* (London, 9 June, 1659)

Heath, James, *Flagellum: or the Life and Death, Birth and Burial of O. Cromwell* (London, 1672 edn)

Jones, Philip, *Articles of Impeachment of Transcendent Crimes* [etc.] *. . . committed by . . . Together with Col. Philip Jones' Answer thereunto* (London, 1659)

Liber Regalis, A Collection out of the book called (London, 1661)

Mercurius Politicus

Monarchy Asserted to be the Best, most Ancient and Legal Form of Government: In a Conference had at Whitehall with Oliver Cromwell and a Committee of Parliament (London, 1679)

Morgan, Bledry, *The Humble Petition of*

Owen, John, *Of the Mortification of Sin in Believers* (Oxford, 1656)

A Perfect Diurnal

Perfect Proceedings of State Affairs

The Picture of a New Courtier drawn in a Conference between Mr. Timeserver and Mr. Plain-heart (London, 1656)

The Public Intelligencer

Proclamation of Richard Cromwell as Lord Protector (London, 1658)

Several Proceedings of State Affairs in England, Scotland and Ireland

Shadwell, Thomas, *The Medal of Bayes: a Satire against Folly and Knavery* (London, 1682)

Ware, Robert, *Foxes and Firebrands: or, a specimen of the danger and harmony of Popery and Separation*, 2nd edn 2 parts (Dublin, 1682)

Warwick, Sir Philip, *Memoirs of the Reign of King Charles I with a continuation to the Happy Restoration of King Charles II* (London, 1701)

Weekly Intelligencer

Whitelocke, Bulstrode, *Memorials of the English Affairs* (London, 1682)

C. Later Publications of Contemporary Diaries, Correspondence, Histories, Memoirs, Official Documents, Records and other works

Abbott, W.C., *The Writings and Speeches of Oliver Cromwell*, 4 Vols.

(Cambridge, Mass., 1937-47)

Acts and Ordinances of the Interregnum, 1642-1660, ed. C.H. Firth and R.S. Rait, Vol. II (London, 1911)

Baillie, Robert, *The Letters and Journals of,* ed. David Laing, Vol. III (Edinburgh, 1842)

Burton, Thomas, *The Diary of,* ed. J.T. Rutt, 4 Vols. (London, 1828)

The Calendar of State Papers: Domestic Series, 1635, 1648-9 to 1661-2

The Calendar of State Papers: Venetian, 1653-4, 1657-9

Clarendon, Edward, Earl of, *The History of the Rebellion and Civil Wars in England,* ed. W. Dunn Macray, 6 Vols. (Oxford, 1888)

The Clarke Papers, ed. C.H. Firth, Vol. III (London, 1899)

A Collection of Ordinances and Regulations for the Government of the Royal Household . . . from King Edward III to King William and Queen Mary (London, 1790)

A Collection of Original Letters and Papers, concerning the Affairs of England, from the Year 1641 to 1660. Found Among the Duke of Ormonde's Papers, ed. Thomas Carte, Vol. II (London, 1739)

Commons, Journals of the House of, Vols. III, VII

Cromwelliana: a Chronological detail of events in which Oliver Cromwell was engaged from the year 1642 to his death 1658 (Westminster, 1810)

Davenant, Sir William, *The Shorter Poems and Songs from the Plays and Masques,* ed. A.M. Gibbs (Oxford, 1972)

Dryden, John, *The Works of,* general eds. E.N. Hooker and H.T. Swedenberg, Jr., Vol. I (Berkeley, Calif., 1956)

Evelyn, John, *Diary of,* ed. William Bray, New edn with life of the author by Henry B. Wheatley, Vol. II (London, 1879)

Fanshawe, Lady Anne, *Memoirs of Lady Anne Fanshawe* (London, 1905)

Fifth Report: Deputy Keeper of the Public Records, Appendix II

Fourth Report: Deputy Keeper of the Public Records, Appendix II

The Harleian Miscellany, Vol. III (London, 1745)

Herbert, Sir Henry, Master of the Revels, *The Dramatic Records of, 1623-1673,* ed. Joseph Quincy Adams (Yale UP, 1917)

Historical Manuscripts Commission, *Second Report* (1871), Appendix

Historical Manuscripts Commission, *Fifth Report* (1876), Appendix

Hobbes, Thomas, *Behemoth, or the Long Parliament,* ed. Ferdinand Tönnes (London, 1889)

'The Inventories and Valuations of the King's Goods, 1649-1651', ed. Oliver Millar, *Walpole Society*, 34th Vol., 1970-2.

The King's Musick; A Transcript of Records Relating to Music and

Musicians (1460-1700), ed. Henry Carte de Lafontaine (London, 1909)

Lords, Journals of the House of, Vol. VI

Ludlow, Edmund, *Memoirs of, 1625-1672*, ed. C.H. Firth, 2 Vols. (London, 1894)

Marvell, Andrew, *The Poems and Letters of*, ed. H.M. Margoliouth, 2 Vols., 3rd edn revised by P. Legouis with the collaboration of E.E. Duncan-Jones (London, 1952)

Nichols, John, *The Progresses, Processions and Magnificent Festivities of King James the First*, Vol. IV (London, 1828)

Nickolls, John, *Original Letters and Papers of State addressed to Oliver Cromwell*, Found among the Political Collections of Mr John Milton (London, 1743)

Owen, John, *The Works of*, ed. W.H. Gould, Vol. VI (London, 1851)

Prestwich, Sir John, *Respublica* (London, 1787)

The Protectorate of Oliver Cromwell and the state of Europe during the early part of the Reign of Louis XIV, ed. Robert Vaughan, 2 Vols. (London, 1838)

Somers Tracts, 3rd Collection, Vol. II (London, 1751)

The Stuart Constitution, 1603-1688: Documents and Commentary, ed. J.P. Kenyon (Cambridge, 1966)

Thurloe, John, *A Collection of State Papers of J.T. To which is prefixed the life of Mr. Thurloe by Thomas Birch*, 7 Vols. (London, 1742)

Wood, Anthony, *Athenae Oxienses*, Vol. III (London, 1817)

Wood, Anthony, *The Life and Times of, 1632-1695, described by Himself*, Collected from his diaries and papers by Andrew Clark, Vol. I (Oxford Historical Society, 1891)

D. Secondary and General Sources

Abbot, W.C., *A Bibliography of Oliver Cromwell* (Cambridge, Mass., 1929)

Akrigg, G.P.V., *Jacobean Pageant, or The Court of King James I* (London, 1962)

Ashley, Maurice, *Cromwell's Generals* (London, 1954)

Ashley, Maurice, *The Greatness of Oliver Cromwell* (London, 1957)

Ashley, Maurice, *Financial and Commercial Policy Under the Cromwellian Protectorate*, 2nd edn (London, 1962)

Aylmer, G.E., *The King's Servants: The Civil Service of Charles I, 1625-1642* (London, revised edn, 1974)

Aylmer, G.E., *The State's Servants: The Civil Service of the English Republic, 1649-1660* (London, 1973)

Beattie, John M., *The English Court in the Reign of George I* (Cambridge, 1967)

Bibliography of British History, Stuart period, 1603-1714, ed. G. Davies, 2nd edn ed. by M.F. Keeler (Oxford, 1970)

Boutells Heraldry, revised by J.P. Brooke-Little (London, 1973 edn)

Butler, Sir Thomas, *The Crown Jewels and Coronation Ritual* (London, 1973)

Carlisle, Nicholas, *An enquiry into the place and quality of the gentlemen of His Majesty's most Honourable Privy Chamber* (London, 1829)

Catteral, R.C.H., 'The Failure of the Humble Petition and Advice', *American Historical Review*, Vol. IX, No. 1 (1903)

Chettle, G.H. (with additions by John Charlton), *Hampton Court Palace* (HMSO, London, 1975)

The Complete Peerage of England, Scotland, Ireland and the United Kingdom, ed. G.E. Cokayne, revised edn ed. by Vicary Gibbs and others, Vols. II, III, IV, V, X (London, 1912, 1913, 1916, 1926, 1945)

Cyclopedia of Painters and Paintings, ed. John Denison Champlin, Jr.; critical ed. Charles C. Perkings, 4 Vols. (pub. 1885-7, New York, 1969 reissue)

The Dictionary of National Biography

Elton, G.R., *The Tudor Revolution in Government* (Cambridge, 1953)

Firth, C.H., 'The Court of Oliver Cromwell', *The Cornhill Magazine* NS, Vol. III (September, 1897)

Firth, C.H., *The Last years of the Protectorate*, 1656-1658, 2 Vols. (London, 1909)

Firth, C.H., *The House of Lords during the Civil War* (London, 1910)

Firth, C.H., *Cromwell's Army* (London, 1962 edn)

Fraser, Antonia, *Cromwell: Our Chief of Men* (London, 1973)

Haynes, Alan, 'The Mortlake Tapestry Factory, 1619-1703', *History Today*, Vol. XXIV, No. 1(January, 1974)

Hennell, Sir Reginald, *The History of the King's Body Guard of the Yeomen of the Guard, 1485-1904* (Westminster, 1904)

Holdsworth, Sir William, *A History of English Law*, Vol. I, 6th edn, Revised (London, 1938)

Holmes, Martin, and Sitwell, H.D.W., *The English Regalia* (HMSO, London, 1972)

Hotson, Leslie, *The Commonwealth and Restoration Stage* (Cambridge, Mass., 1928)

Jesse, J.H., *Memoirs of the court of England during the reign of the*

Stuarts, including the Protectorate, 4 Vols. (London, 1840)

Law, Ernest, *The History of Hampton Court Palace*, Vol. II (London, 1888)

Legg, L.G. Wickham, *English Coronation Records* (Westminster, 1901)

Legouis, P., *Andrew Marvell, Poet, Puritan, Patriot*, 2nd edn (Oxford, 1971)

Loftie, W.J., 'Whitehall: Historical and Architectural Notes', *The Portfolio*, No. 16 (April, 1895)

Andrea Mantegna: The Triumph of Caesar: Hampton Court, Notes by Anthony Blunt (HMSO, London, 1975)

Marillier, H.C., *The Tapestries at Hampton Court Palace* (HMSO, London, 1962)

Munk, William, *The Roll of the Royal College of Physicians of London*, Vol. I, 2nd edn (London, 1878)

Noble, Mark, *Memoirs of the Protectoral House of Cromwell*, 2 Vols. (Birmingham, 1787)

The Oxford English Dictionary

Parliament, Members of: Part I, *Parliaments of England, 1213-1702* (London, 1878)

Peachy, George C., 'Thomas Trapham — (Cromwell's Surgeon) — and Others', *Proceedings of the Royal Society of Medicine*, Vol. 24, Pt. II (1931)

Pearson, Karl, and Morant, G.M., 'The Wilkinson Head of Oliver Cromwell', *Biometrika*, Vol. XXVI (1935)

Pegge, Samuel, *Curialia: or an Historical Account of some Branches of the Royal Household* (London, 1791)

Pinto, Vivian de Sola, *Peter Sterry, Platonist and Puritan, 1613-72* (Cambridge, 1934)

Ramsey, Robert W., *Richard Cromwell, Protector of England* (London, 1935)

The Raphael Cartoons, Introduction by John White (HMSO, London, 1972)

Scholes, Percy A., *The Puritans and Music in England and New England* (Oxford, 1934)

Schramm, P.E. (trans. L.G. Wickham Legg), *A History of the English Coronation* (Oxford, 1937)

Scott-Giles, C.W., *The Romance of Heraldry* (London, 1929)

Shaw, Wm. A., *The Knights of England*, Vol. II (London, 1906)

Stearns, R.P., *The Strenuous Puritan: Hugh Peter, 1598-1660* (Urbana, Ill., 1954)

Stewart, J. Douglas, 'Samuel Cooper: an English Baroque "Man of his

Century" ' in Daphne Foskett's *Samuel Cooper and his Contemporaries* (HMSO, London, 1974)

Tangye, Sir Richard, *The Two Protectors: Oliver and Richard Cromwell* (London, 1899)

Turner, E.R., *The Privy Council of England in the Seventeenth and Eighteenth Centuries, 1603-1784*, Vol. I (Baltimore, 1927)

Varley, F.J., *Cromwell's Latter End* (London, 1939)

Veysey, A.G., *Colonel Philip Jones, 1618-74*, unpublished MA thesis deposited in the University College of Wales, Bangor (1958)

Wagner, Sir Anthony, *Historic Heraldry of Britain*, 2nd impr. reprint (London, 1972)

Wilkinson, B., *The Coronation in History* (Historical Association Pamphlet – General Series No. 23, 1953)

Ward, Charles E., *The Life of Dryden* (Chapel Hill, NC, 1961)

Warwick, Frances Evelyn, Countess of, *Warwick Castle and its Earls*, Vol. II (London, 1903)

Willis Browne, *Notita Parliamentaria*, Vol. III (London, 1750)

Woodward, John, and Burnett, George, *A Treatise on Heraldry* (David and Charles Reprints, Newton Abbot, 1969).

INDEX

John and Waterhouse, Nathaniel
steward of the lands *see* Waterhouse,
Nathaniel
Strickland, Walter: as captain of the
household guard 67, 77, 78, 79,
81, 85, 92, 111, 121, 169; as
Commonwealth councillor of
state 121; as protectoral councillor
16, 18, 28, 30, 33, 42, 43, 85,
91-2; as member of the
Cromwellian Upper House 150;
as member of the Rump Parliament 80; as agent and co-ambassador to the United Provinces 78;
fate of 80
surgeons *see* physicians
Sweden: ambassador of 22, 58,
92-3, 100, 114, *see also* Coyett,
Peter; commissioners of *see*
Fleetwood, George and Von
Tischendorf, H.; king of 93;
Commonwealth's ambassador to
93 *see also* Whitelocke, Bulstrode
Swiss guard, alleged negotiations for
provision of, for the protector 82
Switzerland, Commonwealth's
envoy to *see* Pell, John
Sydenham, Colonel William, protectoral councillor 16, 36, 39,
126

tailor, his Highness's 104, 171
Temple Bar, London 55, 67
Teneriff 139
Thames, River 54, 98, 99, 101;
watermen of 98, 100, 102, 153
Thomas, William, keeper of the
wardrobe at Windsor Castle 29,
120, 121
Thurloe, John: as secretary of state
41, 55, 60, 71-2, 86, 101, 159n;
as protectoral councillor 68, 142
Tillotson, John, archbishop of
Canterbury 108
timber merchant to his Highness 104,
170
tipstaves *see* marshall's men
Titian 109
To His Sacred Majesty (John Dryden)
139
Tower Hill 91
Tower of London 19, 24, 26, 37, 91;
clerk of the records in 101;
keeper of the wardrobe at *see*

Pidgeon, Mr; storekeeper and
master workman of the Armoury
Office at 119; wardens of 78, 79
Tower Wharf 74, 90, 100
Trapham, Thomas, physician to the
protector 110, 112, 169
treasurer of the protector's contin-
gencies *see* Jessop, William
treasury commissioners 39
treasury, his Highness's, the lord
commissioner of 46
Turkey 57
*Two Songs at the Marriage of the
Lord Fauconberg and the Lady
Mary Cromwell* (Andrew
Marvell) 139, 144

Underwood, Mr, gentleman/groom
of the bedchamber 70, 71-2, 169
United Provinces 55, 78, 82, 139;
ambassadors of 22, 55, 56, 60,
77, 91, 94, 100, 124, 140, *see
also* Beveringh, Lord;
Jongestall, A.L.; Nieuport, Lord;
Commonwealth ambassadors to
99; Hogan Mogan or States
General of 78
upholsterer, his Highness's 104, 131,
171
ushers, gentlemen *see* household,
gentlemen of the, and Rolt, Mr

Van Dycke, Sir Anthony 109, 151
Van Somer, Paulus 28
Vane, Sir Henry 160
Vaux, Captain George, housekeeper
at Whitehall 85, 171
Venice: ambassador of 58, 100;
ambassador of, in France 90;
Doge and Senate of 69, 94, 95,
127; resident of, in England *see*
Giavarina, Francesco; secretary
of, in England 86, 89, 90
Verge, Court of the, suggested
existence of during Protectorate
79-80
Verney, Sir Edmund, knight marshall
to Charles I 47
Victory (ship) 152
Von Tischendorf, H., Swedish
commissioner 93-4
Vyner, Sir Thomas, lord mayor of
London 39-40

Index

Wilkins, Dr John (Cromwell's
    brother-in-law), warden of
    Wadham College, Oxford 86
Wilkins, Robina (Cromwell's sister)
    87
William III 97
Windsor Castle 15; St. George's
    Chapel at 136; wardrobe at,
    keeper of see Thomas, William
Windsor Little Park 16
Windsor Park 133
wine, purveyor of 173
wine cellar 36, 173
Wolsey, Thomas 22
Wood, Anthony 110, 112, 137-8
woodyard 36, 173
Worcester, battle of 108
Worcester, Edward Somerset, earl of,
    master of the horse to James I
    56
Worcester, marquis of 49
works, office of 88, 103-5, 119, 151,
    170; staff of 104, 131, 170 see
    also carpenter, master, his
    Highness's; Dallon, Edward, his
    Highness's architect; Embree,
    John, his Highness's surveyor of
    (the) works; ironmonger to his
    Highness; joiner, master, his
    Highness's; mason, master, his
    Highness's; Phillips, Mr, his
    Highness's master carver; timber
    merchant to his Highness
Worsley, Major-General 58
Wren, Sir Christopher 23
Wright, Lawrence, physician to the
    protector 110-11, 169
Wringston, manor of 49
Wynn, Daniel, keeper of the
    Whitehall mews 59, 61, 131, 173

yeomen of the guard see household
    guard
York 64, 120, 121, 132; manor at 15

Zeeland 88n